The Zeebrugge Shipwreck

A forgotten early sixteenth-century merchantman discovered off the Belgian coast

Hendrik Lettany

BAR International Series 2898

2018

Published in 2018 by
BAR Publishing, Oxford

BAR International Series 2898

The Zeebrugge Shipwreck

ISBN 978 1 4073 1604 8

© Hendrik Lettany 2018

COVER IMAGE *Drawings of several types of candlestick stems recovered from the Zeebrugge shipwreck.*

The Author's moral rights under the 1988 UK Copyright, Designs and Patents Act are hereby expressly asserted.

All rights reserved. No part of this work may be copied, reproduced, stored, sold, distributed, scanned, saved in any form of digital format or transmitted in any form digitally, without the written permission of the Publisher.

Printed in England

PUBLISHING

BAR titles are available from:

BAR Publishing
122 Banbury Rd, Oxford, OX2 7BP, UK
EMAIL info@barpublishing.com
PHONE +44 (0)1865 310431
FAX   +44 (0)1865 316916
www.barpublishing.com

For Charlotte and for my parents

Acknowledgements

It has been quite an effort to collect and process all the information presented in this dissertation. I would never have come to this result without some helping hands and support. Therefore, a word of thanks is in place.

First of all I would like to thank my supervisor, dr. prof. Thijs Maarleveld, for his guidance, support and remarks in regards to the presented research.

Special thanks should go to Bart Schiltz, who initiated the excavation of the Zeebrugge wreck and who provided essential information by opening his archives to us and answering our many questions.

We thank the crew of the MAS Museum, where we spent many days recording all available objects from the Zeebrugge collection, for their help. Special thanks goes to Bram Janssens and Jan Parmentier who guided us through the storage facilities and were always available for help.

We thank Leentje Linders for making the xrf-analysis of a large quantity of objects possible.

We thank Maggie Logan, who did an incredible job proofreading this paper on a very short notice.

We also would like to thank the three anonymous reviewers of this paper for their comments and suggestions from which this publication could benefit.

Of course, a special thanks goes to BAR Publishing, for giving me this incredible opportunity to publish my master dissertation in BAR International Series. An additional word of thanks for Dr. Jane Burkowski is here in place, for guiding me through all stages of the process.

I thank Charlotte, for her support and patience, she's the best.

And last but not least, I would like to thank my parents, without whose tremendous support none of this would have been possible.

Many others have helped us as well by sharing thoughts, information or advise. In this regard we also thank:

Jens Auer, Tim Bellens, Katleen Deagan, Yvonne de Rue, Anne-Clothilde Dumargne, Mark Dunkley, Anton Ervynck, Kristof Haneca, Marina Hautman, Ritzo Holtman, Fritz Horemans, Andrea Klomp, Pauline Kulstad, Fien Lettany, Hans Lettany, Jan Lettany, Denis Maly, Dana Piessens, Marnix Pieters, Philippe Probst, Martin Roberts, Rudi Roth, Johan van Heesch, Arent Vos, Alexis Wielemans, Beeldarchief VRT, Centrum voor Religieuze Kunst en Cultuur and Anchor Research and Salvage.

Table of Contents

List of Figures vii
List of Tables x
Preface xi
Abstract xii

Chapter 1. Introduction 1
   1.1. Sources 1
   1.2. Methodology 2
      1.2.1. pXRF-analysis of the Zeebrugge finds 3
   1.3. Status quaestionis 3

Chapter 2. Site and Research 5
   2.1. The discovery of the Zeebrugge wreck 5
      2.1.1. The story of Bart Schiltz, 't Vliegent Hart and the Anna Catharina 5
      2.1.2. Legal issues and the foundation of vzw VOC Anna Catharina 8
      2.1.3. The Zeebrugge wreck and the foundation of vzw Maritieme Archeologie ... 10
   2.2. Location, environment and current state of the wreck 11
      2.2.1. Location 11
      2.2.2. Environment and current state 13
   2.3. Fieldwork 14
      2.3.1. Surveys 14
      2.3.2. Excavation 16
      2.3.3. Post-processing the excavation results 20
   2.4. The paradox of the Zeebrugge site 22

Chapter 3. Finds from the Zeebrugge wreck 24
   3.1. Ship and navigation 24
   3.2. Organic materials 26
   3.3. Ceramics 28
   3.4. Finance-related finds 28
      3.4.1. Nested cup-weights 28
      3.4.2. Coin weights 31
      3.4.3. Venus counters 34
      3.4.4. Coins 35
   3.5. Kitchen- and dining-related finds 35
      3.5.1. Cauldrons and colander 35
      3.5.2. Plates and platters 40
      3.5.3. Salt holders 43
      3.5.4. Flagon 46
      3.5.5. Spoons 46
      3.5.6. Mortars and pestles 48
      3.5.7. Taps 50
      3.5.8. Knife handles and decorations 50
   3.6. Sewing and dress accessories 56
      3.6.1. Pins 56
      3.6.2. Thimbles 56
      3.6.3. Needle cases 58
      3.6.4. Hook-and-eye fasteners 60
      3.6.5. Bells 60

- 3.7. Religious objects 60
  - 3.7.1. Monstrance 60
  - 3.7.2. Devotional medal and mould 62
  - 3.7.3. Holy water fonts? 63
- 3.8. Candlesticks 63
  - 3.8.1. Typological groups 66
    - Type 1 66
    - Type 2 67
    - Type 3 67
    - Type 4 67
    - Type A 67
    - Type B 67
    - Type C 70
    - Type D 70
    - Type E 71
    - Type F 74
    - Type G 75
    - Type H 75
    - Type I 76
    - Type J 77
    - Type K 77
    - Type L 77
    - Type M 80
    - Type N 80
  - 3.8.2. pXRF-analysis 80
- 3.9. Weaponry 84
  - 3.9.1. Mould for musket shot 84
  - 3.9.2. Round shot 85
  - 3.9.3. Ordnance and other weapons 87
- 3.10. Other finds 91

Chapter 4. Discussion 94
- 4.1. Date 94
- 4.2. Origin 94
- 4.3. Cargo 95
- 4.4. Destination: context of trade 96
- 4.5. Further research 98

Chapter 5. Conclusion 99

Bibliography and archival sources 101

List of Figures

Figure 1. Part of the Zeebrugge collection exhibited in showcases at the MAS Museum, Antwerp. 2
Figure 2. Location of the Zeebrugge shipwreck, off the Belgian coast. 6
Figure 3. Plotted wreck locations. 12
Figure 4. Plotted wreck locations after adjustments. The 'original' locations are visible in a lighter grey colour. 12
Figure 5. Buffers for archaeological potential of the different wreck locations. 12
Figure 6. Locations that have been described as being in the proximity of the Zeebrugge wreck. 12
Figure 7. Sediments around the Zeebrugge wreck. 14
Figure 8. Bathymetrical data 1962. 14
Figure 9. Bathymetrical data 1994. 14
Figure 10. Location Zeepipe compared to location Zeebrugge wreck. 14
Figure 11. Impression of the site based upon the 1991 dive survey reports. 16
Figure 12. The red square delimits the area where the multibeam survey was executed. 17
Figure 13. Correspondence between detected concentration and proposed wreck locations. 17
Figure 14. Example of a dive report from the 1994 field season. We can see that at this point, the site still is referred to as 'A.C.' (*i.e.* Anna Catharina). The exact work section is not specified, the earlier reports are more accurate in this regard. The material or method used is referred to as 'M.D.' (*i.e.* metal detector). The report itself specifies the kind of work executed during the dive and mentions some of the recovered objects. Without context, however, the report is difficult to interpret. 18
Figure 15. Impression of the site after the first few months of excavation. 19
Figure 16. Red dots on some of the objects are an apparent indication archaeometrical analysis was executed. 21
Figure 17. A candlestick and a cauldron demonstrating square appertures, probably caused by obtaining samples for material analysis. 21
Figure 18. Anchor with concreted pewter plates (©VRT). 27
Figure 19. 'Single handed' divider. 27
Figure 20. A wooden comb, probably not preserved (©VRT, manipulated by the author). 27
Figure 21. Concreted cask, filled with nails (Images provided by Bart Schiltz). 27
Figure 22. Nested cup-weights. 29
Figure 23. Dimensions of the second-largest weight for each set of nested cup-weights. 30
Figure 24. Little copper-alloy box. 33
Figure 25. Parts of a scale. 33
Figure 26. Coin weights. 33
Figure 27. Coin depicting the *Reyes Catolicos* (not to scale) (Urban Archaeology Department, City of Antwerp (Belgium)). 33
Figure 28. Venus counters. 34
Figure 29. Three nested cauldrons (a, b, c) and a colander (d). 36
Figure 30. Edge of cauldron 29.a. Traces indicate a handle may have been present here. 38
Figure 31. Nested cauldrons from the Punta Cana Pewter wreck (Image provided by ARS Anchor Research & Salvage Inc.). 38
Figure 32. Different sorts of cauldrons from the Zeebrugge wreck. 39
Figure 33. Dimensions of the different kinds of pewter plates. 40
Figure 34. Different sorts of pewter plates from the Zeebrugge wreck. 41
Figure 35. Different pewter marks present on plates and platters from the Zeebrugge wreck (not to scale). 42
Figure 36. Porringer depicted together with other objects recovered from the Zeebrugge wreck (Demerre, Van Haelst and Pieters 2013). 42
Figure 37. Copper-alloy platter. 44
Figure 38. Salt holders (b and d not to scale). 45
Figure 39. 'Last Supper', Dieric Bouts (1464-1468) (left) and detail of type 1 salt holder (right) (M - Museum Leuven © www.lukasweb.be - Art in Flanders, foto Hugo Maertens). 45
Figure 40. Pewter flagon (b and c not to scale). 47
Figure 41. Pewter spoons. 47

Figure 42. Different types of mortars from the Zeebrugge wreck (42.d: Stadtbibliothek Nürnberg, Amb. 279.2° Folio 18 verso (Landauer I)). 49
Figure 43. Pestles of different lengths. 49
Figure 44. Tap and different sorts of tap keys. 49
Figure 45. Different knife handles from the Zeebrugge wreck (images by author and Flanders Heritage Agency, H. Denis). 52
Figure 46. Different types of decorations for knife handles. 54
Figure 47. Two different types of pin heads. It appears some pin heads were finished more poorly. 57
Figure 48. Pins occuring in many different lengths. 57
Figure 49. Histogram showing the dispersal of pin lengths. 57
Figure 50. One large 'pin', made of lead. 57
Figure 51. Different types of thimbles. 59
Figure 52. Needle cases from the Zeebrugge wreck. 59
Figure 53. Hook-and-eye fasteners assembled around a metal wire (a) and individual elements of fasteners. 59
Figure 54. Different sized rumbler bells. 59
Figure 55. Assemblage of objects probably belonging to a monstrance. 61
Figure 56. 16th century monstrance of probably (South) German origin (Rijsmuseum, Amsterdam). 62
Figure 57. Stone carved mould for devotional medallion (a) with detail of the medallion's image (b). 62
Figure 58. Type 1 bases. 68
Figure 59. Type 2 bases. 68
Figure 60. Type 3 bases. 69
Figure 61. Type 4 bases. 69
Figure 62. Dimensions type C stem. 71
Figure 63. Type A stem. 72
Figure 64. Type B stem (a) and pieces of damaged type B stems. 72
Figure 65. Type C stems. 72
Figure 66. Type D stems (a) with detail of wide, square apperture (b) and a detail of de Nuremberg *Hausbücher* (1528) (c) (Stadtbibliothek Nürnberg, Amb. 279.2° Folio 18 recto (Landauer I)). 73
Figure 67. Type E stem. 73
Figure 68. Type F stems. 73
Figure 69. Dimensions type D stem. 74
Figure 70. Dimensions type F stem. 75
Figure 71. Dimensions type G stem. 76
Figure 72. Type G stems. 78
Figure 73. Type H stem (a) and similar stem types from Nuremberg (b) (Stadtbibliothek Nürnberg, Amb. 279.2° Folio 9 recto (Landauer I)). 78
Figure 74. Type I stem. 78
Figure 75. Type J stem (a) and a similar stem from the early 16th century (b), excavated at the site of Concepción de la Vega (Dominican Republic), featuring elements from botht he type I and J stems from the Zeebrugge wreck (Florida Museum of Natural History, University of Florida). 79
Figure 76. Type K stem. 79
Figure 77. Type L stems. 81
Figure 78. Type M stem (a) and a stem excavated at the site of Concepción de la Vega (Dominican Republic), featuring similar characteristics, yet it is not identical (b) (Florida Museum of Natural History, University of Florida). 81
Figure 79. Type N stem with base. 82
Figure 80. Normalized spectra for all candlestick samples. We can see consistent peaks for the same elements (©Flanders Heritage Agency, image: Leentje Linders). 82
Figure 81. Overview of main elements of all sampled stems, grouped per type. 83
Figure 82. Overview of main elements of all sampled bases, grouped per type. 83
Figure 83. One part of a mould for casting musket shot. 84
Figure 84. Different sizes of iron shot from the Zeebrugge wreck. 84
Figure 85. A basket filled with iron shot and a container filled with stone shot (©VRT). 84
Figure 86. One of two stone shot owned by Bart Schiltz. 84
Figure 87. Number of stone shot per recorded size. 85
Figure 88. Histogram showing the dispersal of diameter size for the recorded iron shot. 85
Figure 89. Histogram showing the dispersal of weight for the recorded iron shot. 85
Figure 90. Damaged shot and shot concreted together (left) (©VRT) and a peculiar aperture (right). Are these possible indicators for a use as bar shot? 86

List of Figures

Figure 91. Shot featuring 'crossed ribs'. 86
Figure 92. A dagger's guard? 86
Figure 93. Sketch of first recovered cannon (P.A.B.S., F.C.T., "schets bombarde"). 89
Figure 94. Wrought iron breech loader, shortly after excavation (images provided by Bart Schiltz). 89
Figure 95. Drawings of the wrought iron breech loader and carriage. According to Schiltz the actual length is about 275cm (images provided by Bart Schiltz). 89
Figure 96. (continues on next page) Wrought iron bombard with carriage, probably the only preserved cannon from the Zeebrugge wreck. 89
Figure 96. (continued) Wrought iron bombard with carriage, probably the only preserved cannon from the Zeebrugge wreck. 90
Figure 97. Pullring or handle of an unkown object (a), parts of chain (b) and a copper-alloy ring (c). 91
Figure 98. Copper-alloy handles, possibly belonging to holy water pails or similar objects. 92
Figure 99. Copper-alloy door or lid, possibly of a lantern (a). 92
Figure 100. Unidentified objects. 93
Figure 101. Comparative perspective of *termini post quem* based on study of the Zeebrugge finds. 94
Figure 102. Some of the finds from the Zeebrugge wreck that demonstrate the similar nature of cargo (Martin Roberts 2013a; other images provided by ARS Anchor Research & Salvage Inc.). 97

List of Tables

Table 1. Within the frame of this research collected coordinates for the Zeebrugge wreck. 12
Table 2. Overview of finds studied by the author. 25
Table 3. Overview of finds mentioned in other sources. 25
Table 4. Overview of the different types of candlestick bases recovered from the Zeebrugge wreck. Information is given about the total number of pieces, how many pieces are attached to a stem, and the stem type to which they are attached. 65
Table 5. Overview of the different types of candlestick stems recovered from the Zeebrugge wreck. Information is given about the total number of pieces per type, the total number of objects to which these pieces belong, how many pieces are attached to a base, and the type of base to which they were attached. An estimation is made about the variations per type as well, yet this is a rather arbitrary and debatable contribution since all are unique handmade objects. 65
Table 6. Relative elemente concentration small shot 86

Preface

The research presented in this volume was originally conducted and written as a thesis in partial fulfilment of the requirements for the degree of Master of Arts in Maritime Archaeology at the *Syddansk Universitet* (University of Southern Denmark) and was supervised by Prof. Dr. Thijs Maarleveld. The topic for this thesis was proposed to me by Dr. Marnix Pieters (Flanders Heritage Agency). He had been part of the reading committee for my previous dissertations, both at bachelor's and master's level, at the *Vrije Universiteit Brussel* (Free University of Brussels) where I had earlier graduated as Master of Arts in Art History and Archaeology. As he is an authority in the field of Belgian maritime archaeology, I contacted Marnix to ask him for subjects that might mean a useful contribution to the current state of research. It was during a meeting in August 2014 that he first suggested the Zeebrugge shipwreck, a site discovered off the Belgian coast in 1991, as a possible topic. Although this site was unknown to me up to that moment, it soon became clear that both the recovered assemblage as well as the history of the excavation project itself did allow for an interesting paper. As Thijs was familiar with this site –he was contacted for advice several times during the initial excavation- it went without saying that he would be supervisor.

Both Marnix and Thijs emphasized, however, that a thorough study of this topic would not be without obstacles since it was unclear what information would be available 25 years after excavation. Although obstacles did occur, and even caused frustration or despondency from time to time, we were able to track down a large amount of data. The collection of finds recovered from this site, present at the *Museum aan de Stroom* (MAS, Antwerp, Belgium) and made available by Jan Parmentier, as well as archives related to the excavation made available by Bart Schilz in particular were essential to the success of this research. This data triggered the enthusiasm to keep digging into the past of what turned out to be an exceptional site.

After I had completed and submitted my dissertation it was Thijs who encouraged me to publish it. Different possibilities were looked into, and soon it became clear that BAR Publishing would be the perfect partner in this regard. Some minor changes were made to adapt the paper for publication. Useful feedback was incorporated and data that was previously not included due to time restraints could now be added. Unfortunately, not all images from the original paper could be included in this volume because of copyrights. The omitted images, however, are limited to iconographical sources that were added to illustrate parallels for some of the finds. When appropriate, these iconographical sources are still mentioned in the text.

I would like to thank everyone who made this publication possible. For me, this research has been an incredible experience. I hope the Zeebrugge shipwreck will fascinate you too and I hope this publication will finally give this remarkable site, 25 years after its initial discovery and excavation, a place in the (maritime) archaeological discourse.

Rik Lettany

Abstract

In the early 1990's large quantities of mainly metal objects were recovered from a wreck-site discovered off the Belgian coast, near the port of Zeebrugge. Since then, only a limited number of rather brief contributions on this topic have been published. These articles propose a date for the wreck in the late 15th or early 16th century, yet statements about the wreck are not substantiated with an exhaustive archaeological material analysis. Now, 25 years later, the site still is absent in the maritime archaeological debate and its data remain to be assessed.

By focusing on the analysis and assessment of the archaeological data recovered from this particular wreck-site, this research aims to add it to the maritime archaeological debate. The exhaustive (re-)assessment of the actual archaeological finds combined with information about the excavation project obtained by means of archival research and oral history, allowed us to appreciate the available data within its own limits and to propose a substantiated interpretation for the context of what became known as the Zeebrugge shipwreck.

Chapter 1

Introduction

In September 1990, a wreck was discovered off the Belgian coast near the port of Zeebrugge. In the following years, spread over four field seasons, hundreds of mainly metal objects in excellent condition were recovered from this site, which became known as the Zeebrugge shipwreck. Preliminary research did propose a date for the assemblage in the late 15th or early 16th century, and the rich collection of finds clearly demonstrated the archaeological potential of this discovery. However, to start this paper with a perhaps bold confession, I should admit that the first time that I ever heard of this site was when Marnix Pieters proposed it to me as a thesis subject in 2014. This was peculiar for a number of reasons. First of all, the finds from the Zeebrugge wreck provide a unique assemblage of hundreds of well-preserved artefacts from one single, closed archaeological context. Secondly, this site was discovered over 25 years ago, and excavation took place in the early 1990's, so the data has been available for quite some time. Moreover, it was the first Belgian underwater excavation in territorial waters. Yet very little attention has been given to this site over the years and its existence overall appears to be lacking in the international (maritime) archaeological debate. This hiatus, however, strongly contrasts with the apparent importance of the site. Although no wreck remains as such were recorded, a large and well-preserved cargo of metalware was present on site, as well as ordnance and round shot. With this research we hope to give this collection of finds the attention it deserves and to include the available data in the further academic debate.

The main focus of this research will be the presentation, analysis, and assessment of the many finds recovered from the Zeebrugge shipwreck, in order to propose a general yet substantiated interpretation of this site and its context. Such an assessment, however, did prove to be more challenging than expected. Although the main body of (preserved) finds from the Zeebrugge site is currently located in the MAS Museum (Antwerp, Belgium), this collection does not include all recovered finds and it is unclear where some of the other finds are located. Furthermore, this collection does not provide any contextual information, essential for the archaeological study of these objects. Therefore, in the frame of this research, an attempt was made to collect all available finds as well as all available information related to the excavation of the Zeebrugge site. In order to understand the collection of available finds, it was necessary to first understand the excavation process of this site. The excavation of the Zeebrugge wreck can be considered the first official Belgian underwater excavation in Belgian territorial waters and was executed by amateur-archaeologists in a time before any appropriate legislation for such procedures existed. Therefore, we are only able to understand the excavation process of this site by looking at the history of its discovery and the following legal developments coinciding with the attempts to excavate within a legal and scientific framework. These additional requirements did broaden the scope of this research considerably, yet they are important to appreciate the data available for this research and they are considered essential for the accurate and substantiated discussion of the Zeebrugge site as such.

One main hiatus in this research will be the discussion of construction features of the actual ship. Testimonies about the extent of preservation of any ship remains on site are vague and inconsistent. Based upon the available information, we can assume that, although possibly very limited, structural parts of the ship were still present when the excavation started. However, it appears that the excavation team was less interested in these bits and pieces of timber and focussed mainly on the excavation of cargo. Therefore, through absence of data, we unfortunately were not able to include the important aspect of the ship's construction in our discussion. It is clear, if any data in this regard were still to exist, whether in a private archive or on the site, this would mean a tremendous contribution to the research presented here.

1.1. Sources

It was a challenge to find and collect the necessary data to achieve the above-mentioned goals. Since a legal framework was missing during excavation, and appropriate organised procedures did not exist, the available data related to the excavation is now privately owned by former members of the excavation team, which operated under the name '*vzw Maritieme Archeologie*'. In this regard we were confronted with three main problems. First of all, the available data is not located in one place, and different former members of *vzw Maritieme Archeologie* seem to possess different sorts of data. Secondly, a general overview of which data exists, and who possesses this data, is lacking. Finally, some of these former members are reluctant to share any information in their possession. Therefore, although we were able to locate most data, not all data was available for this research, nor could the actual value of this data be estimated. It was mainly this lack in transparency that caused a challenge for the comprehensive study of the Zeebrugge wreck.

Figure 1. Part of the Zeebrugge collection exhibited in showcases at the MAS Museum, Antwerp.

Nevertheless, a considerable amount of data was collected in the frame of this research. We should mainly thank Bart Schiltz in this regard, discoverer of the Zeebrugge wreck, initiator of the excavation and of *vzw Maritieme Archeologie*. In the frame of this research we were granted access to his private archive related to the excavation of the Zeebrugge wreck. These documents include personal correspondence, meeting reports, and dive reports, all of which provided essential information to understand the context of this project. Another important document is the official excavation report of 1991. This document, provided by the Dutch Cultural Heritage Agency, contains a complete list of finds recovered that year. Furthermore, a considerable amount of information was retrieved by means of interviews and oral history. This approach and the combination of these different sources proved to be essential for understanding the context of this excavation project, and for the further interpretation of the available archaeological data.

The actual assessment of archaeological material focuses mainly on the collection of finds present in the MAS Museum. Part of this collection is exhibited in the museum's permanent exhibition (*fig. 1*), yet most finds are kept in storage. Another number of finds is present at the Flanders Heritage Agency, and a very limited number of objects is in possession of Bart Schiltz. These objects were included in our research as well. Although the existence of a considerable number of other finds was demonstrated, they were not available to us for different reasons. These missing finds will nevertheless be mentioned when appropriate and any available information on these objects will be included.

1.2. Methodology

This research can be divided into three main chapters. First, we will make an assessment of the excavation project as such, in which we will elaborate on the discovery, location and environment of the site, executed fieldwork including surveys and excavation, and previous post-processing of any excavation data. The information in this chapter is mainly based on archival research, oral history, and GIS analysis.

In a second chapter, we will discuss the actual collection of finds recovered from the Zeebrugge site. In the frame of this research we developed a database for all finds registered by the author. This database contains, among others, information about dimensions for each object and allowed us to analyse variables per object category. For each object category, we will discuss the registered and analysed data. For a number of finds, portable xrf-analysis was executed as well. This data is included when appropriate. Visual data is included as well, as representative finds for each object category were photographed by the author. When photographs could not provide sufficient information about the nature of the object, cross-section drawings were made as well. This is mainly the case for objects that are (partly) hollow. For each object category or type of object, parallels are discussed when available. These parallels allow us to determine a preliminary context for each object category.

This inductive approach is continued and elaborated in a following chapter, where we will discuss the Zeebrugge collection in its entirety and propose a date, origin, and possible destination for the wreck, based on archaeological and historical parallels. In addition to the interpretation of the archaeological data, some opportunities for further research will be discussed here as well.

1.2.1. pXRF-analysis of the Zeebrugge finds

Because the majority of finds from the Zeebrugge wreck are made of metal-alloys, it was decided to carry out a limited xrf-analysis (X-ray fluorescence) for some of the objects. The main goal of this analysis was to create qualitative xrf-data for specific object categories. This means we wanted to find out what elements are present in the sampled objects and what alloys were used to create these objects. Generally the results of these analyses will just be referred to as an addition to the description of the object and we will not elaborate on the interpretation of the results. Therefore, we also do not specify these results in specific terminology (e.g. latten, gun metal, muntz metal, leaded bronze, etc.). For reasons of convenience we generally refer to 'brass' for alloys containing mainly copper and zinc (and possible other elements). 'Pewter' is used for objects with a main tin concentration. Since percentages for the normalized concentration of all elements exceeding 1% will be mentioned, the reader will be informed about the actual composition of the objects despite the rather general terminology.

In some rare cases, the qualitative results are used to execute a semi-quantitative analysis. The qualitative data was normalized, to allow comparing of relative element concentrations of sampled objects within this collection. Such a comparative analysis can possibly lead to the identification of individual groups with different relative proportions, and may indicate different workshops or origins for these objects.

Since xrf-analysis only allows measuring the surface layer, we had to be cautious with objects that had been restored by *vzw Maritieme Archeologie* and were covered in coating, to avoid invalid deviations. In order to receive information on many different object categories, but also to process the data within the limits of this research, it was decided to only take one or two samples per object. This allowed us to obtain a broad range of qualitative data. Only for a limited number of objects a comparative analysis of the used alloys has been executed. For a more exhaustive study of the alloys of these objects, the acquisition of additional data is opportune.

The use of xrf-analysis as the method to obtain this data was the obvious choice. First of all, it is a non-destructive technique, which is a strong advantage for the study of archaeological artefacts. Also, accurate measurements can be made relatively fast, in less than one minute, with immediate results. Finally, a portable version of the xrf instrument exists (pXRF), making it a very convincing method to analyse objects *in situ*. We were able to use the Tracer IV pXRF, an instrument manufactured by Bruker and provided by the Flanders Heritage Agency for one day, which made it possible to make about 80 different measurements.[1] These measurements were made at the MAS' storage facilities.

1.3. Status quaestionis

Since the excavation of the Zeebrugge wreck in the early 1990's, several contributions about the site and its finds have been published, mainly in the form of congress papers (Vandenberghe 1997; Parmentier 2000; Schiltz 2006; Vandenberghe 2006; Van Dromme 2006) or exhibition catalogues (Vandenberghe 2007, Parmentier 2011). The site has been included in publications discussing wreck-finds or archaeological finds in the North Sea in general (Termote & Termote 2009; Pieters 2010) and other articles refer briefly to the site in this same regard (e.g. Seys 2001; Demerre and Pieters 2008). Some site-specific information is assembled on the website '*Maritieme Archeologie*', an initiative of the Flanders Heritage Agency (Maritieme Archeologie 2015). To a very limited extent, specific finds from the wreck have been included in material studies (Baumgärtel 1997; Holtman 1999; Vangroenweghe 2015). These latter publications do not focus on the Zeebrugge wreck as such, but rather include some of the finds to support the study of a certain type of object.

When we look at the actual analysis of archaeological data, however, most of these articles refer back to Vandenberghe (1997), who appears to be the only person who has studied the assemblage of finds recovered from the Zeebrugge wreck. In his article, Vandenberghe provides a summary of the recovered finds and gives a brief interpretation. Although the provided information certainly may be correct, Vandenberghe unfortunately neglects to substantiate his statements with visual information, parallels or an academic reference system. Obviously, such a more elaborate discussion may have surpassed the actual aim of this specific article, but nevertheless this article appears to provide the most exhaustive information about the Zeebrugge finds available up to now. Vandenberghe's later articles (2006; 2007) repeat this information concisely, with some adjustments in regards to numismatic data. Parmentier (2000; 2011) mainly elaborates on the history of the project and excavation in two quite similar articles. He provides a limited interpretation of the site based upon historical data rather than a study of the archaeological data as such. When finds are discussed, he refers again to Vandenberghe. Schiltz discusses the excavation of the Zeebrugge wreck as a case study for the development of maritime archaeology legislation, while Van Dromme provides a contribution on the conservation of one of the cannon from the site, but neither author elaborates on the actual archaeological data provided by the excavation. The information provided by Termote & Termote deviates from the other publications and seems to be based upon different sources. All other publications, however, refer specifically to Vandenberghe.

In two of his articles, Vandenberghe (1997, p. 90; 2006, p. 19-20) announces a more profound and detailed scientific publication on the Zeebrugge wreck finds is forthcoming.

---

[1] In this regard we especially would like to thank Leentje Linders from the Flanders Heritage Agency, who executed the xrf-analysis and normalized the received data.

But up to now such a contribution has not been published. We contacted Vandenberghe in this regard, yet it is unclear whether this publication is still to be expected.

Based upon this information it was decided, in agreement with dr. prof. Thijs Maarleveld, a new and independent analysis of the finds recovered from the Zeebrugge wreck, elaborating the actual archaeological data provided by this site to academic standards, was opportune.

Chapter 2

Site and Research

The Zeebrugge shipwreck is located about four nautical miles off the Belgian coast, south of the sandbank "Vlakte van de Raan" (*Fig. 2*). During high tide, the maximum depth of the shipwreck is 14m. The site was discovered by Bart Schiltz, a Belgian salvage worker, in September 1990. Actually, Schiltz was trying to find the wreck of the Anna Catharina, an 18th century Dutch East Indiaman, which, according to historical sources, sank in this same area. Although Schiltz initially believed he had discovered the Indiaman, his find would turn out to be an unknown shipwreck about 200 years older. The context of this discovery, and Schiltz's attempts to excavate this wreck to scientific standards despite lacking legal framework for an undertaking of this type, are not unimportant for our understanding of the archaeological collection in general. The context of these events can clarify the circumstances of the actual excavation and can help appreciate the limits as well as possibilities of the available data. Therefore, in this chapter, we will first elaborate on the discovery of the Zeebrugge wreck since we believe this background context is essential for the substantiated assessment of the actual archaeological data. Afterwards, we will discuss the location and environment of the site as well as previously executed fieldwork and research.

2.1. The discovery of the Zeebrugge wreck

2.1.1. The story of Bart Schiltz, 't Vliegent Hart and the Anna Catharina

The discovery of the Zeebrugge wreck can best be told as the story of Bart Schiltz, a salvage worker, and how the rediscovery of the Dutch East Indiaman 't Vliegent Hart inspired him to go on a quest for the Anna Catharina, the East Indiaman that sank with it. This quest would lead to the discovery of an older ship, now known as the Zeebrugge wreck. The events leading to this discovery are not unimportant, since they create the context for certain choices made during the excavation process, and they help getting a grasp on the view on underwater heritage at that time. After all, much has changed in the field of maritime archaeology over the last 25 years, not only in regard to technology and methodology, but also, and perhaps especially, in regard to legislation. To start our story, however, we have to go back in time much further, to the first half of the 18th century.

The events that started this story took place 3 February 1735, when two ships left the port of Rammekens, near Vlissingen. Both ships, 't Vliegent Hart and the Anna Catharina, belonged to the Dutch East India Company (Dutch: *Verenigde Oost-Indische Compagnie*, or *VOC*) and were heading for Batavia, present day Jakarta. Shortly after departure, however, the ships ran into trouble in front of what is now the Belgian coast. A strong east wind during spring tide made the ships run into sandbanks and despite attempts by the crew to save the ships, they would both sink the same night. Historical sources mention the masts of 't Vliegent Hart were reported sticking out of the water the next day, indicating its exact location (Marnix ET AL. 2010, p. 197). Shortly after the disaster, a failed salvage attempt was made; a second attempt followed in 1736. Although several objects, such as a cannon, bottles of wine and coins, could be recovered, most valuables were lost (Demerre & Missiaen 2010, p. 3). Also shortly after these events, the VOC created a new nautical chart with indication of the sandbanks in this area and the location of both 't Vliegent Hart and the Anna Catharina.

It was cartographer and historian dr. prof. Günter Schilder who, in 1977, while studying charts used by the VOC, rediscovered an important archive with information on the location of these two wrecks (*idem*, p. 4). Based on this information, the Dutch Rijksmuseum invited Rex Cowan, a British lawyer who salvaged other VOC-ships for the Dutch government in the past, as operator to locate and excavate the wreck of 't Vliegent Hart. He made a lucrative deal with the Dutch government, in which he could keep 75% of "profit" from the excavated finds; the other 25% would go to the Dutch State (*Ibidem*). Such an arrangement was not uncommon. In 1795, after the VOC closed down, the (predecessor of the) Dutch State took over its debts and assets, and along with it claimed the ownership rights for all the VOC's former belongings. For quite a few VOC wrecks the Dutch State has transferred these rights to private parties, in exchange for a (small) percentage of the salvaged goods, usually 25% and in some cases only 10% (Maarleveld 2006, p. 164-165).

In 1981 Cowan did indeed discover the wreck of the 't Vliegent Hart. With some intermissions, excavation work continued until 2000 (Marnix ET AL. 2010, p. 197). Initially the Rijksmuseum thought they had made a good deal. They would not have to give financial support to the project since external funding, provided by entrepreneur John Rose and part of the wreck's cargo (now owned by Cowan), would finance the project, and yet they would

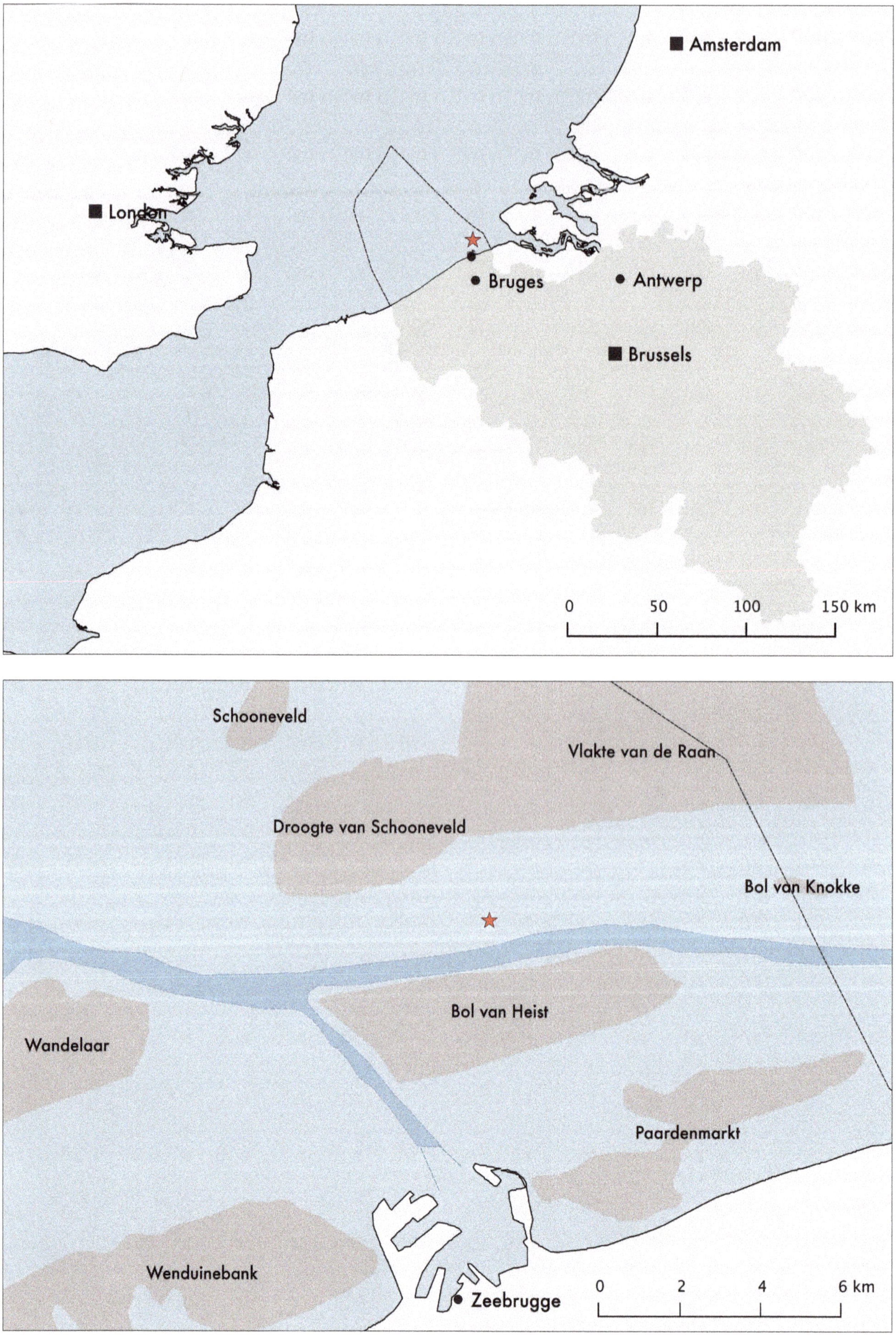

The Zeebrugge Shipwreck

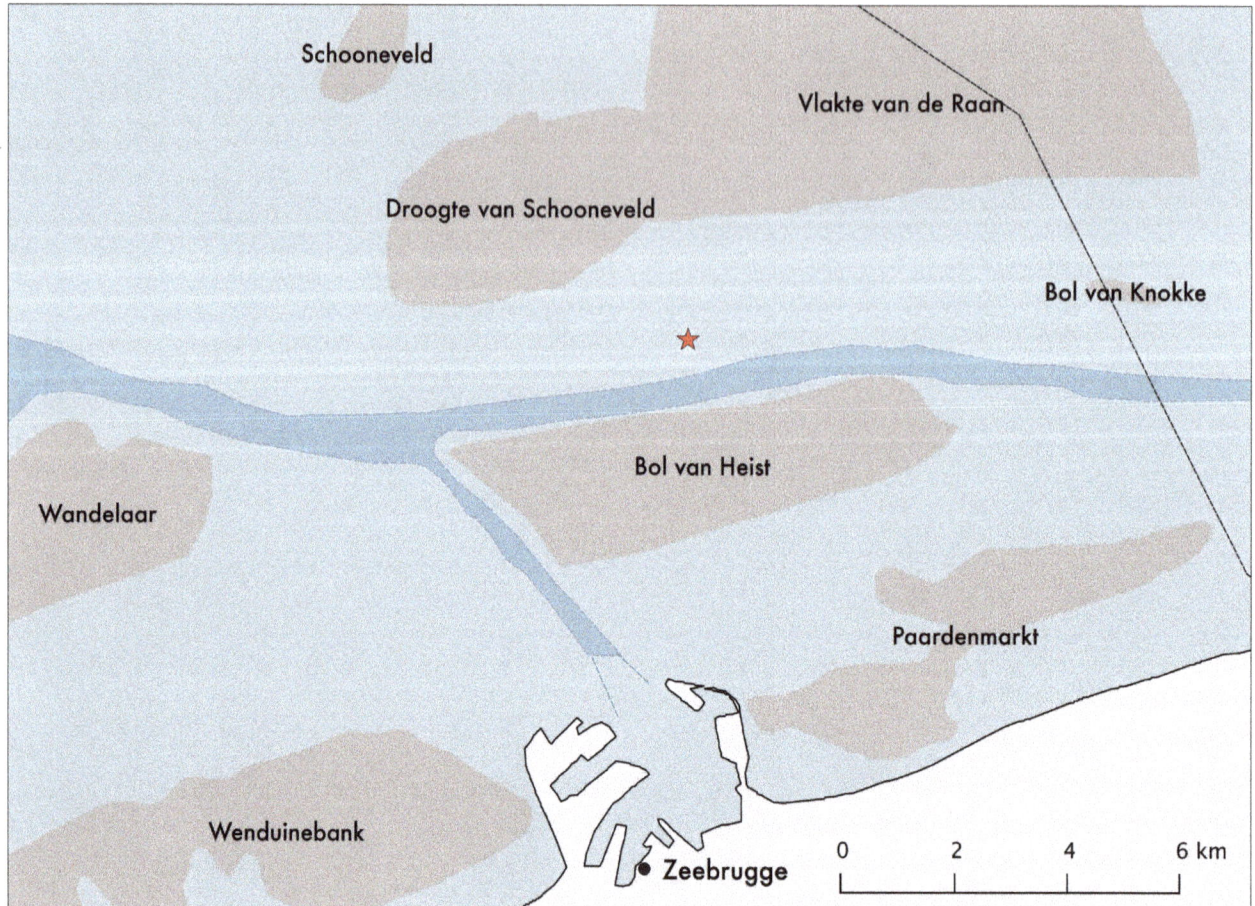

Figure 2. Location of the Zeebrugge shipwreck, off the Belgian coast.

benefit from the results receiving archaeological reports at given moments and they could participate in the project giving scientific advice (Demerre & Missiaen 2010, p. 4, 6). However, things would turn out differently and the excavation of 't Vliegent Hart would go into history as a much criticized project, not only by scholars (e.g. Green 2006) but also by the broader public (Demerre & Missiaen 2010, p. 6) and in the Netherlands it would give rise to a heated debate about ethics and heritage.[2]

Much of the growing critique had to do with unreported finds showing up in auction houses, the lack of excavation reports or reporting to poor scientific standards, Cowan's secrecy about the wreck's exact location and the changing of his percentage with the Dutch Ministry of Finance from 75% to 90% behind the Rijksmuseum's back only shortly before he would discover very valuable goods such as gold and silver (a more detailed version of these events can be found in the above-mentioned publications). This would lead to the Rijksmuseum's withdrawal from the project in 1984. Despite all this, Cowan would continue excavating the wreck, to which he had a legal claim.

In 1985 Cowan moved the project to Zeebrugge, a convenient location for its proximity to the wrecksite (Pieters ET AL. 2008). Bart Schiltz was working in Zeebrugge at that time. Schiltz is a man of many crafts. He initially moved from Antwerp to the Belgian coast to work as a fisherman, later joining the shipping industry. After getting in touch with a group of divers in 1974, he got inspired to become a diver himself. What started as a hobby led him to the salvage industry in 1982 (Personal information Bart Schiltz), and, in 1984, to the foundation of F.V. Submergo, his own salvage company (P.A.B.S., F.V., "Bondig chronologisch rapport over het zoeken naar het wrak van het V.O.C.-schip "Anna Catharina"" (From here on referred to as: P.A.B.S., F.V., "Chronologisch rapport")).

Thus, working as a salvage worker off the Belgian coast, Schiltz was there when Cowan moved his project to Zeebrugge. He describes how he saw Cowan enter the harbour with his boat loaded with archaeological finds on a regular basis. Often Cowan's boat moored along the M.S. Philippe Cousteau; Submergo's working vessel. According to Schiltz he got in touch with Cowan during this time, and he was inspired by his stories of 't Vliegent Hart and the finds he brought to land. When Cowan told Schiltz about a second ship out there to be found, named the Anna Catharina, Schiltz was eager to find this wreck. Despite the misachievements related to the excavation of 't Vliegent Hart, Schiltz stresses his interest for the wreck was purely scientific, and at this time he would not even have known about a contract with the Dutch State in favour of Cowan (*Ibidem*). Schiltz argues it was his ambition to recover finds from the wreck in a scientifically justified way and to exhibit them for the public in a museum. Nevertheless,

he argues, if any objects were to be sold, the finder should be entitled to "a reasonable share of the profits […] if only to cover part of the costs [of the excavation]" (Schiltz 2006, p. 43). In our talks Schiltz would later contend that if objects would have been sold, such a sale would never have fully covered the expenses for a project such as this.

Schiltz started his search for the Anna Catharina in the VOC archive in The Hague, with the same documents that led to the discovery of 't Vliegent Hart. An account in this archive mentions "the Anna Catharina was last seen and heard, firing its guns, at a moment when it was already dark, near the sandbank [Vlakke Raan]" (Parmentier 2000, p. 234). Thus, unlike the wreck of 't Vliegent Hart, the exact location of the Anna Catharina was not known after the disastrous night in 1735, yet there was an indication of where it had sunk. With this information Schiltz delimited a perimeter in which he would look for the wreck.

Friends of Schiltz brought him in touch with Robert Hickson, an entrepreneur from Ipswich who at that time was starting up a business selling magnetometers for private use. Schiltz tells vividly how Hickson advertised his products with slogans such as "find your own wreck". In 1986 he went to Ipswich to buy a MX3 Proton Magnetometer, and to take lessons how to use it. However, the considerable size of his vessel, the M.S. Philippe Cousteau (108 GRT), and the fact that it was made of steel, impeded the use of the devise. Therefore, in 1987 a new boat, made of polyester, was purchased and equipped for the purpose of finding the Anna Catharina. The boat was given the applicable name "Explorer" (P.A.B.S., F.V., "Chronologisch Rapport"). Schiltz explained how the magnetometer would record a signal at regular intervals, coinciding with the magnetic field lines detected underwater. When the intervals became shorter, and the pace of the signal became faster, this indicated a change in the magnetic field, and the detection of an anomaly.

The strategy in practice was rather straightforward. The delimited perimeter was divided into square areas, which were searched systematically with the magnetometer. If an anomaly was detected a small anchor with shot line was dropped and a dive was made to inspect the anomaly. As a former fisherman, Schiltz still had plenty of contacts in this world, and when fishermen and shrimpers alerted him about anomalies, he would focus his surveys on those. According to Schiltz the search was not a fulltime job, but rather a hobby. Nevertheless, at least twenty-three wrecks were discovered during the summer of that same year (*Ibidem*). Continuing his search in 1988, on the 3rd of August he discovered an anchor at a location indicated by shrimpers. They informed him their nets got stuck at this location, and when they lifted their nets they brought up old timber with it. The location of this anchor, however, was too far off from where the Anna Catharina would have sunk, and therefore was not further studied. The search

---

[2] In this regard, we would like to refer to the documentary "40 jaar onderwaterarcheologie, jagen op VOC-wrakken" (2002), which was made and broadcasted by the Dutch Public Broadcasting Company (NPO) and addresses these specific issues.

continued in 1989, albeit less actively, and without success of finding the Anna Catharina.

In 1990 a new proton magnetometer was bought, the MX500, a more advanced type that gave more precise results. This model is still sold by Hickson's company, Planet Electronics Ltd., today. After locating more wrecks in July of that year, a new approach was taken in August. New sources pointed to the idea the Anna Catharina could have sunk more southwards, thus indicating the perimeter of search should be moved southwards as well. From 15 August onwards the area south of the Vlakte van de Raan was surveyed intensely. 15 September, a weak signal was detected within 500m distance of the anchor discovered in 1988. This time, frames were discovered, as well as a "heavy timber construction" which, according to Schiltz, could have been the bow of a ship. 17 September another dive was made and this time a wine bottle was recovered from the silt. When, after a second dive that same day, the small anchor was lifted again, an old piece of net from a shrimper got lifted with it. A brass candlestick was found entangled in this net. Also some small pins were discovered during these dives. Excited about the finds, and about the location which corresponded to the possible location of the Anna Catharina, hopes were high the wreck was finally discovered after three years of research.

The finds were brought to Stéphane Vandenberghe, who at the time was adjunct conservator for the Gruuthusemuseum, Bruges. According to Schiltz, Vandenberge was a contact for divers and fishermen whenever they found something "interesting" in their nets or on the sea bottom. According to Vandenberghe's expertise, the candlestick and pins could be older, but the wine bottle had to be dated to the 18th century. This statement was the confirmation they needed to believe the Anna Catharina was found (Personal information Bart Schiltz).

2.1.2. Legal issues and the foundation of vzw VOC Anna Catharina

The wreck was discovered. However, this was just the beginning, now things had to be set in motion to excavate the wreck. By this time Schiltz must have had found out about Cowan's contract with the Dutch Department of Finance. With the exception of some dives for surveying the site, he stopped all diving activities on site to first arrange a contract with the Dutch State (P.A.B.S., F.V., "Chronologisch Rapport"). Since the wreck was located in Belgian territorial waters, an agreement with the Belgian responsible authorities had to be made too. A project like this had never been executed in Belgium before[3], so without precedent all necessary procedures had to be established for the first time, step by step. Therefore, together with Lino Verbeke, a lawyer acquaintance, Schiltz started to investigate what arrangements had to be made and what problems might arise.

Their first and probably biggest concern was a missing legal framework for such a project. The legal system in Belgium is rather complex. After six state reforms Belgium is now a federal state in which different responsibilities are divided over different governments. Other than the Federal government, acting on behalf of the Belgian State, the country is divided into regions (Flanders, Wallonia, Brussels-Capital) and communities (Flemish-, French- and German-speaking), all of whom have their own governments and specific responsibilities. In the early nineties, when Schiltz needed to make arrangements for his project, no law existed for the protection of archaeological patrimony. A design for such a decree[4] did exist at this time, but would only be enforced in 1993 (VCRO, 07/11/1993). Lino Verbeke, however, had already sent a copy of this preliminary design to Schiltz in 1991 (P.A.B.S., F.C.2, "De Clerck & Verbeke 18/03/1991"), so they were aware of these documents. The decree-draft would enforce a legal framework for the protection of archaeological patrimony in the Flemish Region, since archaeology was (and still is) a responsibility of the regions. The wreck, however, was discovered in the Belgian territorial waters of the North Sea, and the sea was (and still is) a federal responsibility. A law concerning archaeology or cultural heritage in the Belgian territorial sea did not exist.[5] The only law regarding salvaging goods from the sea was the Edict of Charles V, dating back to 10 December 1547 (Deweirdt 2006, p. 60). This law states any lost property recovered from the sea should be declared to the proper authorities within twenty-four hours after recovery, and handed over to these authorities within three days. If, after one year, the rightful owner does not claim his property, the finds become property of the state (P.A.B.S., F.C.1, "De Clerck & Verbeke, 06/12/1990"). Since the Dutch State claimed the ownership rights for all property of the VOC, this would mean all finds recovered from the wreck would go to the Dutch State. This is why Schiltz and Verbeke considered it important to first close a contract with the Ministry of Finance from the Netherlands before starting any salvaging activity. A contract with the Belgian authorities was already closed at this time, but for very different reasons. Soon after the discovery of the wreck,

---

[3] At present, the wreck of 't Vliegent Hart is located within Belgian borders as well. However, Cowan did not share the official location of the wreck for a long time and the concession area established by the Dutch government for finding the wreck in 1981 fell, at the time, within international waters. In 1996, when maritime borders were finally officially agreed upon between Belgium and the Netherlands, this area turned out to be lying partly in Belgian territorial waters. When Cowan finally reported the official location of the wreck, it turned out to be located partly outside the concession area and fully in Belgian territorial waters (Missiaen, Demerre and Verrijken 2012, p. 194). Because of these circumstances, and because this excavation was executed by a Dutch-British team, we believe the Zeebrugge wreck can be considered the first Belgian underwater excavation in Belgian territorial waters.

[4] A Belgian decree refers to a law proposed and enforced by regional or community parliaments from Flanders or Wallonia.

[5] A law for the protection of historical wrecks would not be proposed until 2007, and not unforced until 2014. By that time, and after Belgium's ratification of the UNESCO 2001 convention, the initial law was adapted to the protection of underwater cultural heritage in general[3].

F.V. Submergo was given permission to salvage the wreck Anna Catharina for the official reason it was cumbersome for maritime traffic in this particular area. This deal was closed with Pierre Kerckaert, who in a later stage would become involved with the project as well, on behalf of the coastal department (P.A.B.S., F.C.1, "Dienst de Kust 14/11/1990").

Persuading the Dutch government to make a deal, however, would not be easy, especially after the issues that arose with Cowan's deal. 7 November 1990 Verbeke wrote a first letter to the Dutch Ministry of Finance. In this letter he explains the wreck of the Anna Catharina has probably been discovered in Belgian territorial waters, and he asks for an arrangement in which the Dutch State hands over her ownership rights to the salvage company that located the wreck. He explicitly refers to the "'t Vliegent Hart"-case as an example for the kind of deal he wants to make (P.A.B.S., F.C.1, "De Clerck & Verbeke, 07/11/1990"). The ministry does not seem eager to discuss such a contract, and refers to the fact that the contract for the Anna Catharina has already been closed with Cowan. Nevertheless they seem intrigued and ask for proof that would indicate this wreck is indeed the Anna Catharina, and whether the organisation could guarantee a successful salvage of the wreck (P.A.B.S., F.C.1, "De Clerck & Verbeke, 22/11/1990"). Despite this apparent interest, they decide not to close a contract with Schiltz's company Submergo. The ministry explains that, at this time, Cowan's contract is already expired since he had quit searching for the Anna Catharina because he believed it had sunk in Dutch territorial waters, and therefore was protected by a new law for the protection of monuments (*Monumentenwet* 1988). Surprisingly, however, the main reason for the ministry's decision was to avoid damaging their relationship with Cowan (P.A.B.S., F.C.1, "De Clerck & Verbeke, 25/01/1991").

Yet, Schiltz and Verbeke persevere and they manage to arrange a meeting about a month later to discuss a salvage contract nonetheless. Correspondence between Schiltz and Verbeke demonstrates the efforts to prepare a solid strategy to convince the ministry. There are several focal points among their arguments, such as the location of the wreck in Belgian territorial waters[6] and how to circumnavigate the impediment of salvage contracts by the changed Dutch monuments law. Also, the announced construction of a pipeline in the proximity of the wreck is brought up as a possible threat to the site. The most notable idea, however, is the proposal by Verbeke to set up a non-profit organisation that would maintain the cultural historical interests of the project and guarantee the adequate salvage of wreck and cargo to preserve this heritage (P.A.B.S., F.C.1, "De Clerck & Verbeke, 20/02/1991"). 13 March 1991 the negotiations are put on hold at once by the Ministry of Finance, when an illegal sale of thirteen ducats was discovered in Antwerp.

According to experts these ducats possibly originated from the Anna Catharina or 't Vliegent Hart. Verbeke countered this statement by pointing out salvage work hadn't started yet and all of the wreck was still covered in silt. He informed the ministry he had invited underwater archaeologist Thijs Maarleveld to attend a meeting organised by Submergo to prepare a survey on the wreck-site. Maarleveld had attended the meeting between Schiltz, Verbeke, and the Ministry of Finance as a representative for the department of underwater archaeology from the Ministry of Welfare, Health and Culture (Dutch: *Ministerie van Welzijn, Volksgezondheid en Cultuur*, or *WVC*). Maarleveld was also invited to dive the wreck to make sure it was indeed untouched (P.A.B.S., F.C.1, "De Clerck & Verbeke, 14/03/1991"). Although no dive was made, Maarleveld did visit Submergo 16 March 1991, together with colleague Arent Vos and maritime archaeologist Jerzy Gawronski. Vos (Personal information) recalls how this visit could not convince him this wreck was the Anna Catharina. He was not only doubtful because of the location of the wreck, but also because of the few presented finds that were recovered from the wreck at that time. These could not convince him this was an 18th Dutch East Indiaman. Nevertheless, even if the wreck was older, it could mean an interesting contribution to the field of maritime archaeology. By this time, Jan Parmentier had joined the project as well. He was Historian at the University of Ghent, and, like Arent Vos, was giving guest lectures at the University of Leiden. It was there where he approached Vos and informed him about the "Anna Catharina"-project, asking if Vos would be interested in joining this project with his expertise in underwater archaeology. Vos explains how such a decision was not easy to make, especially in the light of problematic projects related to VOC-wrecks such as 't Vliegent Hart, but also the Amsterdam, Witte Leeuw, Hollandia, etc. In such projects academics were asked by salvage companies to join the project and to lead the scientific activities, while in fact their control would be rather limited. Nevertheless their names would be linked to these projects, creating a scientific backbone for the project as such, but often affecting or threatening the scientific credibility of the academic. Such experiences caused restraint for Vos to participate in the "Anna Catharina"-project. Yet, when Maarleveld, Vos and Gawronski visited Submergo, they explained the conditions for an official cooperation with the department of underwater archaeology and the involvement of their researchers. In addition to a scientific approach towards documentation, consultation and reporting, substantive responsibility for the involved underwater archaeologist was an important prerequisite.

One week after this visit, 23 March 1991, the non-profit organisation (Dutch: *Vereniging Zonder Winstoogmerk*, or *vzw*), brought up by Verbeke, was realized. Under the name '*vzw VOC Anna Catharina*', ten founding members were brought together. With their different backgrounds

---

[6]. After the expansion of the national territorial waters by the Netherlands in 1985 and Belgium in 1988, there was a disputed area. Schiltz and Verbeke were anticipating the Dutch government would see this as a reason to claim the wreck if it would be located here. However, the wreck was located outside the disputed area and unquestionably inside Belgian territorial waters.

and different expertise, they would all have specific responsibilities within the organisation. Bart Schiltz, with his company F.V. Submergo, would be responsible for the actual work on site. André Huyghe and Pierre Kerckaert were approached as officials working for the Belgian customs and the port authority in Zeebrugge, respectively. In their positions they could help with the protection of the wreck, declaration of the salvaged goods, etc. Jan Parmentier was elected president of the foundation and was responsible for the historical research. Stéphane Vandenberghe, conservator, would initially be responsible for the conservation of the objects and would be supported in this task by Martin Van Dromme, a chemist. Later correspondence seems to indicate this task would in the end be mainly Van Dromme's responsibility, while Vandenberghe would rather focus on the study of the finds and their display in exhibitions. Lino Verbeke was responsible for handling the legal procedures in place and to give legal advice. Finally, three businessmen were involved as well; Marie-Jean Pieters, her husband Ignace Becaus, and Mark Beckaert, who were all related to the fish auction in Zeebrugge (P.A.B.S., F.V., "Oprichting VZW "VOC Anna Catharina"", "verslag 22/04/1991").

The association's goal, clarified in the official foundation agreement, was to contribute to the salvage of the wreck and cargo of the VOC wreck Anna Catharina, preserving it from destruction and safeguarding its cultural heritage, and to promote the interest for the VOC in general and the Anna Catharina in particular (P.A.B.S., F.V., "Oprichting VZW "VOC Anna Catharina"").

Three days after this foundation, a letter was sent to the Dutch Ministry of Finance to inform them about this development (P.A.B.S., F.C.1, "De Clerck & Verbeke 26/03/1991"). One month later, 27 May 1991, a letter returns from the ministry, this time to approve the possibility of a contract. According to this letter, the reasons for the ministry's changed position were mainly the fact Cowan's interests would not be harmed and the possible damage threatening the site. Also, the foundation of a non-profit organisation in regard to the preservation of this cultural heritage, as well as the possible involvement, when required, of Maarleveld on behalf of the WVC, were of influence in their decision (P.A.B.S., F.C.1, "Ministerie van Financiën 27/05/1991"). The Ministry of Finance did propose a contract in which Submergo would have to give 25% of the salvaged goods to the Dutch State. Although the members of *vzw VOC Anna Catharina* in response to this proposal tried to negotiate a contract like Cowan in which they would have to donate only 10% of the goods (P.A.B.S., F.V., "verslag 10/08/1991), they would agree with the ministry's condition in the end. This way, 16 September 1991 a contract was closed, one year after the actual discovery of the wreck, between *vzw VOC Anna Catharina*, F.V. Submergo and the Dutch State. Included in the contract was the obligation to ensure any activity on the wreck would be carried out in the frame of scientific archaeological research. Also, scientific reports and scientific motivation for further research had to be presented on an annual basis. The collection of finds had to be conserved and documented adequately and kept together as much as possible. All of this had to happen on a location accessible for other scientists and, if possible, open to the public (P.A.B.S., F.C.2, "Bergingscontract", article 3).

2.1.3. The Zeebrugge wreck and the foundation of vzw Maritieme Archeologie

It is not entirely clear when the members of *vzw VOC Anna Catharina* started noticing the recovered finds did not belong to the Anna Catharina, nor when they fully realized the wreck they were dealing with was actually a much older ship. This realisation would have important consequences. According to the contract with the Dutch State, the Anna Catharina had to be discovered before 1 February 1994. If the discovered wreck would not be the Anna Catharina, the contract would be ended immediately (P.A.B.S., F.C.2, "Salvage Contract", article 11). This would mean they had no ownership rights for the recovered objects anymore. If the contract would come to an end, the only law in place would be the Edict of Charles V. In this scenario, the finds had to be handed over within three days to the local authorities and they would become property of the Belgian State if they were not claimed by the rightful owner within one year. This must have caused some discomfort for the members of *vzw VOC Anna Catharina*. Not only would they lose their ownership rights to the salvaged goods, but many of the finds were also subject to a long-term conservation program and these would incur damage if handed over like this.

A first clear indication of this realisation can be found in a letter the association wrote to the Belgian Ministry of Finance 3 May 1993. This letter mentions the study of certain finds did indicate a possible different origin than the Anna Catharina, although these finds could be personal belongings of the crew too. They also speak of the foundation of a new non-profit organisation, called *vzw Maritieme Archeologie*, which has a broader scope than the previous association. Furthermore the question is raised in this letter, whether, for the purpose of further research and adequate conservation, with the intention to exhibit these objects in a museum, the possibility of a contract similar to the one closed with the Dutch State would be negotiable (P.A.B.S., F.C.2 "VZW VOC Anna Catharina 05/05/1993").

The foundation of this new association, *vzw Maritieme Archeologie*, probably took place in May 1993 (P.A.B.S., F.C.2 "VZW VOC Anna Catharina 30/03/1993). However, a draft of its foundation agreement seems to indicate arrangements were already made in 1992 (P.A.B.S., F.V. "Oprichting VZW Maritieme Archeologie", article 17).

An exhibition and press conference were organised 15 May 1993, to present the finds recovered from the wreck to the public. Arent Vos attended this event and noticed, again, but with more certainty this time, these finds could not originate from a VOC-wreck but probably belonged to an older ship. He also recalls making this suggestion to members of *vzw Maritieme Archeologie*, and how they fully agreed with him. They informed him fairly, however, that for reasons of publicity and sponsorship they decided not to spread this news yet (Personal information Arent Vos). The Dutch Department of underwater archaeology indicated in their 1992 annual report that the wreck was not the Anna Catharina, yet this report was written in 1993 (Maarleveld 1993, p. 4). Nevertheless, in their report of 1993 they mention the cooperation with "*vzw Anna Catharina*" continued that year (Maarleveld 1994, p. 3). In 1994 a meeting with the Dutch Ministry of Finance was planned, related to the contract and the payment of their 25% share (P.A.B.S., F.C.2, "Ambassade van het Koninkrijk der Nederlanden, 29/03/1994"). It is unclear what the outcome of this meeting was, but it seems unlikely they were not aware by this time the ship was not the Anna Catharina. The Department of underwater archaeology does not mention any cooperation in 1994 anymore (Maarleveld 1995a).

An agreement, however, was reached with the local authorities operating on behalf of the Belgian Ministry of Finance. For the purpose of further study and conservation of the finds recovered from what was now called the Zeebrugge wreck, the finds were transferred, as property, to *vzw Maritieme Archeologie*. The only condition for this transfer was the payment of the value-added taxes for all objects. In addition to this arrangement the local authorities advised to estimate the total value of the recovered collection beneath 1.000.000 Belgian francs, an amount roughly comparable to 25.000 euros, since for a higher amount much more administration was needed and the decision would not be theirs to make anymore. The estimation was made by members of *vzw Maritieme Archeologie* itself, making sure to stay beneath this amount. In addition to this arrangement, an oral agreement was made that none of the objects would be sold (Personal information Bart Schiltz). At this point, salvage work had started already.

2.2. Location, environment and current state of the wreck

2.2.1. Location

It is known that the Zeebrugge shipwreck is located about four nautical miles off the Belgian coast, south of the sandbank "Vlakte van de Raan". Yet, the exact location of the wreck has been kept secret for quite some time. This was done, according to Schiltz, to avoid treasure-hunters looting the wreck. Schiltz argues such interest of treasure-hunters was demonstrated when a hammer was discovered on site, not belonging to the actual dive-team. Nowadays, however, the exact location of the wreck can be found on the online "wreck database", an initiative from the Flemish hydrographical service, where the Zeebrugge wreck is included as "Anna Catharina" still (Vlaamse Hydrografie (no date)). For this research, coordinates of the wreck's location were also provided by Bart Schiltz, and other information related to the location could be retrieved from the documents provided by Schiltz. The comparison of these coordinates, however, is not unproblematic, since their locations differ as far as 220m. Because of the specific environment of the wreck (*cf. Infra*) such a deviation could have consequences for our understanding of the current state of the wreck. Therefore, we will briefly discuss the different coordinates and their relation to one another.

The information at our disposal are the coordinates from the wreck database, the coordinates personally provided by Bart Schiltz, and several sets of coordinates from Schiltz' archive (*Table 1*). Most directly referring to the archaeological area is the proposal of a delimited work area, which was sent to the local authorities in February 1991 (P.A.B.S. C1, "Submergo 05/02/1991"). This area is surrounded by four anchored buoys, marked with a cardinal buoy (1) and indicates the location of the wreck as point "alpha" (A). Another map in this folder refers to the same point, but with less accuracy (B) (P.A.B.S. C1, "Map 26/06/1991"). Another set of coordinates is mentioned in an early dive report. This coordinates refer to the actual location of the cardinal buoy (2), which is supposed to be located about 80m east of the wreck site (P.A.B.S. D.R., "22/03/1991"; "27/03/1991"). The coordinates given to us by Schiltz were not present among those in the documents he provided, and deviate from them as well (C). In June 1991, the local authorities are contacted again to inform them the actual excavation will start now, yet the coordinates referring to the wreck are different than the ones mentioned in February (D) (P.A.B.S., F.C.1, "Submergo 18/06/1991"). Finally, there is the location referred to on the wreck-database (E). Another set of coordinates we found refers to a lightbuoy, again for beaconing the site (3) (P.A.B.S., F.C.1, "MVG 11/09/1991"). When we plot these different sets of coordinates on a map, we can see the actual locations are widespread, with distances between them up to 220m (*Fig. 3*). A possible explanation could be the fact the wreck-site is rather scattered and covers a wider area. Also the limited accuracy of the used magnetometer could explain small deviations. However, the present deviations exceed the main archaeological concentration of the site, as well as the limited accuracy of the magnetometer.

A more plausible explanation can be given by examining the spatial reference system used for each coordinate. In 1991 the system commonly used by divers in Belgium was ED50, while today maritime projects more often use WGS84 (Missiaen 2010, p. 1). If we adjust the ED50 coordinates to WGS84, they appear more southwards and the locations correspond a little more to one another (*Fig. 4*). According to Schiltz, location C is most probably in WGS84, which indeed makes it a better fit with the other coordinates. However, he is not entirely

The Zeebrugge Shipwreck

Table 1. Within the frame of this research collected coordinates for the Zeebrugge wreck.

Location		Refers to	Source	Latitude	Longitude	Projection
A	★	Wreck?	P.A.B.S. - C1 "work area"	51°24'55.409"	03°12'45.063"	ED50
1	●	Cardinal Buoy	P.A.B.S. - C1 "work area"	51°24'55.402"	03°12'48.686"	ED50
-	○	Buoy	P.A.B.S. - C1 "work area"	51°24'56.223"	03°12'42.478"	ED50
-	○	Buoy	P.A.B.S. - C1 "work area"	51°24'56.216"	03°12'46.102"	ED50
-	○	Buoy	P.A.B.S. - C1 "work area"	51°24'54.598"	03°12'46.094"	ED50
-	○	Buoy	P.A.B.S. - C1 "work area"	51°24'54.604"	03°12'42.471"	ED50
-	⚓	Anchor	P.A.B.S. - C1 "work area"	51°24'56.225"	03°12'41.443"	ED50
-	⚓	Anchor	P.A.B.S. - C1 "work area"	51°24'56.215"	03°12'46.671"	ED50
-	⚓	Anchor	P.A.B.S. - C1 "work area"	51°24'54.596"	03°12'47.130"	ED50
-	⚓	Anchor	P.A.B.S. - C1 "work area"	51°24'54.606"	03°12'41.436"	ED50
B	★	Wreck?	P.A.B.S. - C1 "map"	51°24'55"	03°12'45"	ED50
C	★	Wreck?	Personal information Bart Schiltz	51°24.88'	03°12.66'	WGS84 (?)
D	★	Wreck?	P.A.B.S. - C1 "Submergo 18/06/1991"	51°24'57"	03°12'40"	ED50
E	★	Wreck?	Wreck Database	51°24.884'	03°12.824'	WGS84
2	●	Cardinal Buoy	P.A.B.S. - D.R. "17/03/1991"	51°24.90'	03°12.83'	ED50
F	★	Wreck?	Derived from location 2	51°24'51.115"	03°12'45.7"	WGS84
3	●	Light Buoy	P.A.B.S. - C2 "MVG 11/09/1991"	51°24.95'	03°12.94'	ED50 (?)
G	★	Wreck?	P.A.B.S. - C2 "Submergo 25/05/1992"	51°23.98'	03°10.42'	WGS84

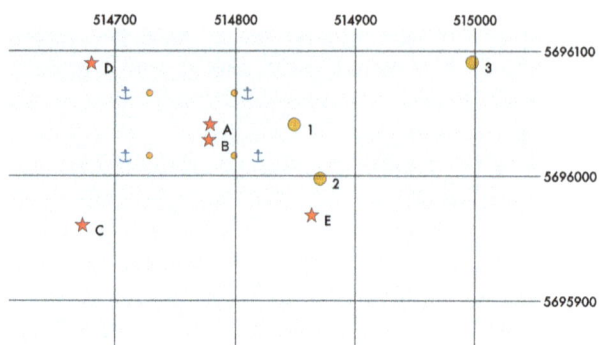

Figure 3. Plotted wreck locations.

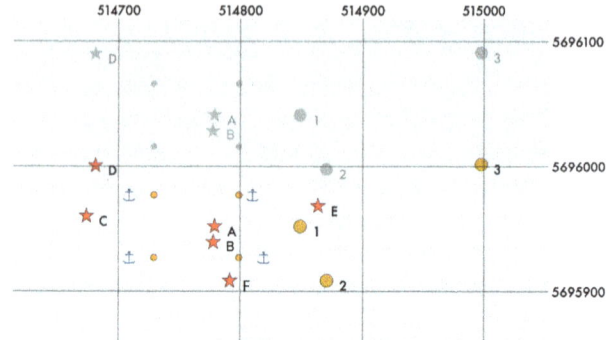

Figure 4. Plotted wreck locations after adjustments. The 'original' locations are visible in a lighter grey colour.

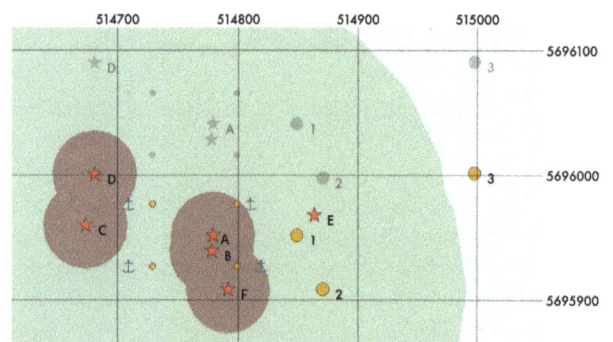

Figure 5. Buffers for archaeological potential of the different wreck locations.

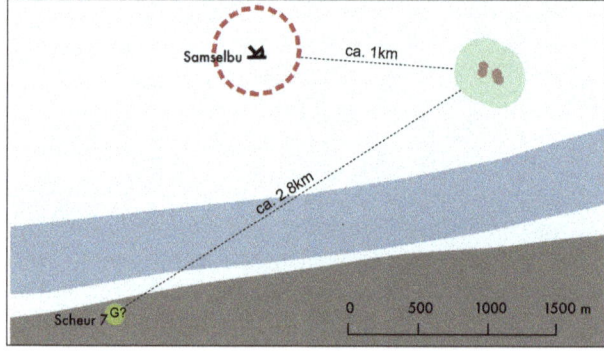

Figure 6. Locations that have been described as being in the proximity of the Zeebrugge wreck.

sure of this, meaning the site could possibly be located even more southwards. This would be the case if we derive the wreck's location from the cardinal buoy (F) (*i.e.* 80m west of location 2). The location provided by the wreck database does deviate notably from the other coordinates, with a location north of the cardinal buoy. According to information on their website, this location was discovered by the Flemish Hydrographical Service (Vlaamse Hydrografie (no date)). They also mistakenly refer to the wreck as Anna Catharina. It seems plausible the survey carried out by the Hydrographical service (in 1994) was based upon the location of the cardinal buoy and does refer to an anomaly detected in this area. This anomaly may or may not belong to the wreck; to our knowledge this has not been verified by means of a dive survey.

But, even if we would ignore location E because of its deviation, the deviation between the other coordinates stays remarkably high as well, with up to 145m between location D and F. With an archaeological area spread over a distance of about 70m, and a core archaeological concentration even smaller (*cf. infra*), not all points can be part of the actual site. However, at least one find was recovered 200m away from the main site area (Personal information Bart Schiltz). This indicates the archaeological remains are dispersed indeed. Based upon this information we created two buffer zones for each possible wreck location. The first buffer has a 70m diameter, corresponding to the extent of the site based upon dive surveys (*cf. infra*) The second buffer is wider and covers a radius of 200m, based upon the maximum known dispersal of objects from the site (*Fig. 5*).

In 1992, local authorities were informed the archaeological project would be partly moved to the area of buoy "Scheur 7", stating "an important part of the wreck was discovered in this area" (P.A.B.S. C2, "Submergo 25/05/1992"). Yet, even including the 200m-radius perimeter around the actual site-area and with a 75m-radius perimeter around "Scheur 7", the distance between both places is approximately 2.8km. Since the dive reports for this period are lacking, we do not know what exactly was discovered here and whether it actually was part of the same wreck.[7] Finally, Schiltz mentioned a warship was located about 300m from the wreck. The closest recorded warship is the WWII wreck SS Samselbu. This wreck is mentioned by Termote (2009, p. 280) as well. He describes how the Zeebrugge wreck was discovered close to the eastern buoy that marks the wreck of the SS Samselbu. But he then refers to the same coordinates as the wreck database for the location of the Zeebrugge wreck; a location over 1km away from the location of the SS Samselbu. Even with a 300m-radius perimeter this ship is located about 1km away from the other coordinates. When we plot all this data, it gives a rather dispersed view of the wreck site (*Fig. 6*). There is only the question of whether the site was indeed so dispersed. For the purpose of this research we will, in this thesis, focus only on the assembled buffers around the original location.

2.2.2. Environment and current state

The environment of the Zeebrugge wreck proved to have advantages and disadvantages for its preservation through the years. Due to the wreck's proximity to the Scheldt estuary, there are strong currents and a huge transportation of sediments. This transportation does not only impede underwater visibility (often close to none), but also is cause to a changing underwater landscape covering and uncovering parts of the site on a regular basis (Parmentier 2000, p. 235; P.A.B.S. D.R.). During one tide up to 60cm of sand can be moved (P.A.B.S., F.V., "verslag 18/05/1991"). Although these conditions make it a difficult environment in which to work, they also succeeded in keeping the wreck well-hidden from potential looters. The upper layer of the seabed in the area of the Zeebrugge wreck is composed of silty sand (*Fig. 7*). Underneath this silt a harder, clay-like soil is present (Personal information Bart Schiltz). This clay is probably of Pleistocene origin (*cf. infra*). The archaeological remains did not penetrate this clay layer and were only covered by silt. This must have created a natural protection for the archaeological remains, and made these remains relatively accessible (P.A.B.S., F.V., "verslag 15/06/1991").

In 1991 the wreck was located along the fairway "Scheur", which creates a passageway between the Scheldt estuary and the North Sea along the several sandbanks and shallow waters in this area. Since the 1960's this fairway has been deepened several times. This has influenced the underwater landscape considerably, and continues to do so. While in 1962 the Zeebrugge wreck was located on the plane seabed (*Fig. 8*), by 1994 this seabed had transformed into a slope and the area where the wreck was located had deepened slightly (*Fig. 9*). According to Schiltz most of the site is probably destroyed by now because of the widening of the fairway through the years.[8] It is uncertain to what extent the site still may exist, yet we believe the continuous dredging work related to the deepening of the fairway does cause a threat to the site

---

[7] We contacted Schiltz to ask about this discovery, with the specific questions why they believed a part of the same wreck was discovered, and whether excavation reports of this period are available to verify what was discovered. Schiltz only informed us the wreck turned out to be a different, younger wreck.

[8] If the current location and dimensions of the present fairway could be ascertained, including if and how the dimensions and/or the location have changed over the last 25 years, then it might be possible to estimate the current state of the Zeebrugge wreck and its potential. To this end, we contacted provincial, regional, and federal authorities, yet none of the contacted institutions could inform us about the actual situation and all referred to one another for further information. We know the fairways are a responsibility of the Flemish region and should be managed by the division 'Maritieme Toegang' from the department 'Mobiliteit en Openbare Werken' (Van den Eynde et al. 2015, p. 102). Yet, they did not claim responsibility either and referred to the federal department of 'Mobiliteit en Vervoer' for further information. This department in turn referred back to 'Maritieme Toegang', causing a stalemate.

The Zeebrugge Shipwreck

indeed, now or in the future. Also fishing activity with trawlers impacts the seabed in this area. Considering the current Belgian legislation in regards to underwater heritage, and the Belgian ratification of the UNESCO 2001 Convention, it seems opportune to carry out further surveys in the near future to determine the present archaeological potential of this area in order to allow for protection and/or further excavation of any site remains if desirable. The Zeepipe, which was brought up as a threat while negotiating the salvage contract, did not, in the end, have any influence on the area under discussion (*Fig. 10*).

2.3. Fieldwork

2.3.1. Surveys

The official excavation of the Zeebrugge wreck started mid-July 1991. Prior to the excavation some surveys were executed by Submergo to get a better understanding of the environment and extent of the site. There seem to be no official reports of these surveys, yet some information on this matter is listed in early meeting reports. In February 1991, some first dive surveys were carried out. During one of these dives, sedimentation was lifted in which several object were discovered. Also, attempts were made to lift

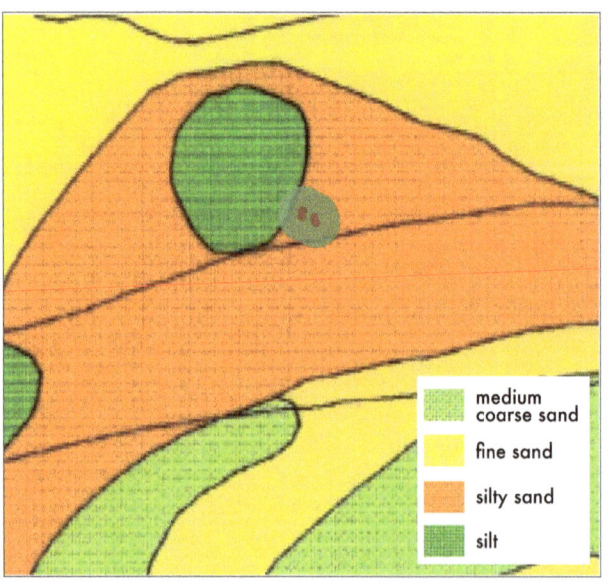

Figure 7. Sediments around the Zeebrugge wreck.

Figure 8. Bathymetrical data 1962.

Figure 9. Bathymetrical data 1994.

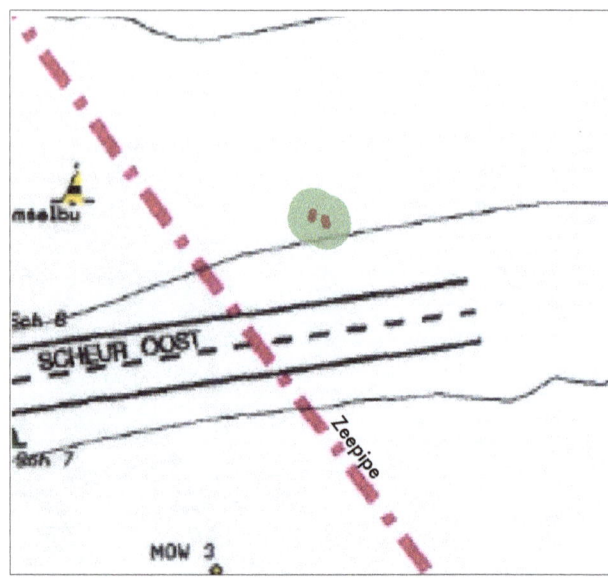

Figure 10. Location Zeepipe compared to location Zeebrugge wreck.

some timber pieces from the site for further analysis, but they were too firmly embedded in the sediment to lift at that point (P.A.B.S., F.V., "Chronologisch rapport"). On 15 March, a second and more profound survey started and continued until the actual excavation began. Although here again official survey reports are lacking, there are dive reports available from this period onwards (P.A.B.S. D.R., "15/03/1991" – "07/06/1991"). Despite being rather scant, these reports give insight into the worked methodology and allow us to get a rough impression of the site.

To start this survey, first a reference point was marked with a buoy. This point, referred to as reference point A, may be corresponding to location F, 80m west of the cardinal buoy (cf. supra). Yet, notes in the reports cannot confirm this conclusively. In preparation of the excavation, three more reference points (B, C, D) were appointed. Point A, however, would be the centre of focus, given its location within a high archaeological concentration. Further organisation of the site would also be based on Point A, and it would be the main reference point during the dive surveys as well.

The main methods for surveying the site were compass swimming and circular searches. In the dive reports, one refers to a heading and a distance compared to point A, and what is located there (e.g. "36m from A (75°): beam and possible frame"). The surveyed areas were searched by eye, touch, and in some cases by means of a pricker to search for objects or structures covered by sand. Loose finds were lifted during the surveys, and bigger finds such as timber, stones, or heavy lumps of concretion were referred to in the dive reports. Based upon this data we were able to create an impression of the site at this point (Fig. 11). However, this site plan should be viewed with certain restraint. First of all, the entire area has not been surveyed at this point. In some cases the reports do refer to areas without finds, but most often they only mention the location where finds were present. This way, the site plan does inform us about where to expect archaeological remains, but it does not (or to a lesser extent) tell us where there are no remains. Additionally, the reports do refer to a general location rather than specific coordinates. For instance, in some cases the heading and distance to a certain object was corrected in a later report, which indicates currents and poor visibility probably did influence the accuracy from time to time. Therefore, even when locations are given, the position on the map could deviate from the actual position. Also, the exact angle between points C and D is not given in the reports; only a sketch indicates their positions making the exact location of D, and objects along this line, uncertain. Finally, the reports are based upon the personal, first impression of the diver underwater. This could lead to misunderstandings. We do know, for example, that some of the cannon were first reported as ship timber and possible masts (probably misled by wooden carriages of the cannon and the general strong concretion). Only later in the project it would become clear these objects were actually cannon, while early sketches do refer to them as masts. These examples indicate caution should be used with the interpretation of this survey plan.

Nevertheless, the plan does give us a basic understanding of the site and the dispersal of the archaeological remains. Although we do not know to what extent exactly, we can see a considerable amount of ship timber was still present in 1991. Also, a considerable amount of stones was present. The dive reports interpret these stones as ballast stones, which seems a reasonable explanation. The stones are concentrated in one specific area and could be considered anomalies in this silt environment. The site plan also indicates the wreck is scattered and the archaeological remains are spread over a considerable area. It is difficult to say whether this dispersal is due to the wrecking process or because of later impact on the site. The net of a shrimper that was recovered when the site was first discovered, along with some heavily dented metalware, do indicate at least some later impact. The fact that stones are concentrated south while most finds were recovered north of the stones leads to the hypothesis the wreck may have been oriented east to west and the hull tilted over in a northern direction.

In addition to dive surveys, remote sensing was also applied to survey the site, by means of side scan sonar and magnetometer. The survey with side scan sonar, which was provided by Kerckaert, was executed over an area of 500m x 500m. A printed role of (part of?) these images was at our disposal, but there were no anomalies present on this print (P.A.B.S., S.S.I.). Nevertheless, the original scan should have shown a concentration of finds spread over an area of 70m^2. Further surveys with a magnetometer would indicate metal objects were present as far as 120m from this concentration (Parmentier 2011, p. 32). As said before, at least one object was discovered at a 200m distance from the site. This object, a mortar, was discovered in 1997 when Schiltz returned to the site after the official excavations were finished.

Later on, other surveys were carried out by different operators. We already mentioned the survey of the Flemish Hydrographical Service in 1994, during which anomalies were detected, yet north of the cardinal buoy. An intense survey with different techniques was carried out in 2010, by the Flanders Heritage Agency and the Renard Centre of Marine Geology (a research unit from the University of Ghent, Belgium), in the frame of the Interreg-IV project "Archaeological Atlas of the 2 Seas". Other than side scan sonar, this time also multibeam and seismic measurements were made. Side scan images were made in an area of about 1.2 x 1.2km, around the location provided by the Flemish Hydrographical Service (location E). Multibeam measurements were made in an area of 220 x 250m around the same position (Fig. 12). Several targets were located, yet none of them could be attributed to a wreck conclusively and further dive surveys are necessary in order to find out what these anomalies are (Missiaen 2010, p. 1-5). It should be said, however, that among these anomalies, there is only one concentration where several targets are grouped

The Zeebrugge Shipwreck

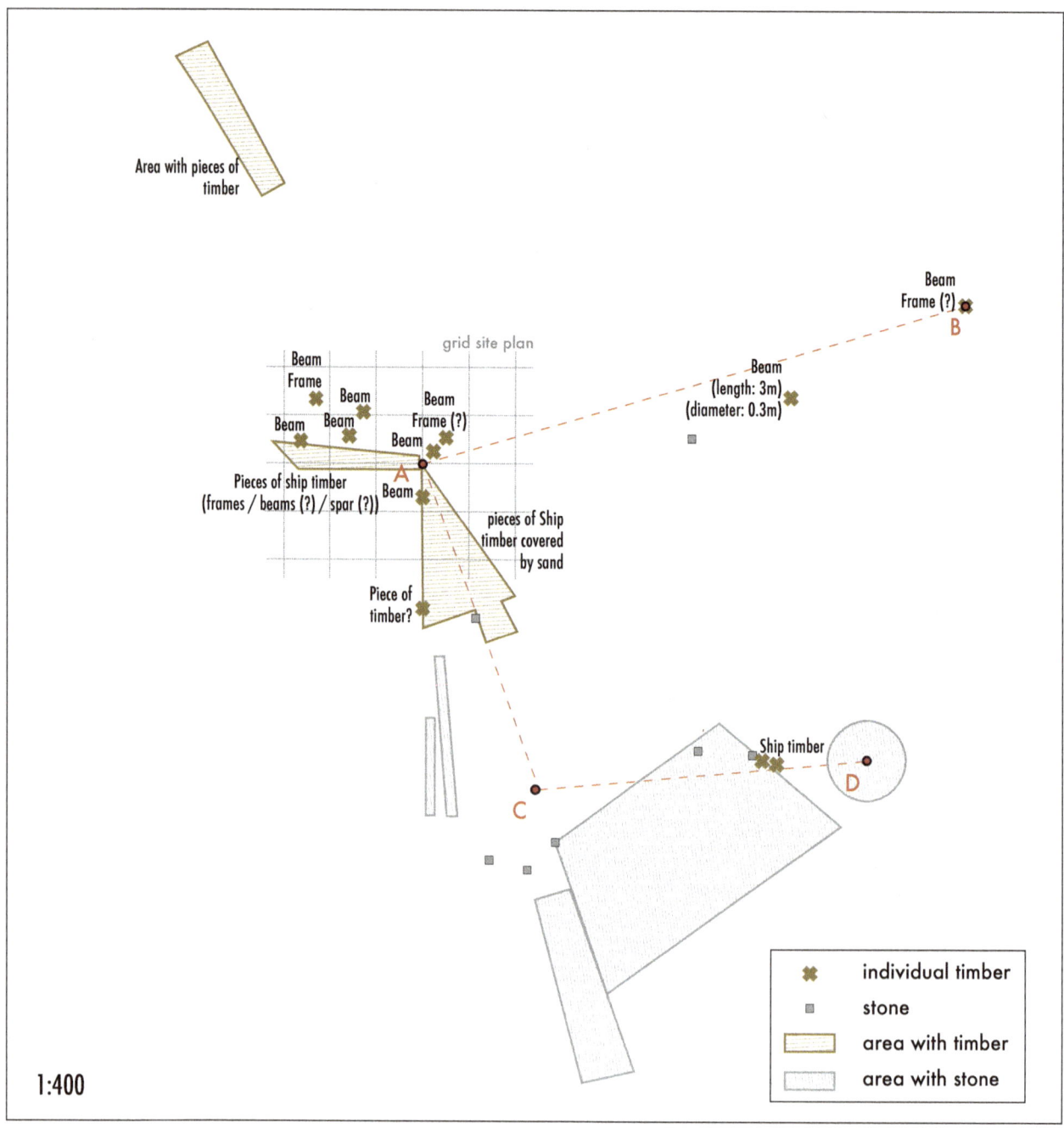

Figure 11. Impression of the site based upon the 1991 dive survey reports.

together, which according to Missiaen may indicate the presence of wreck remains. When we plot these targets on the possible wreck locations we proposed earlier, there is a clear correspondence between this concentration and the 70m-buffer of locations C and D (*Fig. 13*). Missiaen argues target 499 could be one bigger object, or several smaller objects next to one another, while target 500 would be a "long object" (*Idem*, p. 4). It would be interesting to verify what these objects actually are by means of a dive survey. Finally, anomalies were detected by means of multibeam "in the proximity of the Zeebrugge wreck" in 2013 (Maritieme Archeologie 2015). We do not know the exact location of these anomalies, nor were they conclusively identified as wreck remains. We do know, however, further surveys for the identification of wreck remains from the Zeebrugge wreck are planned in the (near) future by the Flanders Heritage Agency (Personal information Marnix Pieters).

2.3.2. Excavation

The excavation of the Zeebrugge site was spread over four field seasons (1991, 1992, 1993 and 1994). To organise the actual excavation of the site, the archaeological area was divided in four parts with reference point A as centre. Each of the four parts was provided with a grid of 3 x 3m squares. According to meeting reports and correspondence, the official excavation was planned to start 15 or 16 June 1991 and first dive reports do appear from 17 June onwards. Yet, the dive reports as such do not indicate a clear difference in approach between survey and excavation. The removal

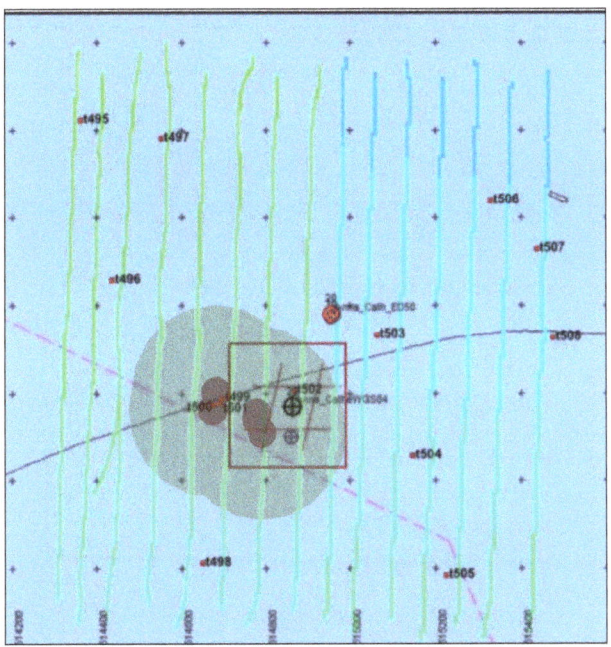

Figure 12. The red square delimits the area where the multibeam survey was executed.

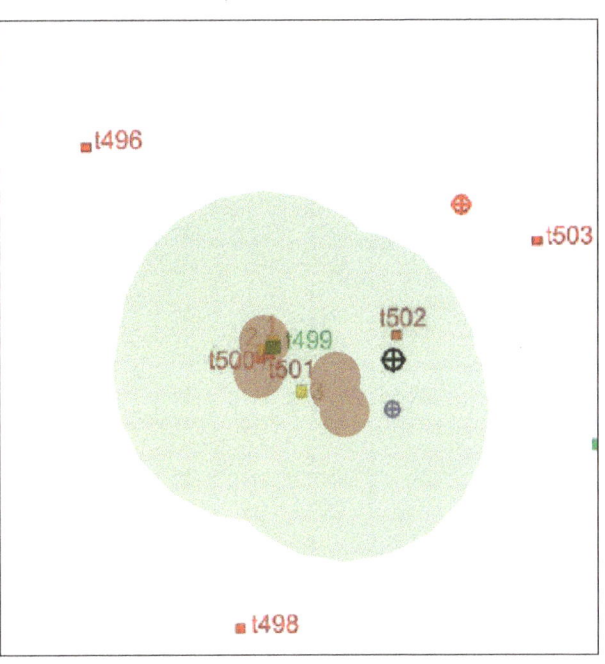

Figure 13. Correspondence between detected concentration and proposed wreck locations.

of silt and lifting of big, concreted lumps of archaeological material had already started before this date and it appears the process just gradually continued. Nevertheless, from this moment on weekly reports appear, giving updates about the salvage work for every corresponding week. Also, the reports are standardised with references to the section(s) worked, as well as which tools were used (*Fig. 14*).

Often this tool is a so-called "jet pump", a system developed by Schiltz and his colleagues, similar to a water dredge. The jet pump was desirable since it allowed for the gentle and controlled removal of silt. Its tube was outfitted with a grid to catch small, loose finds. The jet pump was chosen over the airlift, which at this depth had a stronger, more aggressive suction and therefore was more difficult to control. The airlift was used as well, but less frequently, to search the more dense, clay-like sediment underneath the silt for traces of the wreck (Personal information Bart Schiltz). An actual water jet was used next to the jet pump during excavation. In this case the jet would blow away silt, which was then carried away by the current. The system was developed in such a way the diver could easily switch between jet pump and water jet. Also a metal detector was used from time to time to recover finds from the silt. Although initially the jet pump was the tool of choice, the use of the metal detector gradually replaced it by the end of the first field season.

Finds recovered from the site were either lifted manually or with lifting bags. Once out of the water, every find was photographed, plotted on the site plan and given a unique reference number consisting of the date it was lifted and a follow number for that day (*i.e.* DDMMYY/xx). The photographs and list of registered finds were not

at our disposal for this research. Although finds are often mentioned in the dive reports as well, they do not have a reference number here and the location is only referred to by naming the grid from which it was recovered. Since these grids are 3 x 3m we cannot retrieve the exact location from this data. For the further treatment of the objects once they were out of the water, a hand-out with some basic rules for temporary preservation was put together by Martin Van Dromme. This document, called "first aid after excavation", was based upon Pearson's "Conservation of Marine Archaeological Objects" (1987) (P.A.B.S., F.V., "verslag 15/06/1991", "verslag 27/07/1991"; Personal information Bart Schiltz).

The dive reports and weekly reports can give us an idea of the worked methodology and can create an impression of the site, but do not provide a structural overview of the site. This is due to different reasons. First of all the amount of detail in each report depends strongly on the individual diver/writer. While some of them only mention the grid worked in and the objects recovered (e.g. "worked in section II A2, recovered stone, round shot, candlestick"), others try to add more detail to the reports. In more elaborate reports, one does refer to working conditions (visibility, current), location of objects in relation to one another, or even dimensions of objects. A systematic description of the underwater situation is lacking, however. The first few months this is, to a certain limit, compensated by sketched site plans. These are often to scale and do give a good indication of the situation at this point. However, the last sketch added to the reports dates from 6 August 1991, while the excavation season did not end until October, and three further seasons were planned. Site plans from later on probably do exist. Week reports 15, 16 and 17 (October 1991) do mention the site is systematically searched by

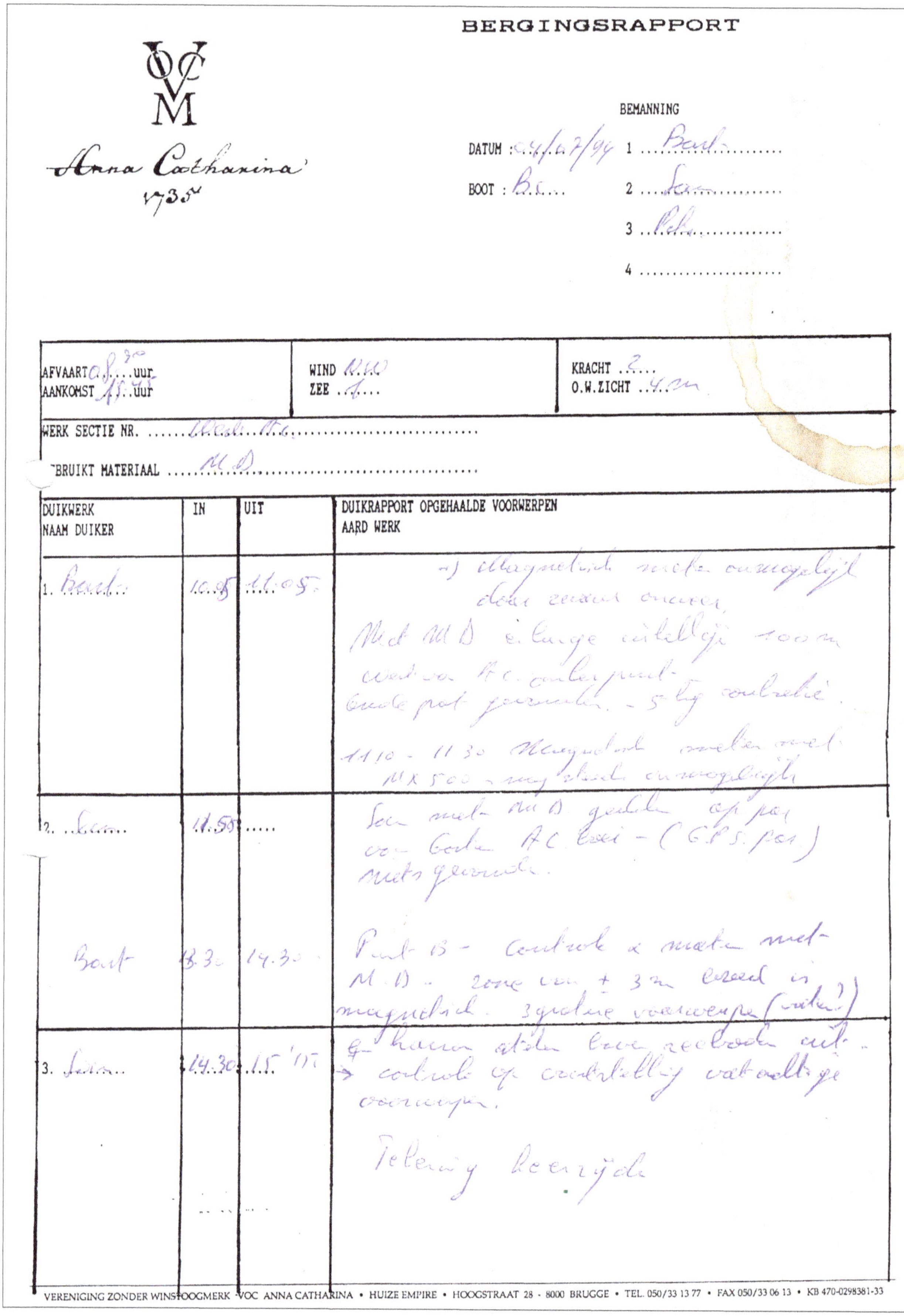
BERGINGSRAPPORT

VOC

Anna Catharina 1735

BEMANNING

DATUM : 04/07/94 1 ......Bart......

BOOT : B.C.... 2 ......Sen......

3 ......Pels......

4 ....

AFVAART 08.30 uur AANKOMST 15.45 uur	WIND N.W. ZEE ..1....	KRACHT ..2.... O.W.ZICHT ..4 m

WERK SECTIE NR. ....

..BRUIKT MATERIAAL ......M.D.........................

DUIKWERK NAAM DUIKER	IN	UIT	DUIKRAPPORT OPGEHAALDE VOORWERPEN AARD WERK
1. Bart	10.05	11.05	
2. Sen	11.55	.....	
Bart	13.30	14.30	
3. Sen	14.30	15.15	

VERENIGING ZONDER WINSTOOGMERK · VOC ANNA CATHARINA · HUIZE EMPIRE · HOOGSTRAAT 28 · 8000 BRUGGE · TEL. 050/33 13 77 · FAX 050/33 06 13 · KB 470-0298381-33

Figure 14. Example of a dive report from the 1994 field season. We can see that at this point, the site still is referred to as 'A.C.' (*i.e.* Anna Catharina). The exact work section is not specified, the earlier reports are more accurate in this regard. The material or method used is referred to as 'M.D.' (*i.e.* metal detector). The report itself specifies the kind of work executed during the dive and mentions some of the recovered objects. Without context, however, the report is difficult to interpret.

Site and Research

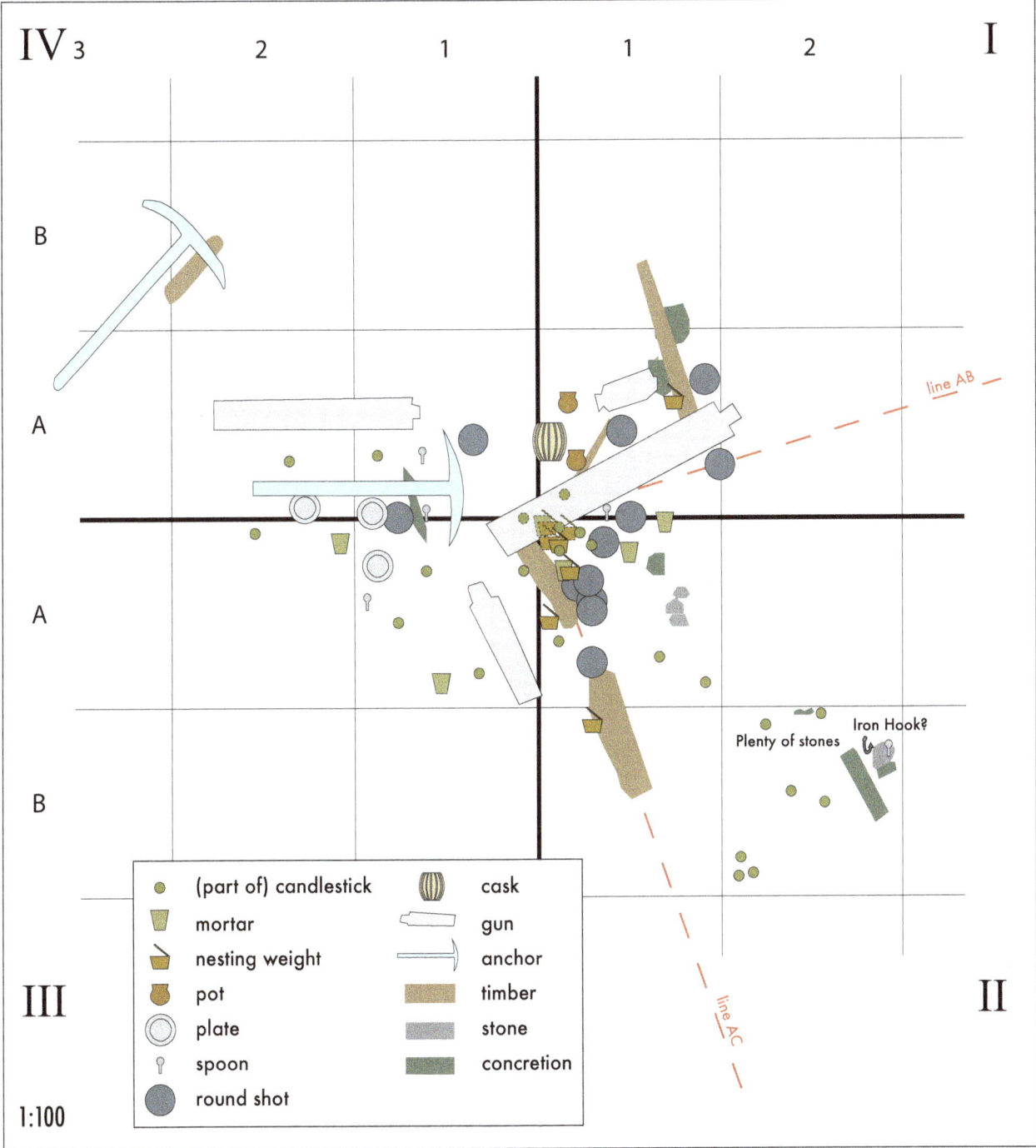

Figure 15. Impression of the site after the first few months of excavation.

means of metal detector, and that all targets are mapped. Unfortunately, this data was not included in the folders at our disposal. Based upon the few sketches that were included, however, we were able to create an impression of the excavation results in the first few months (*Fig. 15*). Once again, this is just an impression and not the exact situation, since none of the sketches did fit exactly on top of one another. The sizes and places of the guns vary in every sketch, as do other objects that are represented in several sketches. Also, these sketches only represent part of what has been excavated and is no indication of the actual distribution of all archaeological material. Nevertheless, this site plan gives us the opportunity to get an impression of the situation during the first months of the excavation period. Notable is the high concentration of very diverse objects in a rather small range. Not represented on the site plan is the abundance of small pins spread over most of the area. Guns, a cask, nesting weights, candlesticks, mortars, and round shot are recovered in high numbers from an area of only a few square meters. Whether this concentration is due to the actual organisation of cargo, due to the wrecking events, or due to later human and/or environmental impact on the site cannot be said. The site plan is too limited to allow for further interpretation of distribution of the finds either. If more data from the excavation were still available (and according to the earlier-mentioned dive reports, this should be the case) this would mean an important contribution to our further understanding of the Zeebrugge wreck.

2.3.3. Post-processing the excavation results

It appears there occurred an ad hoc selection soon after the excavation, or perhaps even during excavation, of objects related to the site and those from earlier or later periods. According to Schiltz lots of intrusive material from many different periods was present at the site. A first example would be the wine bottle dating from the 18th century, which led to the belief that this wreck was the Anna Catharina. Schiltz, however, also mentions ammunition from the world wars and says there were other intrusive finds too. At one point during the excavation animal bone was recovered from the clay-like soil underneath the silt. At first, it was believed this material came from on-board livestock, as a forethought of nutrition during a long voyage. The finds were brought for determination to Anton Ervynck, researcher at the Flanders Heritage Agency. Ervynck identified this material as the rib of a woolly rhinoceros and antler from red deer, both dating to the Ice Age (P.A.B.S., D.R., "week 10"). This indicates the clay-like soil underneath the wreck is of Pleistocene origin. Although this find in itself is a very interesting discovery, and more bone could possibly be present where this was found, it was deemed irrelevant at the time since it did not belong to the wreck. It is uncertain what happened to the material afterwards. According to Schiltz it was thrown away, but according to Ervycnk it may have been preserved in the Flanders Heritage Agency's depot. We contacted the depot to ask about this find, but due to a current reorganisation at the depot it could not yet be traced back. The post-processing of the excavation results executed by members of *vzw Maritieme Archeologie* seems to focus only on those objects that were believed to be part of this particular wreck.

Once the objects were lifted out of the water, most of them were subject to a long-term conservation program. We tried several times to contact the person responsible for this conservation program, Martin van Dromme, but never achieved any response. Yet his input might have meant an important contribution to this research. Van Dromme might have been able to give further insight to the actual conservation process, as well as, even more importantly, an overview of all finds recovered from the wreck including those objects captured in concretions as well as those objects that may not have survived up to today. Bits and pieces of the conservation process can be retrieved from Schiltz' archives, but a full overview is missing.[9] Insight into the conservation process would be interesting because it could inform us about what happened with the objects between the original state they were excavated in, and the state we see them in now. This could lead to the answer to the important question of what original information we can glean from these objects, as well as what information may be lost or was added.

This question is central since several objects demonstrate traces of intense conservation. An example of such an object would be one of the many pewter plates, which shows traces of crude repair. Original repair could tell us something about its long-term use or value, yet this repair seems to be a recent addition. Other plates are strongly affected by corrosion. Is this a consequence of taphonomical processes, or of the use of corrosive substances during conservation, such as strong acids? This is not unimportant, and has consequences for our understanding of the collection. Some of the plates still present a maker's mark, yet most plates lack any kind of marking. It is necessary to understand in what condition these plates were recovered and in what way they were preserved in order to understand whether any marking may or may not have been present originally. Other objects show thick coatings covering the original surface of the object. These additions seem to be irreversible and influence the potential of analysis of the original material. The conservator may have had good reason to believe these treatments were appropriate, and we do not judge any of these choices, especially because of our lack of expertise within this field. Yet the motivation for the conservator's choices is considered an important contribution to our understanding of the original situation of the finds.

Not all objects were conserved immediately, because adequate technical and financial means were not available at the time. This was the case for several of the bigger objects, such as cannon, anchors, and casks. Once recovered from the site, these objects were deposited again under water in the Brittannia dock, in the Zeebrugge outer port. In preparation of "Sail Brugge 2002", a tall ship event in Zeebrugge, it was decided to conserve one of the cannon from the Zeebrugge site and to exhibit it at this event. With financial support from the Port of Zeebrugge, conservation of the cannon started in 2001. When it came time to retrieve it from the Brittannia dock, the cannon had sunk about 4m into the port's soil. The cannon, a bombard, turned out to be in great condition and was still attached to its original wooden carriage with the original rope. For conservation, the bombard was separated from its carriage and placed in a sodium hydroxide solution. The carriage was treated with a solution of polyethylene glycol (Van Dromme 2007, p. 21). The original ropes seem not to have been preserved. Four years later the process was completed and the cannon was tied on to the carriage again. It is since exhibited in the Pierre Vandammehuis, headquarters of the Port of Zeebrugge.

Whether the other objects are still preserved in the Brittannia dock is uncertain and testimonies are inconsistent. When asked about the casks, which could

---

[9] A list of chemicals used for the conservation of finds is mentioned in correspondence between Van Dromme and Schiltz. Among the chemicals are sodium hydroxide, sodium carbonate, sodium bicarbonate, sodium sesquicarbonate, silica gel, benzotriazole, fungicide, thiourea, distilled water and citric acid (P.A.B.S., F.C.1, "Van Dromme 31/08/1991").

make an interesting dendrochronological contribution to this research, Schiltz informed us these probably were still present somewhere in the Brittannia dock. Parmentier as well believed most objects still had to be present there, since only the bombard had been conserved so far. Yet, in later testimonies Schiltz would say no finds were left in the Brittannia dock and all objects that once were there, had now been scrapped. The reason for scrapping the objects was because they were either incomplete or damaged. One cannon was in good condition, with the original rammer still protruding from the barrel. According to Schiltz it was decided to drill this rammer out of the barrel. This procedure heavily damaged the cannon, enough for it to be scrapped. We do not know the motivation for the scrapping of other finds such as casks or the anchor, but it is a shame all this information seems to have been destroyed. Indeed, to think that these objects were lifted from underneath 4m of sediment, just for the purpose of scrapping them after all these years seems quite an inconvenient endeavor, an endeavor that seems to conflict with the original intentions of *vzw Maritieme Archeologie* to "preserve and safeguard the wreck's heritage from further destruction and disappearance" (P.A.B.S., F.V. "Oprichting VZW Maritieme Archeologie", article 3).

Several objects show traces of probable archaeometrical analysis. Many objects feature four red dots around a small area where the upper layer of the original material was scratched off (*Fig. 16*). This seems to be the preparation for some kind of analysis of this material. The surfaces of other objects demonstrate odd square perforations (*Fig. 17*). We believe these squares were cut out to use the material as a sample for further analysis as well. Schiltz did inform us electron microscope analysis was executed by Van Dromme, who could use this device at the Catholic University of Leuven where he had studied.

It seems plausible that the cut-out samples were used for this analysis. A more exact date for the wreck was the goal with this analysis, but according to Schiltz the results did not allow for better dating. Whether the other preparation, with the red dots on the objects, was meant for the same kind of analysis, is unknown.

Dendrochronological analysis was carried out too, again to get a more detailed date for the wreck. Samples were taken from some beams, recovered from the site for this specific purpose. According to Schiltz these samples were sent to an institute abroad, probably in Sweden. Yet, these samples did not allow any further dating either. The results from neither this analysis, nor from the electron microscope analysis or any other analysis, were at our disposal for this research. Both Schiltz and Parmentier refer to Van Dromme and Vandenberghe for this data, but neither of them responded to our inqueries.[10]

The collection of finds recovered from the wreck has, to our understanding, been elaborately studied as well. This was mainly done by Vandenberghe, who published a few short contributions on the material recovered from the wreck (*cf. supra*). Vandenberghe did announce an upcoming, exhaustive final report in 1997 (Vandenberghe 1997, p. 90) and a detailed study in preparation in 2006 (Vandenberghe 2006, p. 19), yet no report or study containing a systematic overview of the Zeebrugge wreck has been published so far. Nevertheless, Schiltz did inform us Vandenberghe did thoroughly study the finds from the excavation and made detailed drawings of several objects. Schiltz also suggested that most of the original data, such as detailed site plans and the systematically recorded data of objects immediately after excavation, are probably in Vandenberghe's possession for further research. We contacted Vandenberghe several times, informing him of

Figure 16. Red dots on some of the objects are an apparent indication archaeometrical analysis was executed.

Figure 17. A candlestick and a cauldron demonstrating square appertures, probably caused by obtaining samples for material analysis.

---

[10] We do not have a name of the company where the dendro samples were sent to, but we did contact several specialists who were active in the field of dendrochronology in Sweden in the 1990's. We did receive answer from Hans Linderson (Dendrokronologiska laboratoriet, Sveriges Lantbruksuniversitet) and Alf Bråthen, as well as from Thomas Bartholin and Olafur Eggertsson, former heads of the same laboratory. According to Bartholin several amateurs did offer dendrochronological analysis in Sweden in this period too, making it more difficult to trace back any results.

our research and asking him to what extent a contribution to his work could still be beneficial, but only received a reply once. In a brief mail he informed us he did have all information related to the Zeebrugge collection, but was not willing to share any of this information (Personal mail Stéphane Vandenberghe).

This creates a very intriguing situation. Great effort was put into finding this wreck in the first place. Although the wreck turned out not to be the Anna Catharina, further effort, not to mention time and private financial investment, was then put into excavating the wreck. Afterwards, the excavation results were studied and even archaeometrical analysis was executed. And yet, despite all this work and despite the intentions to excavate this wreck scientifically, no results have ever been published or shared. It is even more surprising that despite the great interest from the academic world in these results, some of the former researchers are reluctant to share any information at all. This paradoxical situation is problematic, and to a certain extent it has influenced the general perception towards the activities of *vzw Maritieme Archeologie* in a negative way. Since it appears the study of the integral excavation data is a pursuit for which the outcome depends on the goodwill of the former members of *vzw Maritieme Archeologie*, we believe it is opportune to include this paradoxical situation into the discussion.

2.4. The paradox of the Zeebrugge site

Although the initial aim of this research was to study the Zeebrugge site and its finds, assembling the raw data related to the excavation became just as challenging -if not more- as the actual analysis of this data. We know, at the time of excavation and afterwards, objects have been registered and analysed by different means. Long-term conservation was applied to most objects and catalogues including all finds must have been created. This data, however, was not available for our research. Several attempts to pursue information about this data for the purpose of this research were either ignored or rebuffed by the persons holding this data. This situation creates an enormous contrast with the initial setup of the excavation project, and contradicts the original aims as expressed in the documents we had at our disposal. The paradox, however, does not only lie within the high efforts of research versus the lack of sharing the research results. There is also the pioneering credit of this project versus the public unawareness, or the archaeological potential of this site versus its absence in the archaeological debate. This is an absolute shame, since all the effort, the pioneering credit and the archaeological potential of the site, do deserve a wide audience and people talking about it. Most intriguing of all, however, is the fact that this situation does not seem to be just a matter of unfortunate circumstances. A quarter century after the excavation started, some researchers are openly reluctant to share any information as a contribution to the international archaeological debate. Many scholars from different nationalities have tried to retrieve bits and pieces of information from the Zeebrugge site, but were either rebuffed or ignored.[11] Yet, the publication of results has been on the agenda of *vzw Maritieme Archeologie* for a long time, and there was even initiative to institutionalise their work.

The idea to create a book or film for presenting the results of the excavation existed from the very beginning (P.A.B.S., F.V., "verslag 02/03/1991"). We know of meetings in 1993 and 1995 in which the publication of scientific results was discussed[12] (P.A.B.S., F.C.2, "Verbeke 05/10/1993", "Verbeke 29/03/1995") and according to Marnix Pieters, senior adviser maritime and underwater heritage at the Flanders Heritage Agency, there have been talks between members of *vzw Maritieme Archeologie* and the Agency about publishing the results. Yet, no agreement was made and Pieters never saw the results of the excavation either. According to Schiltz no publication was made since there was no more money for such an investment. Even the possibility to sell one of the candlesticks from the excavation, to finance a publication, was proposed and agreed upon by members of *vzw Maritieme Archeologie*, yet not pursued (Personal information Bart Schiltz). From this information we understand the publication was meant to be a nicely illustrated, independent book, and not a contribution to a scientific journal.

However, a publication was not the only intention of *vzw Maritieme Archeologie*. Correspondence and other documents reveal clear intentions for the foundation of a museum or centre for maritime archaeology (P.A.B.S., F.C.2, "Verbeke 05/10/1993", "Verbeke 08/03/1994"). In September 1993 the province of West Flanders was approached to discuss the possibility for such an initiative (P.A.B.S., F.C.2, "Kosten Berging Anna-Catharina"). Acquaintances from the National Fishing Heritage Centre in Grimsby, Great Britain, were even visited and given a questionnaire covering practical and financial issues related to maintaining such a centre (P.A.B.S., F.C.2, "Schiltz 18/11/1993"). Already in 1992, the idea was raised to institutionalise this project. Parmentier contacted Maarleveld in this regard and received exhaustive information about the foundation of the underwater archaeological service in the Netherlands (P.A.B.S., F.V., "verslag 15/02/1992"). And yet, despite this eagerness to

---

[11] We know of at least three such examples. Information about the excavation or about specific finds was requested by researchers from Belgium, the Netherlands and the United Kingdom, but all were rebuffed and/or ignored after several attempts of contact. During this research, interest was shown by researchers from, a.o., France, The Netherlands, the United Kingdom and the United States. These international cooperations and information exchanges have proven worthwhile for all parties.

[12] We do know about the topics of these meetings because they were mentioned in correspondence between members of vzw Maritieme Archeologie, however, the meeting reports as such from this period are not at our disposal.

share their project with the world, the initiatives were not pursued for unknown reasons, and the general attitude changed to a more secluded one. The finds were still exhibited at different temporary expositions, and were finally donated on basis of a permanent loan to the MAS Museum, yet the initial attitude of collecting and sharing knowledge, seems to have disappeared over time.

The reason for this apparent radical change in attitude is uncertain. The tendency towards seclusion, however, may have negatively influenced the perception of this project in the academic world. The seclusion of information and the lack of any transparency that coincides with such an approach may have tempted scholars to believe things were kept secret for possibly sinister reasons. Then again, criticism of this nature may have been the cause of seclusion of results as well, and it is not unlikely both have influenced one another. Also possible critique towards methodology may have been the cause of the reluctant attitude of some of the projects researchers. We noticed questions in this regard have been raised in academic circles, mainly because only nice objects appeared from the excavation, not sherds or pieces of timber, and no archaeological data accompanied these nice objects. Maybe this critique, and fear to fail academic expectations, influenced the sudden reason for seclusion as well. Again, it is not unlikely academic expectations and criticism have influenced the seclusion of information and vice versa. In 2003 the Flanders Heritage Agency instituted a research unit in maritime and fluvial archaeology (Pieters & Schietecatte 2003, p. 3), an initiative that may have impeded plans of *vzw Maritieme Archeologie* to found their own maritime archaeology centre. After all the work they had put in the excavation of the Zeebrugge wreck, and by that time also in the surveys of many other wrecks, the foundation of this new research unit could have been perceived as competition rather than support, with whom they were not willing to share the information they collected over all these years.

Whatever the reason may be, the present situation is problematic and frustrating, since valuable archaeological information has become private property of the lucky few who were there to analyse it first. It seems here, a fundamental mistake is made by mixing up the appropriation of excavated goods on one side, and of assessment and research on the other side; an issue discussed in the past by Maarleveld (2013). The fact the excavated goods are privately owned is in this case not a problem in itself, yet the consequent privatising of information related to the excavation is problematic. As every archaeologist knows, the excavation of a site means the destruction of it and therefore is an unrepeatable and irreversible action. This means the data collected by excavating the site is unique and cannot be obtained again by anyone else. By privatising this data, not only a conflict arises with the own goals of *vzw Maritieme Archeologie*, but the purpose of the excavation to scientific standards becomes meaningless. The public interest is essential in archaeological heritage management and archaeological research, and heritage is or should be a common good. By privatising excavation results, all that is left for the public is a destroyed archaeological site.

If indeed data is guarded because of criticism from the academic world, we can say this project should not be criticised for the above-mentioned reasons. This was a pioneering project without precedent in Belgium. Without any legal framework or legal requirement, *vzw Maritieme Archeologie* decided to carry out this excavation to scientific standards, and to get informed about such undertaking by professionals abroad. Yes, possibly the excavation was object-oriented and possibly the excavation was not up to today's standards, but then again maritime archaeology is now a much more developed discipline, while back then no legal framework existed and excavation contracts were expressed in percentages of recovered finds. However, by hoarding excavation data, the archaeological site seems to be destroyed not for public but personal interest and the archaeological finds recovered become just antique objects without context; a context essential for archaeological research. Therefore, the excavation as such should not be criticised, but we can and should criticise the privatising of excavation data as currently performed by some members of *vzw Maritieme Archeologie*. Transparency about the excavation results would not only be beneficial for the academic debate, but would also be a positive influence on the current academic perception of this project.

Although the private data can probably mean an interesting contribution to this research, it was not possible to include this information. Therefore, we cannot estimate its exact scientific value nor to what extent it could have contributed to this research. Nevertheless, a large quantity of archaeological data was available for this research nonetheless. This data, including the actual archaeological material as well as additional information, will be discussed in the following chapter.

Chapter 3

Finds from the Zeebrugge wreck

Many of the registered finds recovered from the Zeebrugge wreck are currently present at the MAS Museum, Antwerp. Yet, the collection in the MAS Museum does not include all finds from this site. Some finds are located elsewhere, other finds were lost due to decay or damage. Some objects were stolen, while others have been thrown away or destroyed, either by accident or purposefully. Finally, there are some objects we were not able to trace, although they still should exist.[13] Although not all objects were at our disposal to study, we should not ignore these missing finds since they intensely contribute to our understanding of the Zeebrugge wreck. As discussed before, complete overviews of all the finds recovered from the Zeebrugge wreck should exist in private possession. Since this information is currently not available, we tried to create an overview of objects recovered from the Zeebrugge wreck over time from the sources that were available.[14] Although this list may be incomplete and more finds may have been recovered from the Zeebrugge wreck, we did collect information for a significant number of finds not present in the MAS Museum. By bringing all these finds into consideration we hope we are able to discuss the Zeebrugge site in the most comprehensive way possible for now. It is clear any future contribution of excavation data could add significantly to our understanding and interpretation of this site and its finds.

We grouped the finds from the Zeebrugge wreck into two tables. Table 2 gives an overview of the objects the author was able to study. Table 3 shows the finds mentioned by other sources, but which were not available for study. To discuss the total of finds, we divided them into different categories, based upon the general function of the object. This arbitrary division into functional categories may conflict with the object's original function on-board, such as cargo, equipment, or personal belongings. Nevertheless we will address any site-specific context when possible. Although available information is limited for objects from Table 3, we will briefly discuss the information we could retrieve from the different sources when appropriate.

Some finds in Table 3 are only referred to by material, and therefore are difficult to add to a functional group, such as bone or ceramics. Also timber pieces are mentioned, referring to ship timber. Before discussing the functional groups, we therefore will first briefly discuss the available information related to the 'ship and navigation', 'organic materials' and 'ceramics'. The other finds will be discussed according to function within the categories 'finance-related finds, 'kitchen- and dining-related finds', 'sewing and dress accessories', 'religious objects' and 'weaponry'. A significant number of candlesticks was recovered from the site, with a total of several hundreds of pieces. Therefore, these will be discussed in a seperate category. A limited number of finds could not be included in any of the previous categories because they were either incomplete or their function could not be defined. These objects will be discussed separately in the category 'other finds'.

3.1. Ship and navigation

Little is known about the shipwreck as such, and data in this regard is lacking. According to several testimonies, no significant structural parts of the ship were encountered on site. Nevertheless, we know organic materials were recovered from the site, and some of these objects proved to be in excellent condition, such as the carriage and ropes of the bombard. Yet, most organic materials were either not preserved, or did not survive attempted preservation. Also, contrary to given testimonies, ship timber must have been found on site as well. We know at least some pieces were lifted for dendrochronological analysis (*cf. supra*), yet there seems to be no documentation or registration of these finds. It has been argued the ship was either a carrack or a hulk (Parmentier 2011, p. 34), yet this interpretation is based upon historical sources for ship types in this period, rather than on the actual study of any ship remains. Therefore,

---

[13] Although there is insufficient information to create a full pedigree of the objects, there is ample evidence the collection has travelled a lot over the last 25 years. The collection successively resided with Bart Schiltz, then at Van Dromme's company Deco Diving, in the Gruuthusemuseum with Vandenberghe and finally in the MAS Museum with Parmentier. In the meanwhile objects were exhibited in several temporary exhibitions, among others in Leuven and Raversijde (Belgium) and Dunkirk (France) (Personal information Jan Parmentier).

[14] These sources are mainly the few short publications by Vandenberghe (1997, 2006, 2007), an official list of salvaged goods provided to the Dutch authorities in 1991 (Maritiem Erfgoed Archief RCE archiefnummer 1.853.3.16 (from here on referred to as: MEA 1991)) and inventories related to restoration, exhibitions and study (P.A.B.S., F.C.2, "Geschatte inventaris Herent", "Inventaris tentoonstelling Sint Jan 29/12/1993", "Lijst objecten Zeebrugge 25/04/1993", "Objecten Brugge Vandenberghe"). Additional information was obtained by photographic documentation and short contributions in other publications about the Zeebrugge finds (e.g. Baumgärtel 1997, Holtman 1999, Termote & Termote 2009).

Finds from the Zeebrugge wreck

Table 2. Overview of finds studied by the author.

Objects registered by author	
Object type	N° of objects
Bell	2
Bombardelle	1
Bowl	3
Candlestick (max.)	292
Cauldron	3
Chain (part of)	3
Coin weight	9
Colander	1
Divider	1
Flagon	1
Hooks (bulk)	32
Knife decoration	23
Knife handle	97
Little box	1
Mould for bullet	1
Mould for seal	1
Monstrance (part of)	5
Mortar	3
Needle-case	4
Nested cup-weight	13
Pestle	7
Pin	1729
Pin (large)	1
Plate	46
Platter	6
Pull Ring	4
Round shot	188
Salt holder	7
Scale	1
Spoon (max.)	17
Support bracket	4
Tap (max.)	9
Thimble	27
Venus counter	2
Unknown	7

Table 3. Overview of finds mentioned in other sources.

Objects mentioned in other sources	
Object type	N° of objects
Anchor	2
Ballast stone	x
Beads	≥13
Bell	1
Bone etc.	11
Bottle	1
Brick	2
Candlestick	>3
Cask	4
Ceramic sherds	x
Chiselled stone	1
Coins	2
Comb	1
Copper wire	1
"Crenelated cover"	1
Frame (ship)	x
Hinge	1
Iron objects	6
Iron wire	3
Jar	2
Key	1
Knife decoration	41
Lace chape	x
Lead objects	≥27
Marlin spike	1
Measure instrument?	1
Medallion	1
Mortar	4
musket	1
Nails	x
Nested cup-weight	6
Ordnance	6
Pestle	2
Pewter jug	1
Pickaxe	2
Pin	x
Plaiting (reed)	1
Platter	2
Porringer	1
Roundshot	x
Scabbard (leather)	10
Sounding lead	1
Stone roundshot	x
Timber pieces	x
Venus counter	3?
Wooden plug	2

in archaeological terms, linking this site to such a type has rather little value (Maarleveld 1995b, p. 6). Although no large coherent parts of the shipwreck may have been preserved, the presence of structural ship remains, such as planks, beams and frames, was attested. A thorough analysis of construction details on these objects could have contributed to our understanding of this specific ship. Especially with the proposed hypothesis that these timbers could have been part of a hulk, it would have been interesting to study these remains, since the hulk is a type almost unknown in nautical archaeology (Greenhill 2000, p. 4). Unfortunately, no information on these objects is available, and may not even exist anymore. Furthermore a large quantity of supposed ballast stones is mentioned in different dive reports, as well as in the survey reports (*cf. supra*). These finds, again, do not seem to be recorded.

At least two anchors were present on the site. One of these anchors was lifted when a crew of the Flemish Broadcasting Organisation (then BRTN, now VRT) was visiting to shoot a news item about the excavation (*Fig. 18*). The anchor was heavily concreted and we can see pewter plates included in this concretion as well. Unfortunately the anchor was, to our knowledge, not scientifically recorded or described so no information about its design or construction is available. The only references to the anchor we could find are mentioned in dive reports. Here, one states the anchor is a stocked anchor with long stem and an estimated weight of 500kg (P.A.B.S., D.R., 26/07/91). It was argued the anchor could not be preserved (MEA 1991), and according to Schiltz it was demolished together with other finds that could not be preserved. This is unfortunate, and one can question why the anchor was lifted in the first place if not for study or preservation. One dive report does mention some pewter plates are concreted to the anchor and cannot be separated from it, and they argue the anchor should be lifted for this reason (P.A.B.S., D.R., 03/09/91). This indicates the pewter plates we see in the picture were the actual reason this anchor was recovered from the site. The second anchor was not lifted from the site and is only known from site plan sketches.

Only one item related to navigation was discovered on site. This object is a well-preserved divider (*Fig. 19*), an instrument used to plot courses and distances on navigational charts. The divider is made of two separate legs with interlocking half-circles on top. The circular top allows for conveniently using the object with only one hand. Therefore, this type of divider is known as the so-called 'single handed' divider (Hicks 2005, p. 273). It has a total length of 14cm and a width of 3.1cm. Each leg measures 11.1cm. The upper part of both legs features a decorative pattern of reversing triangles. Traces of a decorative pattern on the circular top seem to be present as well. The object is made of an alloy of copper (86.1%), lead (4.5%), zinc (4.2%) and tin (2.7%). Very similar brass objects have been recovered from other wreck sites such as the Mary Rose (1545), where four almost identical dividers were found (*Idem*, p. 273-274), or the Portuguese Oranjemund wreck (1530's) (Chirikure et al. 2010, p. 50). Such dividers may have been produced in the Low Countries, Germany, or France (Hicks 2005, p. 274).

3.2. Organic materials

As we have said before, many organic finds were recovered from the wreck, yet most of these finds are only referred to by the material of which they are made. Among these objects are pieces of timber and bone. The pieces of bone include at least six vertebrae from the spinal column as well as five undefined bones (P.A.B.S. P.C.2, "Marinebasis 15/05/1993"). Whether any of these bones are human, is unknown. Neither do we know whether these bones refer to the Pleistocene finds mentioned earlier (*cf. supra*). Furthermore a bead made of horn with a circular protrusion in the middle is mentioned (MEA 1991).

When timber is mentioned, this most often refers to pieces of ship timber. Yet, some other objects are mentioned as well such as wooden plugs. At least one comb, made of wood or bone, was recovered from the wreck as well, and according to Vandenberghe (2006, p. 20) several combs were recovered. The comb is toothed on both sides, with very fine teeth on one side and larger teeth on the opposed side. Although the object appears not to be preserved, it is shown in a news item broadcasted in 1991 (*Fig. 20*). Although not mentioned in any of the find reports or inventories, several casks were present on site too. Three casks of pins and one cask of nails are mentioned by Termote & Termote (2009, p. 280) and Schiltz did confirm several casks were present on site indeed. At least one of the casks was lifted and stored in the Brittannia dock (Personal information Schiltz). According to the dive reports, at least one cask was lifted in 1991 (P.A.B.S., D.R., "21/07/1991"). In 1994 at least three more casks were discovered and we know two of them were lifted (P.A.B.S., D.R., "04/07/1994"; "06/07/1994"; "10/10/1994"). A picture of one of these casks demonstrates these objects were heavily concreted. This cask contained relatively large nails with flat heads (*Fig. 21*). Possibly these nails were brought on board for eventual reparations. Other tools that were recovered, such as strongly damaged pickaxes made of timber and iron, may be interpreted in the same light. A peculiar find is a part of reed plaiting, which was found together with a piece of pottery underneath a cannonball (MEA 1991). Unfortunately, neither a description nor image of this find was available to the author. Furthermore, at least ten leather scabbards are mentioned among the finds. A small number of organic finds was actually preserved and will be discussed later, such as knife handles and the carriage of the bombard.

Finds from the Zeebrugge wreck

Figure 18. Anchor with concreted pewter plates (©VRT).

Figure 20. A wooden comb, probably not preserved (©VRT, manipulated by the author).

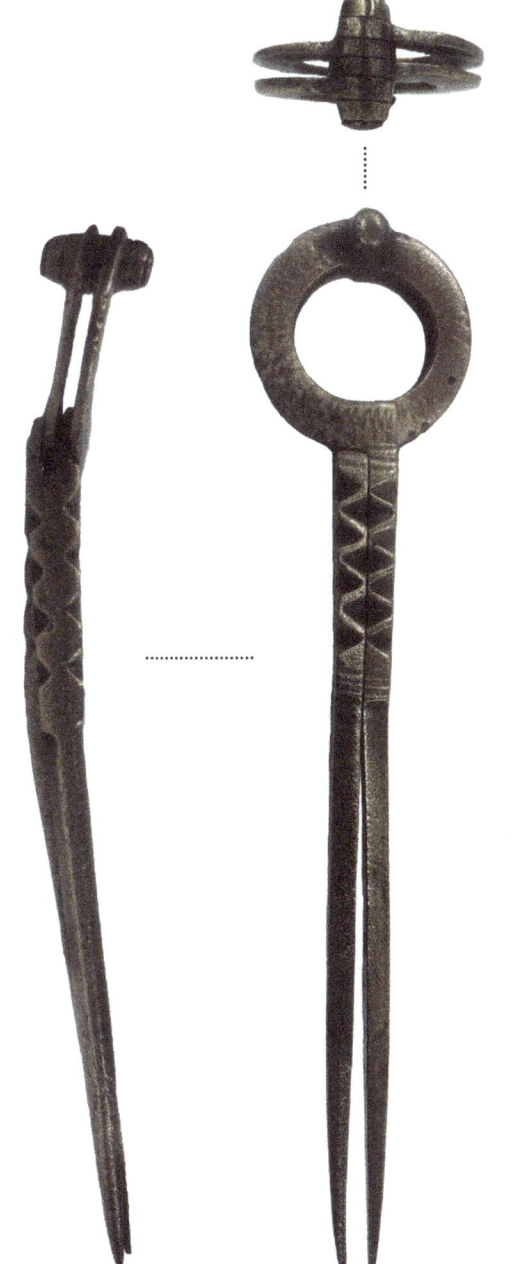

Figure 19. 'Single handed' divider.

Figure 21. Concreted cask, filled with nails (Images provided by Bart Schiltz).

3.3. Ceramics

Although one would expect ceramics to be present on a site like this, no such objects are present among the finds in the MAS Museum. There is a lot of uncertainty about actual finds in this regard, and testimonies are conflicting. Van Dromme does mention the presence of "numerous sherds" in the conservation laboratory in Herent in 1993 (P.A.B.S., F.C.2, "Geschatte inventaris Herent"). Schiltz, asked about these finds by the author, argues this information is incorrect and only one sherd was recovered from the Zeebrugge wreck, a piece of a so-called Bartmann jug. Yet, the official list of salvaged goods provided to the Dutch Authorities in December 1991, after the first field season, does mention at least twelve sherds as single items, plus another undefined number of sherds as one item (MEA 1991). Among these finds they distinguish potsherds (eight) and sherds of earthenware (one + undefined number), although it is uncertain whether this nuance was made intentionally. One piece is described as "sherd from a jug with a piece of stamp", another as "earthenware tile with angular profile". In addition to these finds, two incomplete bricks were recovered separately from one another. A brick is also mentioned in the inventories of two separate exhibitions (P.A.B.S., F.C.2, "Inventaris tentoonstelling Sint Jan 29/12/1993", "Lijst objecten Zeebrugge 25/04/1993").

The second inventory also mentions "a big jug" and "a small *Rahren* jug". The latter may refer to the city of Raeren, located in present-day Belgium. Raeren was an important production centre for stoneware in the late 15th and early 16th centuries, with a wide and international distribution of its products (Gaimster 1997, p. 224). Rheinish stoneware in general was recovered from several wrecks from the 16th-18th century (Gaimster 1992, p. 340-341). Raeren ware was, among other wares, recovered from the Cattewater wreck[15] (ca. 1530)(Redknap 1984, p. 68) and the Mary Rose (1545) (Gaimster 1992, p. 340). The Raeren jug mentioned in the inventory could possibly be the Bartmann jug referred to by Schiltz. In the early 16th century, mugs, jugs, and bottles produced in Raeren were often decorated with facemasks. These were incised (stabbed) and applied to the necks of the objects (Gaimster 1997, p. 224; Hurst 1986, p. 194). Unfortunately, we cannot confirm the identification of this Raeren[16] stoneware, since no material or visual evidence is available. It is clear that a study of the ceramics recovered from the Zeebrugge wreck would contribute significantly to our understanding of this wreck, since, in contrast to many of the metal objects recovered from the site, ceramics are much better documented and could add significant contextual information. We can only hope the sherds do still exist, available for future research.

3.4. Finance-related finds

Quite a few finds from the Zeebrugge wreck are related to financial business. These finds form an important category in this research, since they generally allow for a better determination and therefore provide more precise contextual information. Some of these finds are provided with marks or carry numismatic information, factors that can help determine a relative date for the site. Among the finds in this category are nested cup-weights, coin weights, counters and other related objects.

3.4.1. Nested cup-weights

A set of nested cup-weights comprises a series of tapered, cup-shaped weights. They decrease in size and fit exactly into one another (*Fig. 22.a*). The biggest cup has a lid and is used as a housing for the smaller weights. Every cup weighs twice as much as the next smaller cup. Only the smallest piece, called the "pill", is not cup-shaped but discoid-shaped. The pill fits exactly in the smallest cup, to which it is equal in weight. Therefore, the weight of every cup is equal to the total of pieces it holds (Wittop Koning & Houben 1980, p. 102). The production of nested cup-weights is often associated with Nuremberg, although they probably have been produced in other places too (Holtman 1999, p. 6).

Several sets of nested cup-weights were recovered from the Zeebrugge site, and they have been discussed in different publications. The exact number of sets varies, depending on the author, from "about 20" (Vandenberghe 1997, p. 88), "20" (Vangroenweghe 2015, p. 17) or "19" (Holtman 1999, p. 25)[17] to "12 complete sets" (Parmentier 2000, p. 235). In the MAS Museum currently 13 sets are present (based on the number of housings), and 10 of them are complete. It is unclear where the missing sets are located and why they are not included in this collection.

All sets from the Zeebrugge wreck have a similar design. The housing features a hinged lid with three struts and a handle. The handle is not present for all objects; these objects feature holes where the handle once was attached. The handle itself is horseshoe-shaped with a small protruding part on the top. Two of the struts, arranged in a V-shape, support the hinge to the lid. On top of the struts and on the inside of the lid, riveting points are visible. The V-shaped struts have one riveting point each. The third strut is positioned opposed the V-shaped struts and features a hinged clasp. The clasp may represent a stylized zoomorphic figure. It fits over the pin protruding from the housing cup, serving as a lock. The third strut has two riveting points. The lid features concentric circles both underneath the struts as well as on the inside. Possibly,

---

[15] The Raeren ware from the Cattewater wreck was dated to the 16th century, yet according to Redknap's (1984, p. 19, 21, 68) stratigraphy for this site, a direct association with the wreck is uncertain for the layer from which the Raeren ware was retrieved.
[16] Both Gaimster (1997, p. 225) and Hurst (1986, p. 194) argue the fabric and typology of Raeren ware in this period is virtually identical to the products of Aachen at that time. Products identified as Raeren ware therefore may best be attributed to the more general Raeren-Aachen region.
[17] This is an independent and revised version of Holtman's publications in Meten en Wegen 97 (March 1997) and Meten en Wegen 101 (March 1998), which can be requested at gmvv@planet.nl. The nested cup-weights from the Zeebrugge wreck are included in this article.

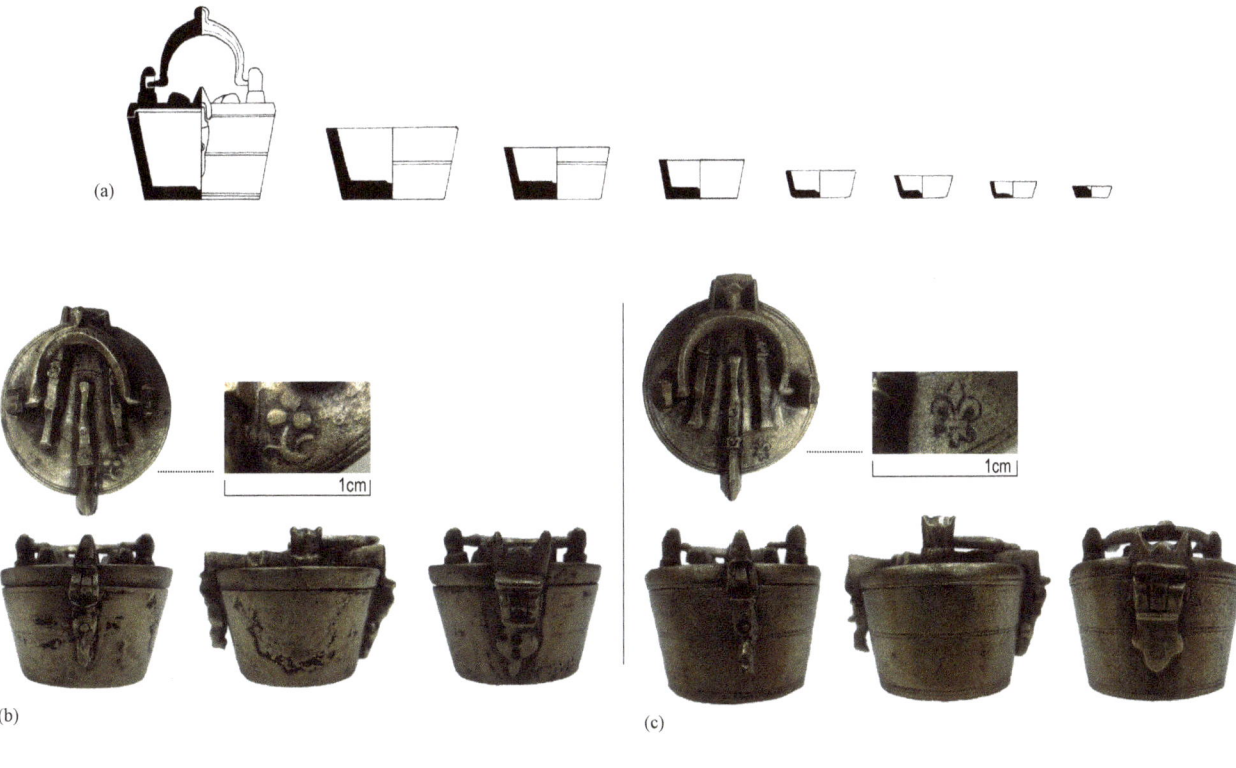

Figure 22. Nested cup-weights.

these rings served to verify no one had tampered with the thickness of the object to decrease the actual weight of the object (Holtman 1999, p. 4). For most sets, both the housing and the two biggest cup-weights feature a double engraved line along the sides, both on the inside and outside. This, again, could be a means to control the authenticity of the weight. All weights feature a small concavity in the centre of the bottom. This is an indication the weights were lathe-finished after they were casted (*Ibidem*). The specific design of these weights is associated with the city of Nuremberg (Houben 1984, p. 26).

All housings feature a mark on the right side of the single strut. We can distinguish the mark of a clover (6x) (*Fig. 22.b*) and the mark of a lily or so-called *fleur-de-lys* (6x) (*Fig. 22.c*). One lid that suffered substantial erosion does not feature a mark, although it may also have featured one. The clover and lily are, indeed, known makers' marks from Nuremberg, yet known examples of these marks deviate in design from the ones encountered in the Zeebrugge collection. The clover can be associated with weight-maker Hans Gscheid (Lockner 1981, p. 272). Gscheid became master in 1507 and died in 1540. However, the mark is also associated with Balthasar Gscheid (son of Hans) and Sebald Gscheid (son of Balthasar) (Houben 1984, p. 53), two weight-makers who used this mark later on in the 16th century as well (Lockner 1981, p. 272-273). Although there is no weight-maker directly associated with the *fleur-de-lys* as such, we would like to mention candlestick-maker Heinrich Geiger, who is associated with both the clover and the lily. His products should be dated before 1542 (*Idem*, p. 39). According to Houben (1984, p. 65) the lily on Nuremberg nested weights should not be considered a master mark. He argues the lily was punched in later at other places (e.g. France, the Netherlands), but unfortunately he does not further clarify this statement. Both Holtman (1999, p. 27) and Vangroenweghe (2015, p. 52) assume the clover mark present on the Zeebrugge weights should be attributed to Hans Gscheid. Holtman argues deviations in design may be explained by the cutting of new mark-stamps, when the previous stamp became blunt (Personal information Holtman). Vandenberghe (2006, p. 19) does mention the weights have "famous Nuremberg master marks", but does not specify any further.

We wanted to plot the dimensions (length, width, thickness) of the housings in a chart, but due to damage and/or eroded decorations on the lid and hinge, these dimensions were rather insecure. For the width, however, some pattern became visible. Therefore, we decided to plot the dimensions of the second-largest weight (*i.e.* the largest weight in the housing) in a chart (*Fig. 23*). These objects have no applied decorations and were protected from erosion by the housing. The chart allows some interesting observations. First of all, we can see the lily-marked objects make a very homogeneous group. They have an average length of 1.9cm, a width of 3.6cm, an inner diameter of 2.9cm and depth of 1.4cm. The clover-marked objects, on the other side, appear to be much more heterogeneous. Yet, when we take a closer look, for the first four objects one can see the decreasing length and depth are inversely proportional to the increasing width and inner diameter (length: 1.8-2cm; width 3.8-3.6cm; inner diameter 3.2-3cm; depth 1.3-1.4cm). For

The Zeebrugge Shipwreck

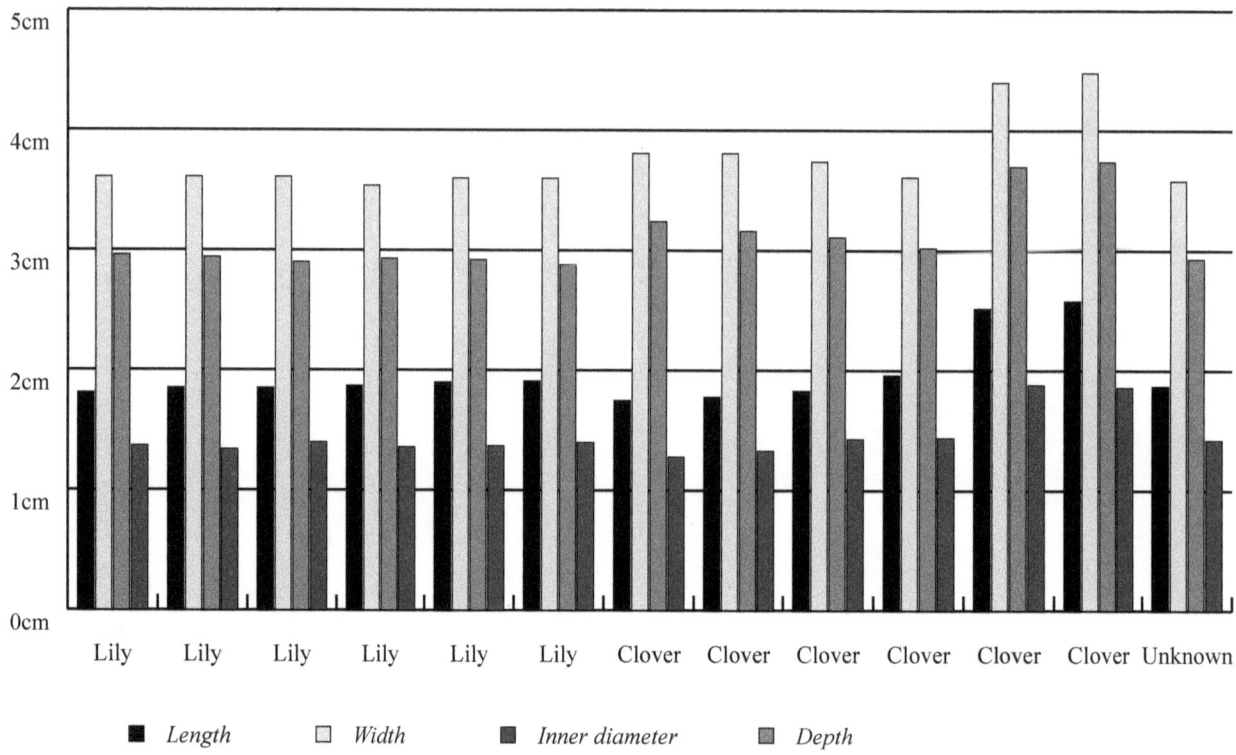

Figure 23. Dimensions of the second-largest weight for each set of nested cup-weights.

the objects where length and depth approach each other the closest, the dimensions correspond to the lily-marked weights. Therefore, we believe these objects were meant to represent an equal weight (*cf. infra*). Also the weight without any mark corresponds to these dimensions. The last two clover-marked objects in the chart seem to form a separate homogeneous group of larger dimensions. All dimensions of these objects vary less than 1mm from one another (length 2.5cm, width 4.4cm, inner diameter 3.7cm; depth 1.9cm). Only one of these larger sets is complete. It is interesting to notice this set is the only one that exists of nine weights (including the housing). All other, smaller sets seem to exist of eight weights (including the housing).

Obviously, the most important aspect of these nested cup-weights would be their actual weight. Unfortunately, the scale at our disposal was too imprecise and unstable to get satisfying results when weighing these objects.[18] We only measured a part of the assembly and, although imprecise, the results are proportional to the different sizes represented in figure 23. The smaller group had a weight ranging between 222-255g. For the bigger weights, the one complete weight measured 455g. For the incomplete set, we could deduce the total weight from the two present weights. This gave a result of 465g. All these results, however, are influenced by the eroded housings. To eliminate this factor, we also deduced the total weight for each set from the second biggest weight. By multiplying this number by four (= its own weight + the weight of its content + twice its weight for the housing), the actual total weight was more accurately achieved. For the group of smaller nested cup-weight sets, the total weight was 240-252g. For the bigger sets, the weight was 480-492. Although the results are imprecise, they seem to indicate the smaller weight sets actually represent about half the weight of the bigger weight sets.

More precise measurements for some of the nested cup-weights were provided by Ritzo Holtman[19], who in the past was given permission by Vandenberghe to weigh a few of the sets, but unfortunately not all of them. The largest object he could measure had a weight of 493.68g. This approaches the weight of the larger sets we measured for this research and, according to Holtman, is related to the Dutch troy pound. Troy weights are mainly used for weighing expensive materials such as silver or gold (Houben 1984, p. 13). Troy pounds did vary from city to city, since most cities used an individual mass unit. The troy pound for Antwerp, for example, was 470.1g. In Amsterdam its weight was set to 494.1g. An interesting note is that troy weights produced for the Netherlands could be recognised by a *fleur-de-lys* punchmark (*Ibidem*; Wittop Koning & Houben 1980, p. 17). Further, Holtman measured one object of ½ pound and three objects of

---

[18] We contacted the Flanders Heritage Agency for more precise measurements and were offered to use the precision scales in their offices. Within the frame of the dissertation, however, it would have been too complex and too time-consuming to fulfill all administrative obligations for moving these objects from the MAS Museum to the Flanders Heritage Agency's offices.

[19] We want to thank Ritzo Holtman for sharing his thoughts on this matter, and for sharing these unpublished results with us for the purpose of this research.

¼ pound. These do not seem to be present among the objects recorded by the author. The weights of these objects, converted to one pound, were about 492.5g for sets marked with a clover, and 497.5g for sets marked with a lily. Although not present in the MAS Museum either, objects of two pounds must also have been recovered from the wreck (Holtman 1999, p. 25). Holtman argues the nested cup-weights from the Zeebrugge wreck were probably adjusted roughly to the Dutch troy weight when produced, and had to be further adjusted to the local pound after they had been transported (Personal information Holtman, Holtman 1999, p. 26).

We executed xrf-analysis for two of the housings with different marks. For the clover-marked housing, the main elements are copper (79.3%), zinc (13%), iron (2.8%) and lead (1.6%). Similar results occur for the lily-marked housing, with main elements copper (77.8%), zinc (16.8%) and lead (2.3%). Here, however, only minor traces of iron are present (0.3%).

For parallels of this type of nested cup-weight in general, we would like to refer to Holtmans typology, where this type is discussed in depth (Holtman 1999, p. 25-28). A classic parallel for these weights, as referred to in many other publications on this subject, would be Flemish painter Quentin Matsys' "The Money Changer and his Wife" (1514), with the depiction of a weight quite similar to those recovered from the Zeebrugge wreck. The type is also not uncommon in archaeology (e.g. Deagan 2002, p. 264, figure 12.23). Yet, the combination of this type of weight with these specific marks seems to be more difficult to find. Objects recovered from the Punta Cana wreck, however, appear to be very similar to the nested cup-weights from the Zeebrugge wreck and carry a (slightly deviating) *fleur-de-lys* mark as well.[20]

3.4.2. Coin weights

A special group of finds are the nine coin weights recovered from the wreck. They are of special interest because they feature iconographical or numismatic documentation, allowing for better identification than many other objects in this collection. Coin weights were used, as the name indicates, to weigh coins. For most of our history, the value of a coin was defined by the intrinsic value of the mass of precious metal of which it was made. By using the coins, however, they started to wear and the value could decrease. Therefore, to verify the actual mass and thus value of the coin, coin weights were used (Pol 1990, p. 9). In general, one side of the coin weight depicts the image of the coin corresponding in mass to the coin weight. On the opposite side, generally a maker's mark was depicted (Wittop Koning & Houben 1980, p. 156). From the 14th century onwards, coin weights were kept, together with a small scale, in a simple wooden or metal box (Houben 1998, p. 9). Other than the nine coin weights, both a box and metal parts of a scale were recovered from the Zeebrugge wreck. For the scale, it is very likely it was used in relation to coin weights. For the box, however, it is more difficult to say whether it indeed was used to store coin weights and scale. Also, several of the weights recovered from the wreck have identical iconography and about the same weight, indicating they were used in relation to the same coin. Normally, a box of coin weights would only carry one coin weight for each type of coin (Personal information Holtman). This seems to indicate these coin weights, or at least a portion of them, were shipped as cargo.

The little box (*Fig. 24*) is made of thin, folded, brass sheets. Both the bottom and the cover of the box have short, folded edges. These edges fit exactly over the separately folded sides of the box. A handle is attached to the cover of the box. Two separate hinges used to attach the cover to the box. Opposed to these two hinges, part of another, centred, hinge is present. This is probably part of a locking system, related to the small protrusion on the side underneath this hinge. The hinges are "spade"-shaped. The handle, attached centrally over the length of the cover, is made of a single strap of brass, and is partly spiralled. The thin surface of the box makes it rather fragile, and the bottom of the object is greatly damaged.

The box has a total length of 11.3cm and a total width of 6cm (including hinges). The height of the box, without handle, measures 2.5cm. The complete height, including handle, would be 4.6cm. The length of the handle (measured at the top) is 6.8cm. Xrf-analysis shows the brass alloy contains 80.3% copper and 16.9% zinc. No other elements reach a relative concentration of 1%.

No parallels for this box were found. However, if indeed this box would have been used as a container for coin weights, this may well be one of the earliest, if not the earliest, known example of such a container.

Two parts of a scale were recovered from the site (*Fig. 25*). The first object is a circular, relatively flat plate (diameter 3.5cm; height 0.4cm). Four concentric circles (grouped per two) are present on the inside of the object. A dot in the middle may indicate the object was lathe-finished. Along the edges, three pierced holes (diameter 0.1cm) are present, positioned to one another as the corners of a triangle.

The other object is triangular-shaped (width 4.8cm; length 4cm; height 0.06cm). On one side a double-lined triangle is engraved along the edges of the object. Towards each corner of this triangle, a small hole is pierced (diameter 0.1cm).

Together, the plate and the triangle are the main part of the scale. A small wire would be fitted through the pierced holes to keep both parts in balance. Such scales are known

---

[20] We would like to thank Martin Roberts, who currently studies these objects, for sharing pictures of these finds and sharing some preliminary thoughts.

from several paintings. Although examples are known of marked scales, these objects do not present any marks.

Most important to discuss are, of course, the coin weights themselves. All of these are square-shaped. We can distinguish three types. The first type (2 items; length 1.5cm; width 1.4-1.5cm; thickness 0.4cm; ±7g[21]; *fig. 26.a*) shows, on one side, the heads of two crowned figures facing each other inside a circle. The other side shows, also in a circle, a crowned coat of arms. The second type of coin weights (4 items; length 1.5cm; width 1.4-1.5cm; thickness 0.3cm; ±4g; *fig. 26.b*) is very similar to the first type. It also depicts two crowned faces on one side, and a coat of arms on the other side. Although the crowned faces are almost identical for the type 1 and type 2 coin weights, the coats of arms are different and for the type 2 weights they are flanked by what appears to be the letter "S" or number "5".

Several coins are known to depict these faces. The oldest coin with this image would be the '*Medio excelente*', ordered by Ferdinand and Isabella, the so-called '*reyes católicos*' of Spain, in 1475 (De Francisco Olmos 1999, p. 93). On the reverse side of this coin, the coat of arms of Castile and León is depicted. This is the exact same coat of arms present on the reverse side of the type 2 coin weights. This indicates two things. First of all, it is clear the type 2 coin weights were used in relation to the *medio excelente* and this provides a *terminus post quem* of 1475. Secondly, these weights do not feature a maker's mark, but depict both sides of the coin instead. This is a rather uncommon feature. The *medio excelente* has a weight of 4.6g, corresponding to the weight of the *Castellano*. In certain publications, this weight is referred to as *Castellano* (e.g. Pol 1990, p. 119), yet according to historical sources the actual name would have been *medio excelente* (Farrés 1959, 227-228).

In 1497, the *reyes católicos* ordered a new series of coins. One of these was the *excelente de la Granada*, with a weight of about 7g. Both the *excelente de la Granada* and the *medio excelente de la Granada* (3.5g) depicted the opposed crowned faces. The other side of these coins depicted the unified coats of arms of Castile and León, Aragon and Sicily, and Granada. For the *excelente de la Granada*, this coat of arms was carried by an eagle (Farrés 1959, p. 231; De Francisco Olmos 1999, p. 100-101). This image corresponds to the coat of arms depicted on the type 1 coin weights, where we can see the wings of the eagle flanking the shield. This means the type 1 coin weight was used in relation to the *excelente de la Granada*. Again, we are dealing with an unusual coin weight depicting both sides of the actual coin, this time providing a younger *terminus post quem* of 1497.[22] As demonstrated by these contemporary finds, the *medio excelente* was still in use at the time of the *excelente de la Granada* (De Francisco Olmos 1999, p. 106). The unusual depiction of both sides of the coin on these weights was very likely an aid to distinguish between these rather similar objects.

A parallel for the type 1 coin weight has been discussed by Houben (1992, p. 1814). He proposes a possible origin in Antwerp and dates the object to the beginning of the 16th century. A parallel for the type 2 coin weight has been reported by Holtman (2002, p. 2791). He argues for an origin of these weights (including the type 1 weights) in the city of Ghent based upon stylistic features, and proposes a *terminus post quem* of 1499.

Although both the *medio excelente* and the *excelente de la Granada* were never minted in the Southern Netherlands (Vanhoudt 2015), archaeological evidence from Antwerp demonstrates these Spanish coins did circulate there nonetheless (*Fig. 27*) (Minsaer 2007). Since these coins circulated in the Netherlands, it is not surprising related coin weights were also produced there. More surprising, however, may be the fact we have a clear indication these weights were produced in Antwerp or Ghent for export, while the actual coins were not minted there.

The third type of coin weight that was encountered in the Zeebrugge collection (3 items; length 1.4-1.5cm; width 1.4-1.5cm; thickness 0.2cm; ±3.5g; *fig. 26.c*) shows, on one side, a figure with cape and crown. The figure is holding an orb and cross (or *globus cruciger*) in the right hand, and what appears to be a stick in the left hand. The figure is flanked by two letters, possibly "N". On the other side of the coin, a hand is depicted. Left of the hand we can see the initial "C". Above the hand another orb and cross is depicted and right of the hand some sort of dot is present. The image of the figure is associated with the Hungarian "*forint*"[23], which has a wide date range of 1325-1848 (Pol 1990). The hand-mark is a maker's mark associated with the city of Antwerp. Unfortunately, the maker of this specific mark is not known and no specific date can be attributed to it, yet it is believed to be a rather "early" mark (Wittop Koning & Houben 1980, p. 185). Possibly it should be dated around 1509, when Charles V ordered makers to mark their weights with the city's coat of arms (Houben 1998, p. 24), yet this is uncertain.

A comparative analysis of the relative element concentration would have been very interesting for these coins and possibly could have answered the question whether all these weights were produced in one workshop. Due to time constraints, however, a qualitative analysis over quantitative analysis was chosen, therefore results for only one of the type 1 weights are available. This

---

[21] The mass presented for the coin weights was measured by means of a kitchen scale, which unfortunately could not present results up to the expected standards. Therefore, the presented masses should be considered approximations of the actual mass.

[22] The opposed crowned faces appear again, later in the 16th century, on the Dutch *dukaat*. This image was inspired by the image of Ferdinand and Isabella, yet adapted to its own context (Pol 1989, p. 95) and does not correspond to the coin weights of the Zeebrugge wreck.

[23] The figure is also associated with the Dutch *dukaat* in the late 16th century. Since this date does not correspond to the relative date of most other finds, we will only discuss the Hungarian Forint.

Finds from the Zeebrugge wreck

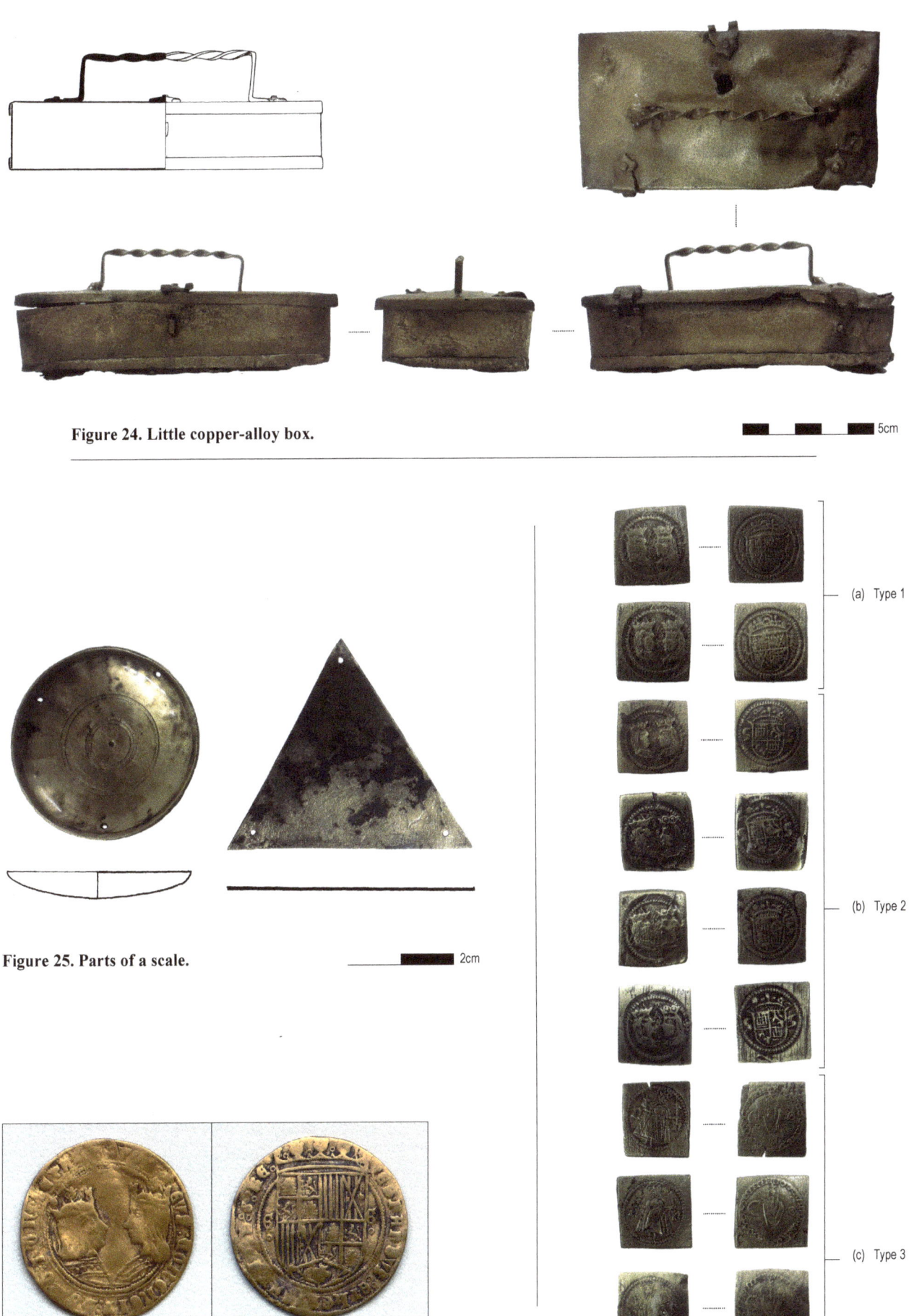

Figure 24. Little copper-alloy box.

Figure 25. Parts of a scale.

Figure 27. Coin depicting the *Reyes Catolicos* (not to scale) (Urban Archaeology Department, City of Antwerp (Belgium)).

Figure 26. Coin weights.

(a) Type 1
(b) Type 2
(c) Type 3

weight was made of a brass-alloy with 77.4% copper, 17.2% zinc and 1.3% lead. Although we do not know the relative element concentration for the other coin weights, it appears they are all made of brass too.

3.4.3. Venus counters

Among the finds related to financial issues, two so-called 'Venus penny' counters are present. A counter, counting token or *jeton*, is the name given to round metal tokens that, in Europe, generally appear around 1400 and are used for mathematical calculations. Historical sources, however, mention the use of such counters in Flanders already in 1284 (Groenendijk 2015, p. 6, 12). The tokens were placed on a so-called *abacus*, featuring different lines representing different values. By adding tokens to a certain line, one could make complex calculations.[24] The counters were used for different trades that required detailed calculations, among others by merchantmen, and offered the advantage of being used with no literacy skills required. The specific type of so-called Venus counters, depicting a naked woman on one side, were minted in several places in the Southern Netherlands, among which was Antwerp, between 1488 and 1512. Copies of these official counters have been produced in the Southern Netherlands as well as in Nuremberg, in the period 1500-1550 (*Idem*, p. 94-95, 98, 213-216).

The Venus counters from the Zeebrugge wreck are relatively similar, yet there are some small differences. Both counters depict a nearly naked woman holding a bird on one side and the coat of arms of Philip the Fair (1478-1506) on the opposed side, and both the naked figure and the coat of arms are surrounded by a legend. These legends feature the mark of an open crown. Both legends appear to be nonsense words, depicting rather a group of random letters than actual words. Differences between both counters can mainly be seen in the attributes depicted around the naked woman. In both cases, she holds a so-called *chantepleure* (a sort of water can) in the left hand, yet the flowers she waters appear in different spots. Also, the cloth she wears over her right arm differs on both counters. The first object (*Fig. 28.a*) has a diameter of 2.9cm and a thickness of 0.1cm. This object is mainly made of copper (89.6%) and a small amount of zinc (6.4%). A close parallel for this object is depicted by Groenendijk (2015, p. 159, nr° 71a/c), and many nearly identical variations seem to exist.

The second object (*Fig. 28.b*) has a diameter of 3.1cm and a thickness of 0.1cm. It is made of copper (86.6%) and zinc (10.1%) as well, with a little higher relative zinc concentration compared to the other counter. Although no exact parallel for this object was found, close parallels with small deviations are depicted once again by Groenendijk (2015, p. 162-165).

The copper alloy for both pennies appears to deviate from the objects discussed by Groenendijk. Although the elements are similar (mainly copper with a small amount of zinc), the relative concentration is different. For the parallel objects discussed by Groenendijk (2015, p. 278), the amount of copper ranges between 94-98%. Similar results are discussed by Mitchiner, Mortimer, and Pollard (1988, p. 122-123), with one exception featuring a lower copper concentration (Cu 80%; Zn 18%). Mitchiner, Mortimer, and Pollard argue the main composition is comparable to latten of the quality used in post-medieval France.

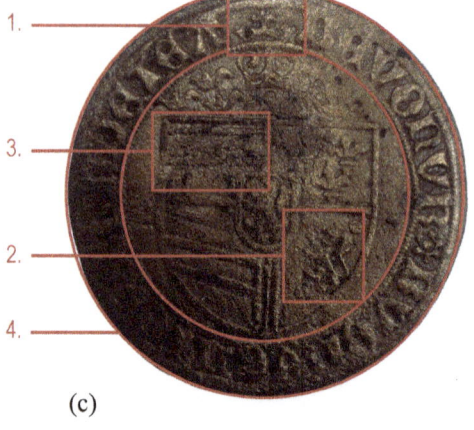

Figure 28. Venus counters. 2cm

---

[24] For examples of this practice, see Groenendijk 2015, p. 7, Figure 3.

Despite the small differences between these two objects, both of them appear to be copies of the official counters. The naked figure holding a bird, with a rounded coat of arms on the opposed side, are typical features for the early copies. Some small yet peculiar details (*Fig. 28.c*) support this identification. First of all, the specific open crown depicted in the legend (1) is a typical feature among the early copies. Also, the less detailed lion, accompanied by two dots in the fourth quarter of the shield (2) is a common feature, as are the three lines in the first quarter (3). Another peculiar detail is the 'fantasy' legend, which is rather a combination of letters instead of depicting any actual words (4). Finally, the diameter of these objects corresponds to the common 3cm diameter of the copies, as opposed to the 2.8cm diameter of the original items. According to Groenendijk (2015, p. 246, 267), these specific copies should be dated to around 1500 and could have been made in either the Southern Netherlands or Northern France.

Venus counters have been discovered in archaeological contexts, not only in the former Southern Netherlands, but also in other places such as England (Barnard 1924, here (mistakenly) interpreted as Nuremberg products). It is hard to tell whether the Venus counters from the Zeebrugge wreck were part of the cargo or were brought for personal use by a merchantman. In both cases one would expect to find more of these objects. According to some of the inventories two or three more Venus counters may have been recovered from the wreck. However, since no other counters are present in the current collection we cannot include their data in this discussion. It is unclear what happened to these objects or where they are located now.

3.4.4. Coins

Although no coins are present in the current collection, several sources mention at least two coins were recovered from the Zeebrugge wreck. Unfortunately, visual data in this regard is missing and the proposed numismatic interpretations are not consistent. Nevertheless, this information would be very valuable, specifically in connection with determining a relative date for the wreck.[25]

Vandenberghe (1997, p. 89) argues both coins are very damaged and proposes, as a preliminary interpretation, they are related to Alfonso V of Aragon (1416-1458), produced in Sicily or Southern Italy. Parmentier (Personal information) did recall a coin indeed related to the Aragonese monarchs. Schiltz informed us an Italian coin (from Genoa?) was found, dated 1481. Later on, however, Vandenberghe (2006, p. 20) would argue the damaged coins were issued by Charles V (1500-1558). Similar information is given by Parmentier (2000, p. 236) who argues "a few coins and coin weights not younger than 1520" could procure a relative dating. He refers to this date again in a later publication (Parmentier 2011, p. 33). Since the coin weights, at best, can provide a *terminus post quem* of 1509, it is likely this date is based upon the coins. Holtman (1999, p. 27) gives a very precise date for the site between 1520-1522. Holtman informed us this date was given to him by Vandenberghe. If we assume this date indeed is based upon numismatic research and we take the earlier information into consideration as well, it is possible the present coins were identified as coins from the second emission by Charles V in 1521 (Vanhoudt 2015, p. 133). But this would not explain the *terminus ante quem* of 1522. Of course, as long as the actual archaeological data is not available, we can only express presumptions on this matter.

3.5. Kitchen- and dining-related finds

The largest and most diverse category is composed of objects related to cooking or dining. A considerable amount of pewterware is present among these finds, such as plates, salt holders, spoons and a flagon. Furthermore there are several types of cauldrons recovered from the wreck, as well as mortars, pestles, taps, and some knife handles and knife decorations. Some of these objects may have had applications other than use in the kitchen, such as mortars, which could have been used by pharmacists. Nevertheless, all objects discussed in this category could have been used in a context of kitchen and dining. Possible other functions will be mentioned when appropriate.

3.5.1. Cauldrons and colander

Different kinds of cauldrons have been recovered from the site, as well as one colander. Peculiar among these objects is one series of three nested cauldrons, made of brass. The one colander recovered from the wreck is very similar to these objects, yet provided with a pattern of puncture holes. Furthermore there is one smaller cauldron of a different type, made of copper, and two heavy tripod cauldrons.

The nested cauldrons are three objects of different sizes that fit into one another and can be stored this way. They were recovered from the wreck assembled together. Traces of straw were encountered in the concretion between the cauldrons (P.A.B.S., D.R., 16/97/1991). Probably the cauldrons were stored in straw to prevent any damage. This seems to indicate these objects were part of the cargo, rather than being used on board. The largest cauldron has a diameter of 33cm and a height of 15cm (*Fig. 29.a*). The next smaller cauldron has a diameter of 30.6cm and a height of 13.1cm. It features slightly tapered sides (*Fig. 29.b*). For the smallest cauldron the sides are more tapered. It has a diameter of 28.5cm and a height of 12.5cm (*Fig. 29.c*). The colander was recovered separately, yet it

---

[25] Many attempts were made by the author to locate these specific objects since there are clear indications these coins can provide the youngest terminus post quem for this site and thus provide the most precise date. Unfortunately, even with the help of several people from the Flanders Heritage Agency, the objects could not be located.

The Zeebrugge Shipwreck

Figure 29. Three nested cauldrons (a, b, c) and a colander (d).

Finds from the Zeebrugge wreck

(c)

(d)

20cm

37

appears to be very similar to the nested cauldrons (*Fig. 29.d*). With a diameter of 33cm and a height of 18.7cm, it is slightly bigger than the largest of the three nested cauldrons. The puncture holes of the colander form a decorative pattern. When this colander was recovered, an iron rim was present along the upper edge to reinforce it and, although highly eroded, traces of two handles could be recognised (P.A.B.S., D.R., 19/09/1991).[26] The iron rim appears not to be preserved, yet we can distinguish a more reddish colour where the rim was connected to the colander. The cauldrons feature a similar reddish colour along the edge and it is very likely these were reinforced with an iron rim too. The edges of the cauldrons are folded, yet on two opposed places they point upwards (*Fig. 30*). This seems to indicate handles were once present here.

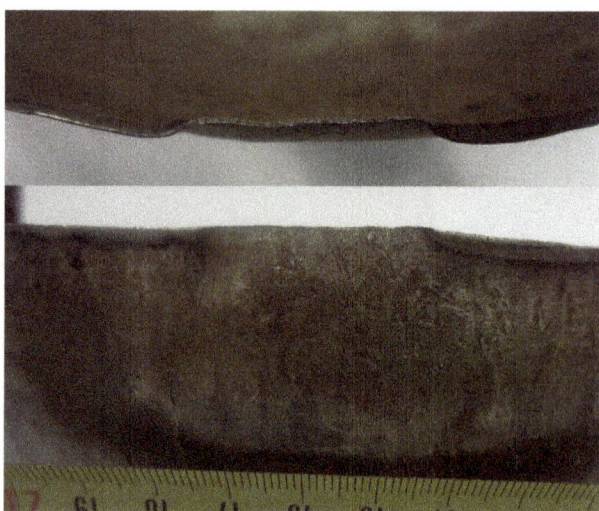

Figure 30. Edge of cauldron 29.a. Traces indicate a handle may have been present here..

Xrf-analysis was executed for the largest cauldron and the colander. Results demonstrate they are both made of brass with a very similar relative element concentration (Cu 80-81.5%; Zn 13.8-13.4%; Sn 2.1-2.2%). All three nested cauldrons show traces of hammer punches on the bottom. This indicates these objects, and probably the colander too, were shaped by hammering a brass sheet. Based upon the similar element compositions and similar production details, we believe the nested cauldrons and the colander were all made in the same workshop. A woodcut print from *Das Ständebuch* (1568) by Jost Amman depicts nested cauldrons in the workshop of a coppersmith. Similar objects were recovered from the Punta Cana Pewter wreck (mid-16th century, *fig. 31*) (ARS Anchor Research & Salvage Inc. 2012a, p. 108). According to Ostkamp (2013, p. 203), wreck-finds for this type of cauldron indicate they were transported without any iron rims and he believes these objects were traded as semi-finished products. Indeed, the cauldrons from both the Zeebrugge wreck and the Punta Cana wreck do not present any iron features, yet similar cauldrons from submerged contexts, featuring repairs indicating use, do not have these iron rims either (Hoss & Grimm *in preparation*). It is not unlikely iron features were actually present but are just missing for simple taphonomic reasons. At least for the Zeebrugge finds this appears to be likely, for the above-mentioned reasons. A parallel for this type of cauldron, with actual iron rim, can be found in the Boijmans-van Beuningen collection in the Netherlands (Dubbe 2012, p. 115; Ostkamp 2013, p. 203).

Figure 31. Nested cauldrons from the Punta Cana Pewter wreck (Image provided by ARS Anchor Research & Salvage Inc.).

A smaller cauldron of a different type was recovered from the site too (*Fig. 32.a*). This cauldron is more bulb-shaped, with a flared rim on top. The upper edge is folded. The object is dented and partly damaged. It exhibits strong traces of conservation. Notable are several round clamps riveted to the cauldron. When the clamps are not present anymore, their location is indicated by a small hole. On opposed sides of the cauldron, two clamps are located next to each other on the rim, and one is located in the middle of the body, beneath the clamps on the rim. The lower part of the body features clamps grouped per three, at three equally interspaced locations. The clamps must have been used to hang the cauldron above a fire. The total height of this object is 15.9cm and it has a width of 19.9cm. The cauldron is made of copper (95.3%). Traces of other elements are present, but do not exceed a relative concentration of 1%. It is uncertain whether this object was part of the cargo or used on board.

Finally, two tripod cauldrons were lifted from the wreck site too. The larger of the two objects (*Fig. 32.b*) has a bulb-shaped body with flared rim on top and a pointed bottom. Triangular handles, pointing sideward, are attached on opposed sides of the cauldron. They run from the upper part of the body to the rim. On the outside of the cauldron's body, opposed to one of the handles, a mark depicting a sort of loop is present (*Fig. 32.c*), yet the meaning of this mark is unknown. One of the three legs is missing. The object has a total height of 23cm and a total width of 24.9cm. It has a depth of 19.2cm. Xrf-analysis of this object demonstrates a composition with a very high

---

[26] The dive report specifically mentions the photographic recording of this feature. Unfortunately the actual pictures were not at the author's disposal.

Finds from the Zeebrugge wreck

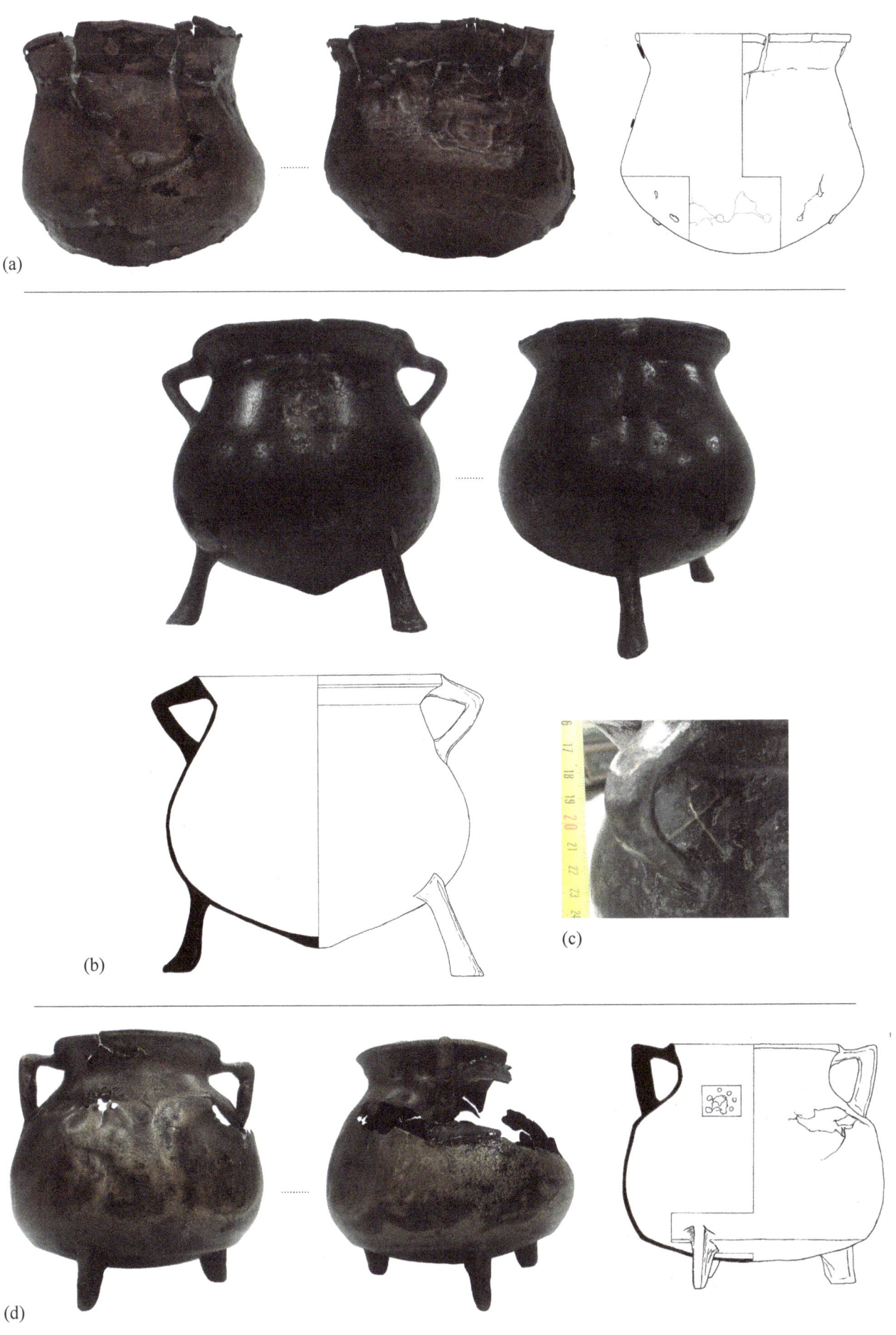

Figure 32. Different sorts of cauldrons from the Zeebrugge wreck.

relative lead concentration (45.2%), and to a lesser extent also copper (33.7%), tin (11.1%) and antimony (6%). The poor material quality of this object compared to other objects in the collection, may indicate this cauldron was present for use onboard the ship.

The last cauldron to discuss also features three legs, yet the shape is slightly different than the previous discussed object (*Fig. 32.d*). It also features a bulb-shaped body with flared rim on top, yet the bottom is more flattened. The hooked handles on opposed sides of the object are pointed upwards and run from the upper part of the body to the rim. A circle of puncture holes in the body indicates a past repair. This peculiar feature indicates this object was already used and was probably not part of the cargo, which in general appears to exist of objects in excellent condition. The cauldron has a height of 18.9cm and a width of 19.3cm. It has a depth of 16.4cm. No xrf-analysis was executed for this object.

3.5.2. Plates and platters

A large quantity of objects in this category is made of pewter. Most of these objects are pewter plates. Forty-five complete (or nearly complete) pewter plates were recovered from the Zeebrugge wreck. Furthermore, five incomplete pieces were recovered, probably belonging to pewter plates too. All but three of the complete plates are round. The three exceptions are deep plates with octagonal-shaped rims. For the round plates, we can distinguish deep plates and "flat" plates in different sizes. Some of the larger plates were probably used as platters rather than dinner plates.

When we plot the dimensions of the pewter plates in a chart, we can distinguish different groups with more or less homogeneous sizes (*Fig. 33*). A first group, with ten items, consists of smaller deep plates (*Fig. 34.a*). They have a height of 3-3.3cm and a width of 21.1-21.4cm. The inner diameter of these plates, which is the width without the rims, measures 11.6-11.9cm. In general, no marks seem to be present on these objects. One plate, however, features a U-shaped imprint (*Fig. 35.a*). This could be a trace of a worn maker's mark, although it could just as well be damage.

Group 2, with eight objects, comprises very similar, but larger, deep plates. With a height of 3.3-4.2cm and a width of 25-25.4cm, they are slightly bigger than the plates of group 1. The inner diameter for this group is 14.1-14.7cm. No marks are present on any of these plates.

The third group exists of sixteen "flat" dinner plates, in size comparable to the deep plates of group 2 (*Fig. 34.b*). They have a height of 1.9-2.3cm and a width of 25.7-26.3cm. The inner diameter measures 14.8-15.1cm. Two of the plates in this group show traces of what may have been a mark depicting a crowned rose (*Fig. 35.b and 35.c*).

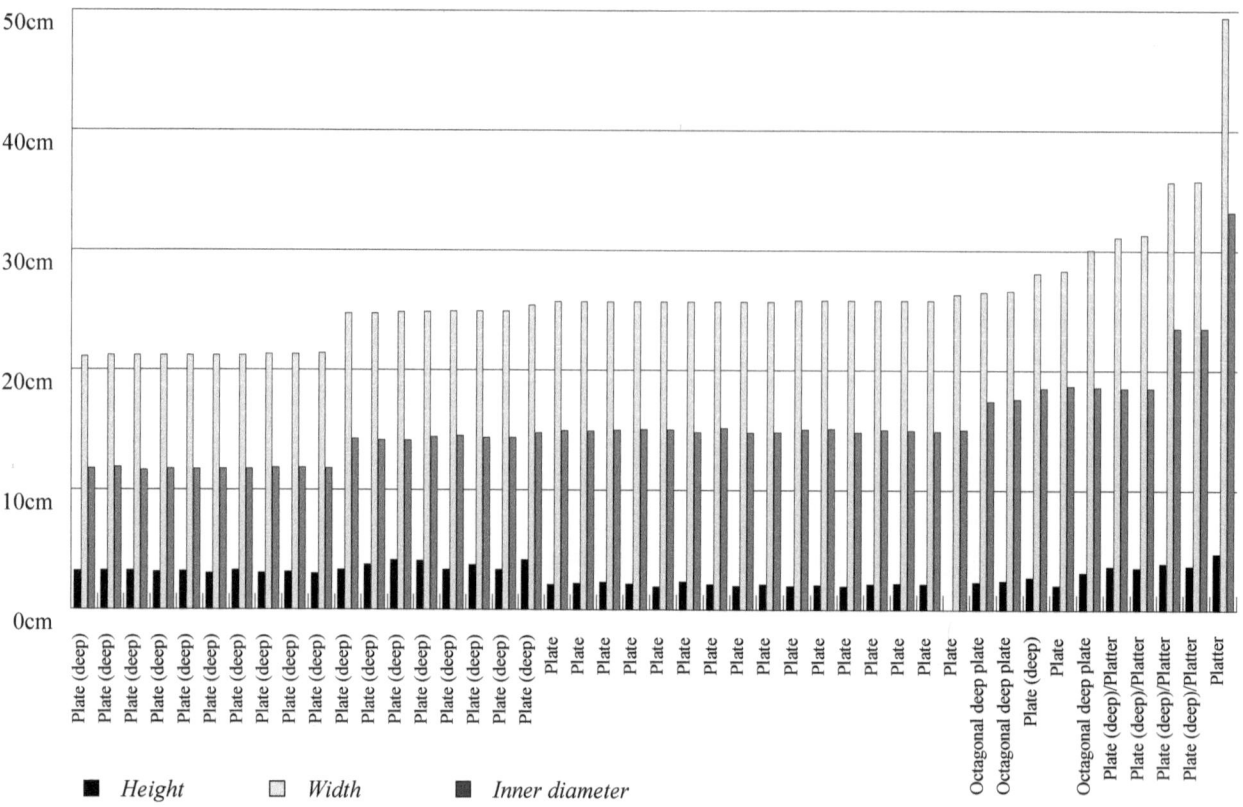

Figure 33. Dimensions of the different kinds of pewter plates.

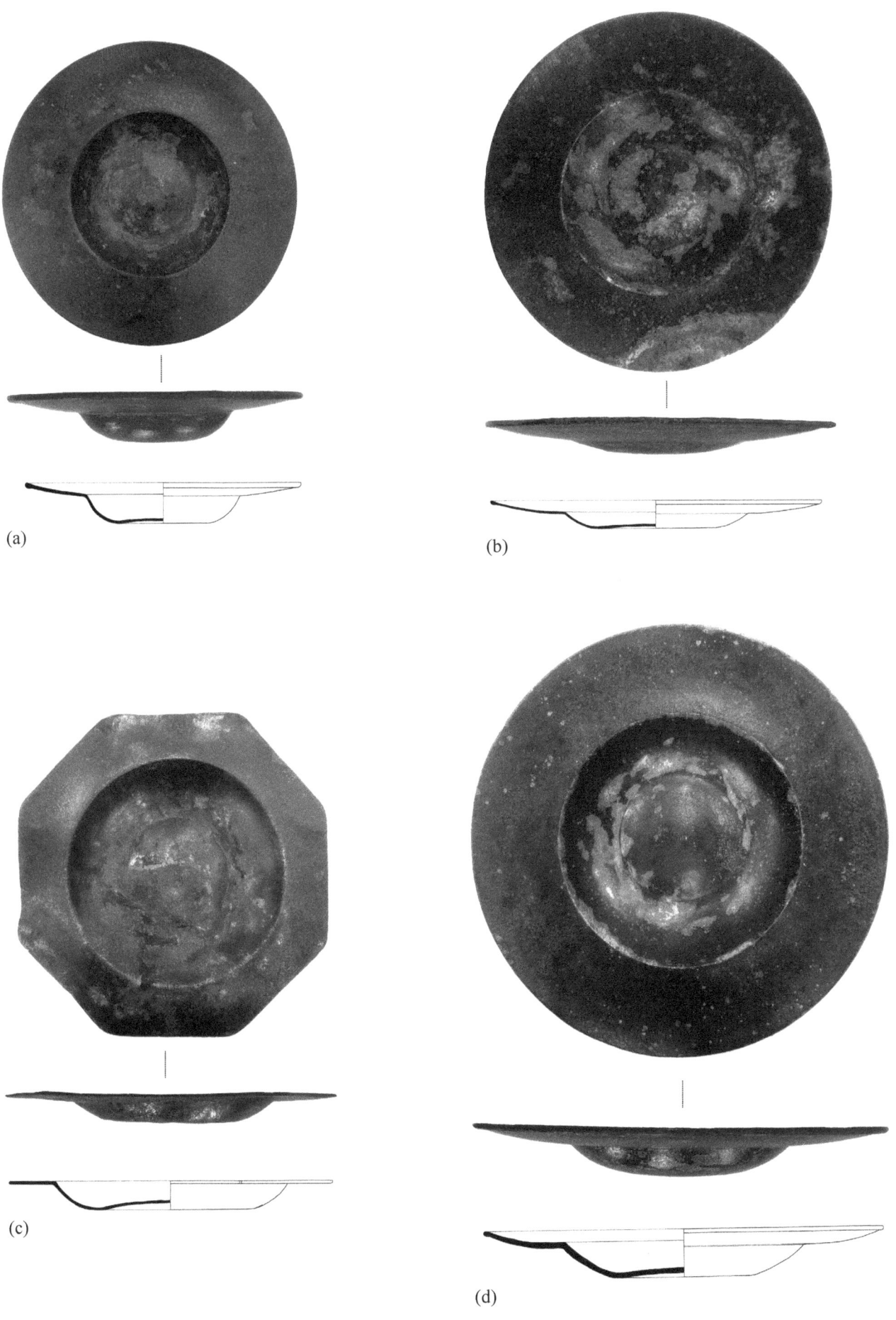

Figure 34. Different sorts of pewter plates from the Zeebrugge wreck.

The Zeebrugge Shipwreck

Unfortunately these plates suffered severe erosion, and they may have been treated with acid products (*cf. supra*). Therefore it is very difficult to determine possible maker's marks exactly.

Group 4 are the octagonal-shaped plates. Although we can distinguish different sizes among these three plates, we grouped them together because of their common characteristic shape. The first two octagonal plates have similar dimensions (height 2.4cm; width 26.5cm; inner diameter 17.5cm). One of these plates features clear traces of a crowned rose, yet the mark is strongly eroded (*Fig. 35.d*). The third octagonal plate is slightly bigger than the first two objects (height 3.1cm; width 30.1cm; inner diameter 18.6cm; *fig. 34.c*). It exhibits a similar mark as the smaller octagonal plate (*Fig. 35.e*). One of the five fragmentary finds may have belonged to a similar plate.

For the seven remaining complete objects we can distinguish four sizes. Since all these plates have considerable sizes, they may have been used as platters rather than plates, although the distinction may be arbitrary. The first two plates/platters have a width of about 28.2cm and an inner diameter of about 18.6cm. Only the height of both objects varies (2-2.7cm). The higher plate shows the mark of a crowned hammer (*Fig. 35.f*). On both sides of the hammer initials seem to be present, yet they are too eroded to recognise what they say.

Next we have two platters of 3.5cm high, a width of 31.2cm and an inner diameter of 18.5cm. No marks are present on these objects (*Fig. 34.d*). Neither do the following two platters (height 3.8cm; width 35.8cm; inner diameter 23.5cm) show any marks. The biggest of all recorded platters (height 4.7cm; width 49.4cm; inner diameter 33.2cm) is marked with a crowned hammer again (*Fig. 35.g*).

Some of the four remaining incomplete fragments may have belonged to a same object, but probably not all of them. One of the items is pierced. Another item, probably part of a large platter, shows the mark of a crowned rose (*Fig. 35.h*).

Among the marks mentioned above, we can distinguish the crowned rose and the crowned hammer, and only a few of them appear to be similar. Detailed literature for the identification of such marks exist (e.g. Dangis 2014) and we attempted to identify these marks ourselves, and with the help from experienced pewter specialists.[27] Unfortunately the marks are too worn to identify them easily. Especially the lack of any initials makes identification difficult. Also, although many examples of the crowned hammer and crowned rose are known in many variations, data for the period consistent with the other finds from the Zeebrugge wreck (*i.e.* late 15th-early 16th century) seems to be very limited. Possibly, further and more thorough study of these marks may result in

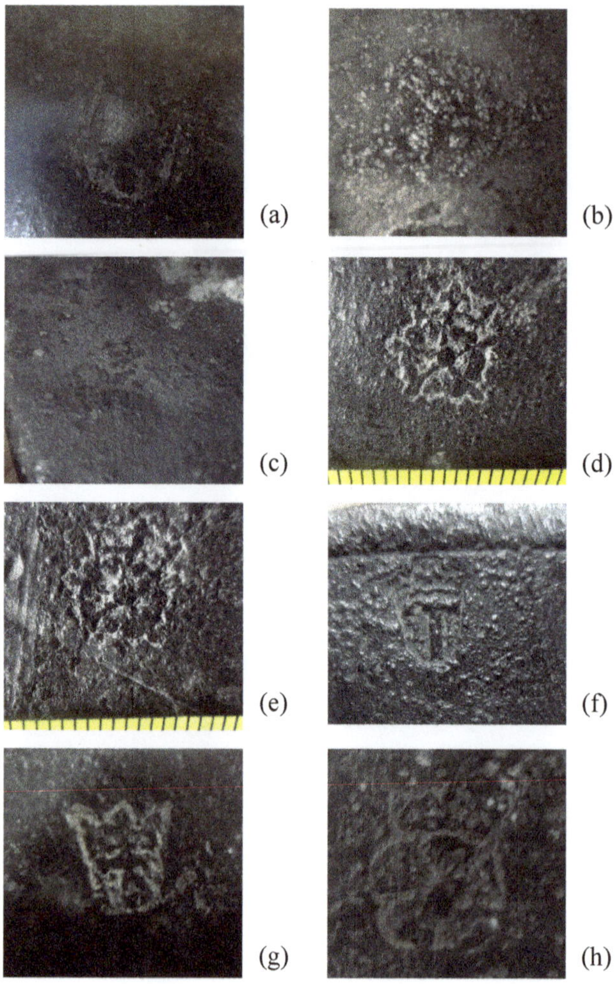

Figure 35. Different pewter marks present on plates and platters from the Zeebrugge wreck (not to scale).

Figure 36. Porringer depicted together with other objects recovered from the Zeebrugge wreck (Demerre, Van Haelst and Pieters 2013).

---

[27] We would like to thank Martin Roberts (The Pewter Society) and Philippe Probst (Vlaamse Tin Vereniging) for their help in this regard.

identification. Although the identification of these marks may provide a more specified origin and date for these objects, the general type of mark as such can give us some information too.

The crowned hammer is considered one of the earliest known quality marks for pewter, dating back to the 14th and 15th century (Roberts 2013a, p. 34). Its origin is uncertain, but it seems to first appear in French and Flemish pewtering regions (Gadd 1999, p. 8). There is also evidence for the use of this mark in England in the 16th century (Roberts 2013a, p. 40; Gadd 1999, p. 8). Although later examples exist, the crowned hammer is mainly associated with objects of the 15th and 16th century. From the 16th century on the mark becomes largely outcompeted by the mark of the crowned rose (Beekhuizen 1998, p. 16).

The use of the crowned Tudor rose as a quality mark is better documented. It has its origin in London where it was a label for high quality pewter of (almost) 100% tin (Gadd 1999, p. 9). Archival sources indicate that, by the early 1520's, Antwerp pewterers must have had adopted the crowned rose as a pewter mark, to compete with English export products (Roberts 2013a, p. 35). From here the use of the crowned rose mark spreads further over the Low Countries. However, different from the English pewter, the alloy here still contained about 10% lead for sadware, and even up to 20% lead for hollowware (Gadd 1999, p. 9). In 1523, the Antwerp magistrats forbade the further use of the crowned rose as a mark. Only from 1535 was the use of this mark allowed again for Antwerp pewterers (Roberts 2013a, p. 36).

In relation to the discussed pewter marks, xrf-analysis of the marked plates in the Zeebrugge collection could possibly lead to a relative date or origin for these objects. Because of time limitations, however, we could only sample four objects for xrf-analysis, and at the time we executed these measurements a more random sample was considered preferable. The samples include one octagonal plate with crowned rose mark, a plate/platter with crowned hammer mark, a "flat" plate without mark and a "deep" plate without mark. Despite different (or lacking) marks, all samples have a relative tin concentration exceeding 90% and a small concentration of copper between 1-2.6%. Considerable traces of lead are only present for the plate with crowned hammer mark (1.9%). For the octagonal plate the relative lead concentration is 0.4% and for the other two plates the lead content is less than 0.1%. Relatively high traces of iron were detected for the unmarked deep plate (2.3%). In general, these results are consistent with English pewter compositions of the 16th century (Roberts 2013a, p. 21), as are the marks. Therefore, we believe an English origin for this collection of plates is very plausible. The plates with the crowned hammer marks may have been produced elsewhere; for now unfortunately the data does not allow a more specified conclusion. Further analysis of this collection of plates certainly may lead to more precise answers of date and origin.

According to Parmentier (Personal information) several of these plates were part of concreted lumps, where they were grouped together. Although this is not described as such in the dive reports, and many of the plates were recovered individually as well (MEA 1991), we can indeed see plates grouped together in figure 18. This seems to indicate those plates were piled together, likely as part of the cargo. Only a few consistent studies of large pewter assemblages from a single archaeological context seem to exist. This is the case for the Mary Rose (1545) (Brownsword & Pitt, 1990) and the Punta Cana Pewter wreck (Roberts 2013a). A comparative study with these assemblages may be interesting for future research. For the latter wreck, a large number of octagonal-shaped plates were present, some of them very similar to the octagonal-shaped plates from the Zeebrugge wreck (Roberts 2013b, p. 17, fig. 8). This particular shape, known as *puntschotel*, was believed to be a creation of silversmiths in the 17th century. However, the large assembly of such plates recovered from the Punta Cana Pewter wreck indicates this type was common in the mid-16th century already (*idem*, p. 19). Based upon this information, it is not unlikely the octagonal plates from the Zeebrugge wreck are among the earliest known examples of this type of plate.

Also, a porringer must have been present among the finds. This object was shown, together with other finds from the Zeebrugge wreck, in a presentation by members of the Flanders Heritage Agency in 2013 (*Fig. 36*) (Demerre, Van Haelst and Pieters 2013). In the finds list provided to the Dutch authorities, a 'flower-shaped dish' is mentioned (MEA 1991). This description may refer to the porringer. This porringer appears to be made of pewter and features two opposed ears with eight-lobed margins. The current location of this object, however, is not known.

In addition to the pewter plates, five large platters made of copper-alloy were recovered from the site as well (*Fig. 37*). They feature a broad, flat rim and a rounded bottom. They all have similar dimensions, and small variations seem to be the consequence of damage (height 3.8-5.1cm; width 39.1-44.5cm; inner diameter 29.7-32.1cm). It is uncertain whether these objects are actually related to kitchen or dining. Another possible use could have been wash basin, since relatively similar copper platters with a similar height are known to have had this function (Dubbe 2012, p. 75-77). Since five similar such objects were recovered we believe these platters were probably part of the cargo.

3.5.3. Salt holders

Further pewterware finds from the Zeebrugge wreck include seven salt holders. Among them we can distinguish two types.

The first type (*Fig. 38.a*), represented by four pieces, is a salt holder with a hinged cover. It features a skirted, circular base with a dotted, decorated collar at the bottom.

The Zeebrugge Shipwreck

Figure 37. Copper-alloy platter.

Both cup and cover have the shape of half a sphere. They are provided with slightly protruding, cross-fitting rims. Along these rims dotted, decorated collars are present. When closed, together they form a complete sphere-shape. The cover is provided with a "spiked" top, which can be used as a handle to open the covered salt holder. At the end of this handle an acorn-shaped finial is present.

One of the four objects is in excellent condition. The other objects are dented, eroded, or incomplete. Nevertheless they appear to have very similar dimensions, when not distorted by these influences. The type 1 salt holders have a height of about 9.3cm and a width of about 5.9cm (or, with hinge included, about 6.4cm). The base has a diameter of 5.8cm. The depth of the cup measures 2.5cm. The length of the acorn decoration on top is 1.3cm.

Three of the four type 1 salt holders show clear traces of a hand-shaped mark, stamped under the base (*Fig. 38.b*). This mark is strongly associated with the city of Antwerp and we can assume these objects were produced here. The hand mark is known from other salt holders too, dated to the 16th century (e.g. Roberts 2013a, p. 16; Dangis 2014, p. 80). However, the hand mark appears on many objects in different periods, and, again, the absence of any initials makes it difficult to attribute these specific objects to a specific maker.

Nevertheless, the particular shape of this object can help us to propose a relative date for this type of salt holder. Examples of this type of salt holder are associated with the 15th and early 16th century (Dubbe 1978, p. 224-226). A relatively similar object, dated to the 15th century,

Finds from the Zeebrugge wreck

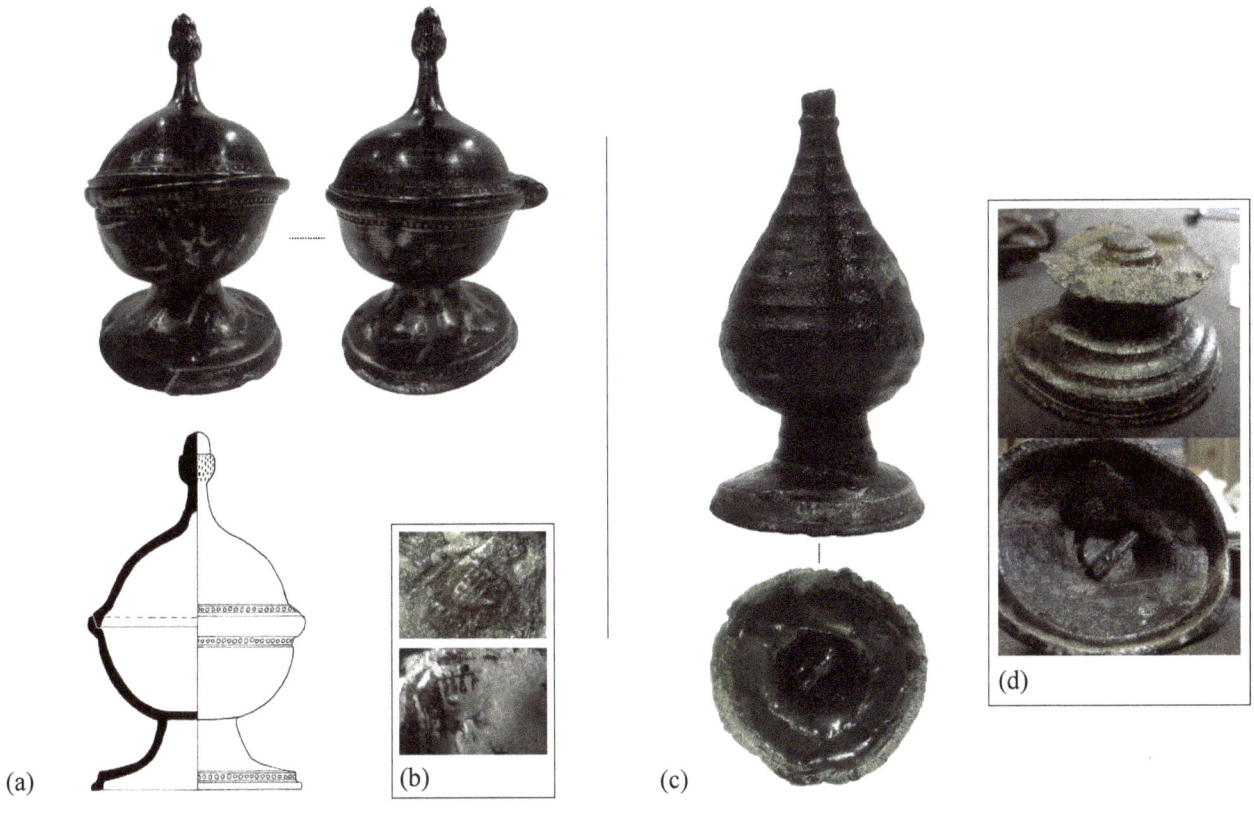

Figure 38. Salt holders (b and d not to scale).

Figure 39. 'Last Supper', Dieric Bouts (1464-1468) (left) and detail of type 1 salt holder (right) (M - Museum Leuven © www.lukasweb.be - Art in Flanders, foto Hugo Maertens).

can be found in the Boymans-van Beuningen museum (Museum Boymans-van Beuningen 1976, p. 29). A very close parallel is depicted on Dieric Bouts' "Last Supper", a painting made in 1464-1468 in Leuven, Belgium (*Fig. 39*). Here we can see the acorn-shaped finial, rims and dotted collars are gilded. Although no traces of such practice appear to be present on the Zeebrugge objects, this may well have been the case initially.

The second type of salt holder (*Fig. 38.c*)[28] features a pear-shaped body resting on a slightly flared discoid base with conical centre. The top of the body is open and functions as a nozzle. The entire object is ribbed. Underneath the base a plug is present to fill the hollow body with salt. This plug, with small handle on the outside, can clearly be seen on one of the objects that is missing the body (*Fig. 38.d*). Another object appears to have been squeezed, possibly as a consequence of trawling activity on site. The third object is the only object in good condition, yet it is covered in a thick coating as a consequence of its preservation. All three objects have similar dimensions with a height of about 12cm and a width of 6.5cm. The top opening has an

---

[28] The closed shape of this object did not permit the author to draw an accurate cross-section. For a cross-section drawing of a very similar object we would like to refer to Dubbe 1978, p. 229.

inner diameter op 0.6cm, and the depth of the body would be about 8.3cm. No traces of marks were encountered on these objects. A very similar object was found at the *Verdronken Land van Reimerswaal*, Netherlands, again dated to the late 15th or early 16th century (Dubbe 1978, p. 229; Museum Boymans-van Beuningen 1976, p. 29).

The relative element concentration was measured for one object of each type. For the first type, the pewter alloy is of relative low quality. Next to tin (66.5%), a large amount of lead is present (17.7%), and considerable amounts of copper (7.2%), iron (4.2%) and manganese (1.4%) were measured too. This result is consistent with the contemporaneous production in Antwerp.

The relative element concentration for the second type of salt holder, however, is more surprising. This object is made of high quality pewter, consisting of mainly tin (91.4%) and minor percentages of lead (2.3%), iron (2%) and copper (1.5%).

When we look at the very different element concentration of both objects, in combination with stylistic differences and marks, it seems reasonable to conclude different makers produced both objects. There is, however, no clear indication for the origin of the type 2 salt holders.

3.5.4. Flagon

One pewter flagon is present among the finds (*Fig. 40.a*). The flagon has a thick pear-shaped body and is provided with a hinged lid and handle. The flagon has a total length of 24.5cm, and measures 12.6cm at the base. The object is dented in the middle, where we measure the maximum width. The dented part measures 12.5cm, but the original width was approximately 13.2cm. The hinged lid is provided with a T-shaped thumb piece. Traces of what could have been a maker's mark seem to be present on top of the lid, yet it is too worn to recognise any image (*Fig. 40.b*). Inside the flagon, however, a medallion on the bottom shows a winged man holding a sword. This image, surrounded by dots, probably represents Saint Michael (*Fig. 40.c*). The presence of this religious medallion reveals that the object was cast vertically, a common practice before 1550 (Beekhuizen 1998, p. 13). The medallion of Saint Michael, including the surrounding dots, does show parallels with many pewter marks from Brussels, albeit from later periods (several examples in: Dangis 2014, p. 115-144). Although to some extent similar marks appear elsewhere too, Saint Michael is known to be patron of the city of Brussels, and possibly the flagon was produced there.

Xrf-analysis was executed at three separately casted parts of the flagon: the body, the lid, and the handle. Although all three parts contain the same elements, the relative element concentration is quite different. The body of the flagon contains mainly tin (70.6%) and lead (24.9%) and traces of mainly iron (1.2%) and palladium (1%). For the lid, however, the proportions are different with only 64.7% tin and 31.4% lead. Traces of palladium (1%) are present as well. For the handle, the relative tin concentration (47.5%) is almost equal to the relative lead concentration (43.8%). Here, traces of mainly iron (2.9%), copper (1.3%) and to a less extent palladium (0.9%) are present. We can conclude the pewter for this flagon is of much lower quality than the pewter plates discussed earlier. This supports the idea the flagon was produced in the Low Countries, possibly Brussels.

3.5.5. Spoons

The last group of pewter finds include spoons and parts of spoons. All together we can count seventeen such objects. Eight of them are complete spoons with decorative finials. Five spoons do not have a finial, yet we believe it is likely these spoons once featured decoration too, since one such finial was recovered from the wreck free from a spoon. Furthermore, two handles with finials but without bowls were recovered from the wreck, as well as one incomplete bowl with part of the handle.

All spoons but one have a similar design. The one exception is an incomplete object, with a different shaped handle (*Fig. 41.a*). This rectangular-sectioned handle has a flat surface on the upper side. Traces of what appears to be a maker's mark are present on the handle, near the bowl just above the drop. Although eroded, an "L"-shape can be recognised (*Fig. 41.b*). Whether this is an initial or part of an image is unclear. The width of the bowl is 5cm. The length of the object is 9.2cm, yet this and other dimensions are rather meaningless since the object is incomplete.

All other spoons present a very similar design and, when still observable, similar marks as well (*Fig. 41.c*). These spoons have a fig-shaped bowl and a square-sectioned handle. The flat sides of this handle are oriented diagonally, thus a rib runs over the length of the upper side of the handle. On both sides of this rib, near the bowl just above the drop, traces of what appear to be crowned hammer marks are present (*Fig. 41.d*). Although crowned hammer marks are not unusual for spoons in this period, the repeated mark on both sides of the rib is a rather unusual feature (Personal information Roberts and Probst). Unfortunately none of the marks are well-preserved, making identification difficult. Among this group of spoons, we can distinguish two sorts of decorative finial (*Fig. 41.e*). The first decoration, present on eight handles, possibly depicts a stylized pinecone. The other decoration, only present two times, depicts a stylized acorn. While the spoons are made of pewter, these finials are made of brass, and have been attached to the spoons afterwards.

Seven complete spoons are decorated with a "pinecone". These objects measure 18.5-19.6cm. One complete spoon is decorated with an acorn and measures 17.4cm. The spoons without decoration have a length of 14.5-17cm. The width of the bowl ranges between 4.7-5.2cm, but

Finds from the Zeebrugge wreck

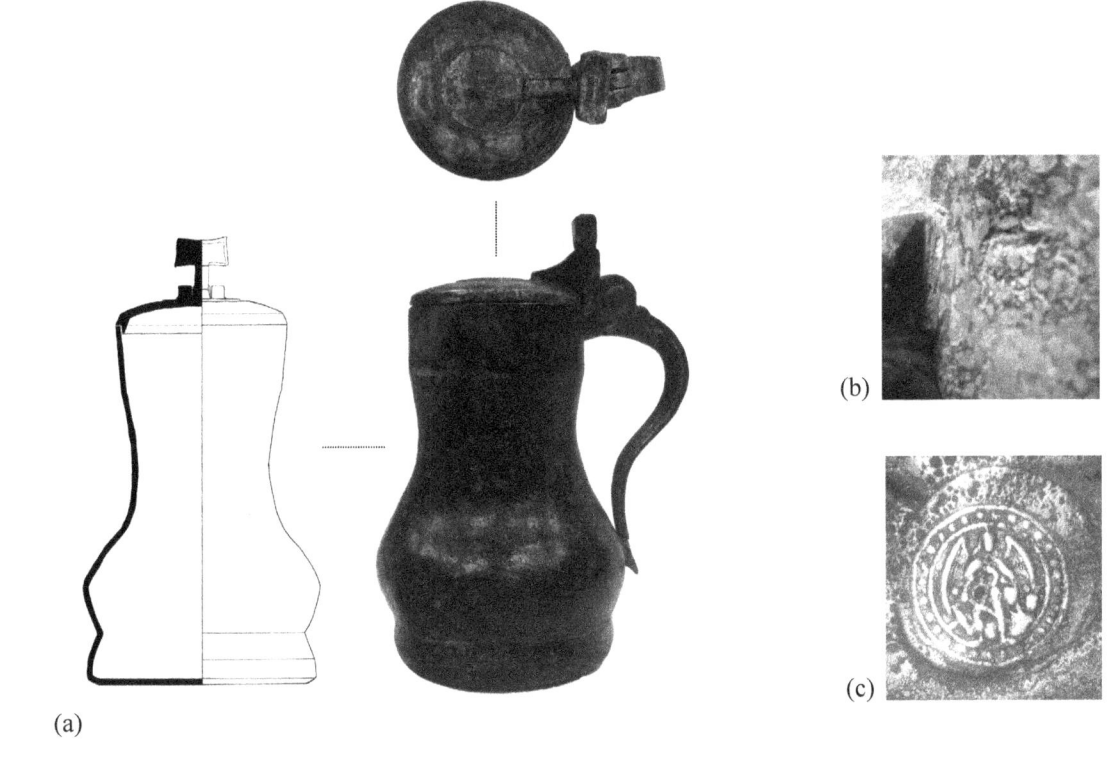

Figure 40. Pewter flagon (b and c not to scale).

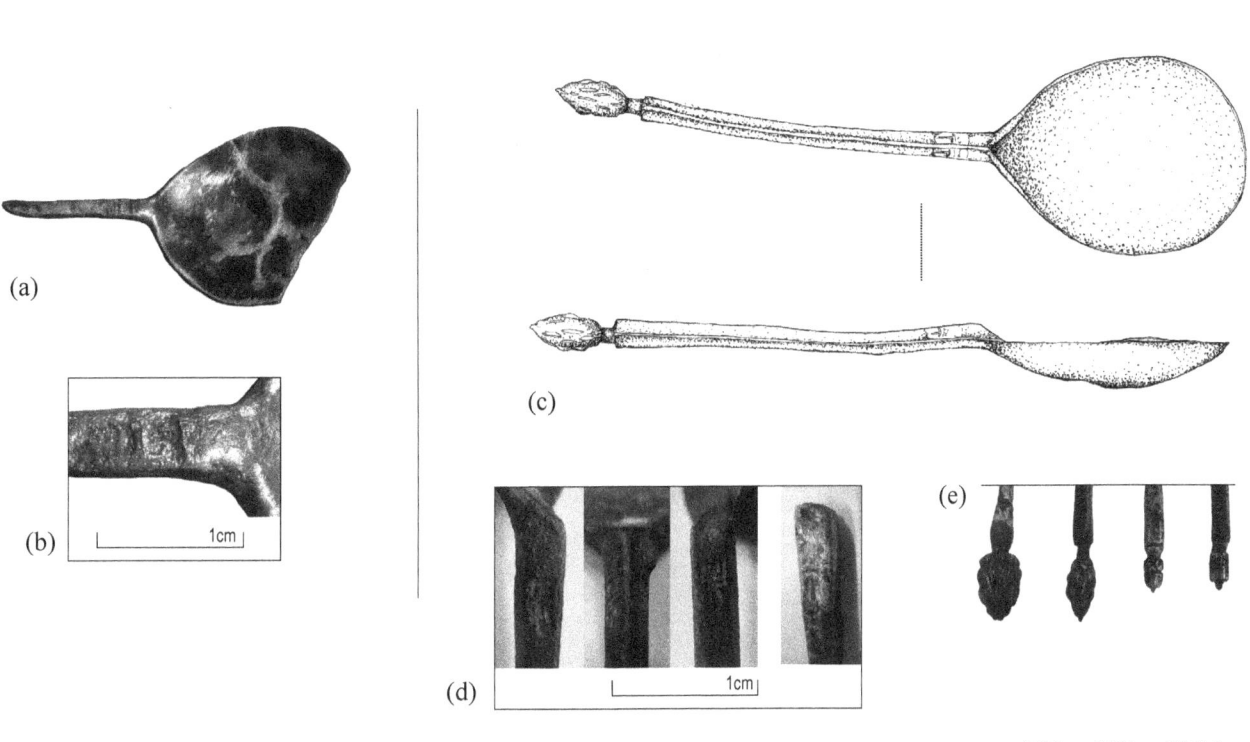

Figure 41. Pewter spoons.

most objects have a width of 5cm. The length of the bowls ranges between 6-7cm. The length of the acorn decoration measures 0.9-1cm. The length of the "pinecone" measures mostly 2.4cm, with one outlier of 1.6cm due to erosion.

Xrf-analysis was executed for two spoons and their "pinecone" finials. The spoons themselves contained mainly tin (68.2-72.7%), although a large amount of iron (15.2-12.6%) and copper (11.4-9.8%) was present as well. Furthermore a small concentration of lead (1.2-1.5%) could be measured. The corresponding decorations for these spoons were composed mainly of copper (74.8-75.5%) and zinc (19.7-20.1%), with a small concentration of lead (1.9-1.2%).

Although no exact parallels for these spoons were found, many sorts of similar spoons with different kinds of finials appear through time. The fig-shaped bowl is known to exist since at least the 16th century (Dubbe 1978, p. 286-287). The very similar alloy used for both decorations seems to indicate these were casted as a series, to add to pewter spoons afterwards.

3.5.6. Mortars and pestles

Among the finds in the MAS Museum are three mortars and seven pestles. More such finds were recovered from the wreck-site, yet two pestles and three mortars were reported to be stolen in 1991. A police investigation was put in motion, but unfortunately the original objects were never found (P.A.B.S., P.C.2, "Ontslag van Ondezoek 17/04/1992"). According to the 1991 finds list, a total of six mortars were discovered on site that year. Another mortar was discovered in 1997, by Bart Schiltz, about 200m away from the original centre of the site. This mortar is still in the presence of Schiltz. The finds list from 1991 further mentions nine pestles, indicating two of them are missing. The considerable number of mortars and pestles recovered from the Zeebrugge wreck seems to demonstrate these objects must have been part of the ship's cargo.

Among the present mortars, we can distinguish two types. The first type (*Fig. 42.a*), represented by two objects, is bucket-shaped with relatively straight sides. Above the slightly flared base three ribs are present, as well as underneath the flared rim on top. Two rectangular handles are soldered to the body on opposing sides. The larger of these two mortars has a height of 10.6cm and a diameter of 10cm. The total width, including handles, would be 11.6cm. The smaller mortar has a height of 9.4cm and a diameter of 10cm. Its width including the handles would be 12cm.

The second type of mortar is also bucket-shaped, but with strongly flared bottom and top, giving the sides of the object a concave appearance (*Fig. 42.b*). The sides feature multiple ribs, and although no handles are present, traces of soldering are clearly visible. The object is missing a part of the upper side. It has a height of 12.8cm and a diameter of 14.4cm. The bottom of this mortar features several concentric circles, a feature not present on the other type of mortars. The mortar discovered in 1997 (*Fig. 42.c*) appears to be relatively similar to this second type of mortar. Notable, however, is the upper edge of this mortar is much thicker. Also, the handles are still present here. These rectangular handles feature concave sides and more pointed corners than the earlier discussed handles. Possibly the mortar without handles had similar handles in the past.

The relative element concentration was determined for all three objects. Both mortars of the first type are made of the same alloy (Cu 79.6-80%; Zn 16.4-16.1%). The second type of mortar appears to be made of a different alloy, containing also lead (Cu 72.2%; Zn 16.8%; Pb 4.4%; Fe 2.7%; Sn 1.3%).

The pestles all appear to be relatively similar, yet none of them are identical (*Fig. 43*). First of all we can distinguish several lengths. The smallest pestle measures 13.7cm. Two pestles have a length of about 16cm, three of about 17cm and the largest one measures 23cm. Their widths vary from 3.1-4cm. All of the pestles feature flared, rounded ends on both sides, and a knop in the middle. All pestles are decorated with double or multiple engraved lines between the ends and the knop. The largest pestle features ribs between one of the ends and the knop in the middle. A small indentation in the centre of each end indicates all pestles were lathe-finished.

Xrf-analysis was executed for three of the pestles. Two of these three pestles feature a similar relative element concentration. Both objects contain mainly copper (70.3-71%), zinc (13.3-14%) and lead (11.4-10%), and to a less extent also tin (1.2-1.3%) and iron (1.1-1%). The third pestle contains a similar amount of zinc (14.4%), but more copper (78.2%) and less lead (4.2%). The alloys used for the pestles do not match any of the mortar alloys.

Mortars were used for many reasons. In some of the *Hausbücher* from Nuremberg we can see these mortars used by pharmacists to produce medicines, but also in the kitchen for grinding spices, grains, or other products (Stadtbibliothek Nürnberg (no date)). They were common trade goods and were found as part of the cargo in both the St Anthony wreck (1527) and the Punta Cana Pewter wreck (mid-16th Century). Nicely decorated mortars with concave sides, featuring texts, figures, or information about their maker, are known to have been produced in the Low Countries (Wittop Koning 1953). Mortars, more similar to the type 1 mortars from the Zeebrugge wreck, appear in a Nuremberg *hausbüch* (1528) as a product of the coppersmith (*Fig. 42.d*). Although the mortars and pestles from the Zeebrugge wreck do not feature any information about where they were produced, it is not unlikely they were made in the Low Countries or Southern Germany.

Figure 42. Different types of mortars from the Zeebrugge wreck
(42.d: Stadtbibliothek Nürnberg, Amb. 279.2° Folio 18 verso (Landauer I))

Figure 43. Pestles of different lengths.

Figure 44. Tap and different sorts of tap keys.

3.5.7. Taps

Several taps were recovered from the wreck. These taps comprise two separately casted parts; the tap and the tap key (*Fig. 44.a*). Two of the recorded taps consisted of a matching tap and tap key. Four objects were taps without a tap key, and three objects were individual tap keys. Some of these taps and tap keys may have belonged together, but it is also possible they originate from different sets. This means the actual number of taps, based on these recordings, may vary between a minimum of six objects and a maximum of nine objects.

Each tap consists of a spout, a key house, and a pipe. The spout is square-sectioned and features projecting triangular "ears", a shape interpreted by some as a stylized, zoomorphic head (Pieters ET AL. 2013, p. 494; Portable Antiquities Scheme (from here on referred to as: P.A.S.), find SF-07F127). The key house, octagonal on the outside, has a central, vertical, circular aperture to fit the tap key. The aperture narrows down a bit towards the bottom. The round-sectioned pipe is the last part. It is basically a hollow tube that narrows down toward the end. This side was plugged into a barrel. The taps vary in size, with a length of 16.9-19cm, a width of 2.1-2.5cm and a height of 2.5-3cm.

One tap was sampled for xrf-analysis and main elements are copper (78%), zinc (16.5%) and lead (2.7%).

The tap key consists of two parts. The first part is a cylindrical plug that fits into the key house. Just like the aperture of the key house, the plug narrows down a bit towards the bottom. The plug is pierced horizontally. By turning it, the plug either connects the pipe and the spout of the tap, or it separates them. The second part of the tap key is the head. For three of the five tap keys, the head is openwork trefoil-shaped (*Fig. 44.b*). The two other tap keys have a similar head, but with openwork double rings instead of the trefoil-shape (*Fig. 44.c*). All of the tap keys feature a mark with the lowercase letter "m" underneath the openwork. The two double-ringed tap keys have lengths of 6.5cm and 7.5cm. For the trefoil-shaped tap keys, only one object is complete, with a length of 8cm. For the two other tap keys we cannot give the actual length since they are incomplete, but even so they are bigger than the one complete object, having lengths of 8.5cm and 9.3cm. The width of the tap keys varies between 3.9-4.4cm, the thickness ranges between 1.9-2.3cm.

Also one tap key was sampled to determine the relative element concentration. We can see the composition is somewhat different compared to the tap (Cu 82.2%, Zn 7.5%, Sn 3.7%, Pb 2.9%). For the tap, tin was only present as a trace element, with less than 1%.

Tap keys with trefoil-shaped heads appear in the 15th century and seem to stay in use from that moment onwards (Baumgärtel 1997, p. 106). An object very similar to the Zeebrugge taps was recovered from a late medieval context (15th century) near Ostend, Belgium (Pieters 2013, p. 496). The "m" mark can be associated with an early tradition of Nuremberg marks on taps depicting a lowercase letter. The exact meaning of the letter is unknown. It may have been an initial of the maker, but it also could have been a kind of trademark. The lowercase "m" was used by an unidentified master and dates to the late 15th-early 16th century (Baumgärtel 1997, p. 110-111).[29] Similar taps are depicted on several images of the Nuremberg *Hausbücher* too (16th-17th century).

3.5.8. Knife handles and decorations

According to the available inventories, almost 100 knife handles were recovered from the wreck, and 64 separate items used for decorating knife handles were found as well. In the current collection, however, only 23 such decorations appear to be present. From the many complete handles a large quantity still remains. These handles are currently kept at the Flanders Heritage Agency for material analysis.

Wood analyses of the different knife handles by Kristof Haneca (Haneca and Pieters, 2016) lead to the identification of six different wood species as well as the identification of horn and bone. Each material type represents one or multiple designs of handle. We will briefly discuss the different species and the designs they represent. Most of these knife handles are made of two separate pieces of timber, riveted together. The space between these two pieces deviates strongly depending on the preservation of the objects. Therefore, when we refer to thickness of the object, we only measured the thickness of one piece of timber. The complete thickness would then be twice this number, plus the thickness of the iron shaft in the middle. When the object is only made of one (cleaved) piece, we will refer to the complete thickness.

Thirteen handles were identified as maple (*acer*). Based upon anatomical features it is difficult to specify between *acer pseudoplatanus*, *acer platanoïdes* or *acer campestre*. However, all three maple species are native to Europe and know a relatively similar distribution (Euforgen (2016)). We can distinguish at least three different designs among the maple handles.

The first design is made of one solid piece of timber that is partly cleaved in length, and features an angulated end (*Fig. 45.a*).[30] These handles are among the largest recovered from the Zeebrugge wreck, with a length of 11.7-14.9cm. They have a width of 1.8-2.9cm and a thickness of about 1cm. The smallest of these objects are damaged and

---

[29] Baumgärtel refers, among others, to the Zeebrugge taps to demonstrate the statement he makes.

[30] We opted to only depict a selection of handles in this paper. For a more complete overview of all handles recovered from the Zeebrugge wreck, we would like to refer to Haneca and Pieters (2016).

probably do not represent the actual full dimensions of the handle. Near the top of the handle the object is pierced, to rivet it to an iron blade.

Another design of handle made of maple comprises two separate pieces of timber riveted together with four rivets (*Fig. 45.b*). The handle narrows towards the top. Four such objects were recovered from the wreck, yet only two of them are more or less complete. These complete objects have a length of 13.5-13.9cm. The maximum width of these objects is 2.5-2.8cm. At the top they measure only 1.4-1.9cm. Their thickness is 0.8-0.9cm.

The other handles made of maple are somewhat smaller. They consist of two timber pieces, riveted together with three rivets. They have a length of 6.2-6.9cm and a width of 1.1-1.6cm. Their thickness is 0.3-0.4cm.

Nineteen handles are made of European yew (*Taxus baccata*), a tree species common in Europe. Although minor differences in length and shape occur for some of the handles (e.g. in some cases the top is slightly flared, in other cases not), in general they all appear to be relatively similar, made of two pieces of timber assembled with four rivets (*Fig. 45.c*). The lowest of these four rivets is slightly larger than the others. These handles have a length of 8.2-11.1cm. Their width ranges from 1.3-2.1cm and they have a thickness of 0.6-0.9cm. One exception in this group features only three rivet apertures, which are notably larger than the ones present on other yew handles.

Six handles are made of box (*buxus*), a genus with species in Europe, but also Africa, Asia and Central-America (Haneca and Pieters, 2016). Three of the box handles are notable for their decoratively-shaped ends (*Fig. 45.d*). It is likely these objects once featured a decoration similar to the ones depicted in figure 46.b, also recovered from the Zeebrugge wreck. These handles have a length of 7.9-8.1cm and a width of 1.7-1.9cm. Their thickness is 0.3cm. All three handles feature five rivets or rivet apertures.

Two other box handles do not feature a decorative end. They are provided with six rivets and have a length of 8.5-8.8cm. They have a width of 1.9-2.2cm and a thickness of 0.3-0.4cm. The final box handle is distinct because of its more circular cross section. It features three rivets. It is 6.7cm long, 1cm wide and 0.4cm thick.

Two handles are made of oak (*quercus*). Based upon anatomical features this could be either *quercus robur* or *quercus petraea*, two similar species very common in Europe. The handles consist of one single piece of timber which is cleaved to fit an iron shaft. Both objects feature multiple rivets. For one object with 19 rivets, 13 of them are organised in one line over the length of the handle. Underneath this line, five rivets are organised around one sixth rivet. This appears to be part of a decorative pattern.

The other handle features 12 rivets. The end of both handles features a decorative shape, and for one of them a small strap of copper-alloy metal is attached to the bottom of the handle (*Fig. 45.e*). These objects have a length of 9.8-10.3cm, a width of 1.3-1.9cm and are 0.8-1.1cm thick. For one of the objects, a very small part of iron shaft appears to be present on the inside of the handle, probably a part of what used to be the blade.

Another thirteen handles are made of a *millettia* species, either *millettia laurentii* (wengé) or *millettia stuhlmannii* (panga panga). Both these hardwood species grow exclusively in (Central-)Africa. Five handles feature a slanting end and have bevelled edges at the top. They feature three rivets (*Fig. 45.f*). They have a length of 7.9-8.1cm, a width of 1-1.1cm and a thickness of 0.3-0.4cm. Around some of the rivets the timber has a slightly different colour in a circular shape. This seems to indicate some sort of decoration was applied here in the past.

Three other handles feature four rivets and are rather oval-sectioned. They have a length of 6.8-7cm, width of 1.2-1.3cm and thickness of 0.4cm.

Two more *millettia* handles taper towards the top and feature a small gully in the centre from top to bottom on each side. Five rivets are present in this gully (*Fig. 45.g*). These handles have a length of 7.8-7.9cm and a thickness of 0.2-0.4cm. At the bottom they are 1.8cm wide, at the top 1.4cm. The gully has a depth of about 0.06cm.

Finally, three more objects are made of a single piece of *millettia*. One of them is cone-shaped; the other two are rather oval-sectioned and have more straight edges (*Fig. 45.h*). All of these objects feature openings on top and in some cases these run to the bottom through the entire object. Their lengths vary between 5.2-6.9cm, their width between 1.2-1.6cm and their thickness between 0.8-1.2cm. Traces of corrosion indicate a metal object was assembled to these handles once. Whether this was a knife, or rather a bodkin or other tool, is unclear.

Four handles are made of one single piece of yet unidentified timber (*Fig. 45.i*). Preliminary analysis seems to indicate that European species, and probably African species as well, can be excluded. It might be an Asian species, although another origin (e.g. Central-America) is also possible.[31] The handles have a tapered cylindrical shape, and feature a perforation on top. Their lengths vary between 5.3-7.2cm. They have a maximum width of 1.4-1.8cm and a thickness of 0.9-1.2cm.

The largest number of handles, a total of 36 objects, is made of *bovinae* horn. The identification of this material was complex because of its very dense structure, an indication the objects are made of the uppermost part of the horn (Personal information Haneca). Five peculiar objects

---

[31] At the time of research one of the handles was relocated for examination at the Royal Museum for Central Africa (RMCA, Tervuren, Belgium). This handle could therefore not be included in this research.

The Zeebrugge Shipwreck

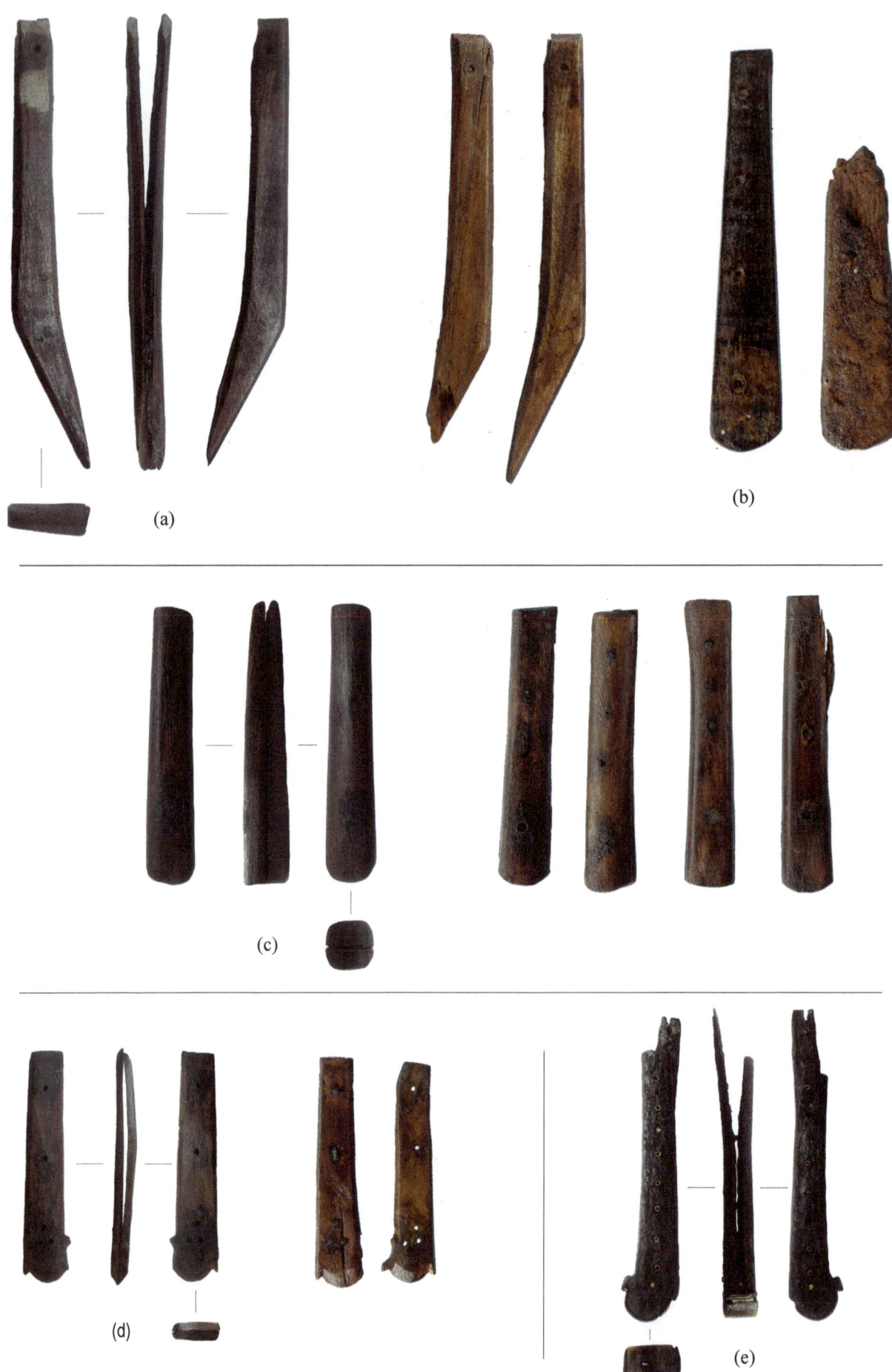

Figure 45. Different knife handles from the Zeebrugge wreck (images by author and Flanders Heritage Agency, H. Denis).

Finds from the Zeebrugge wreck

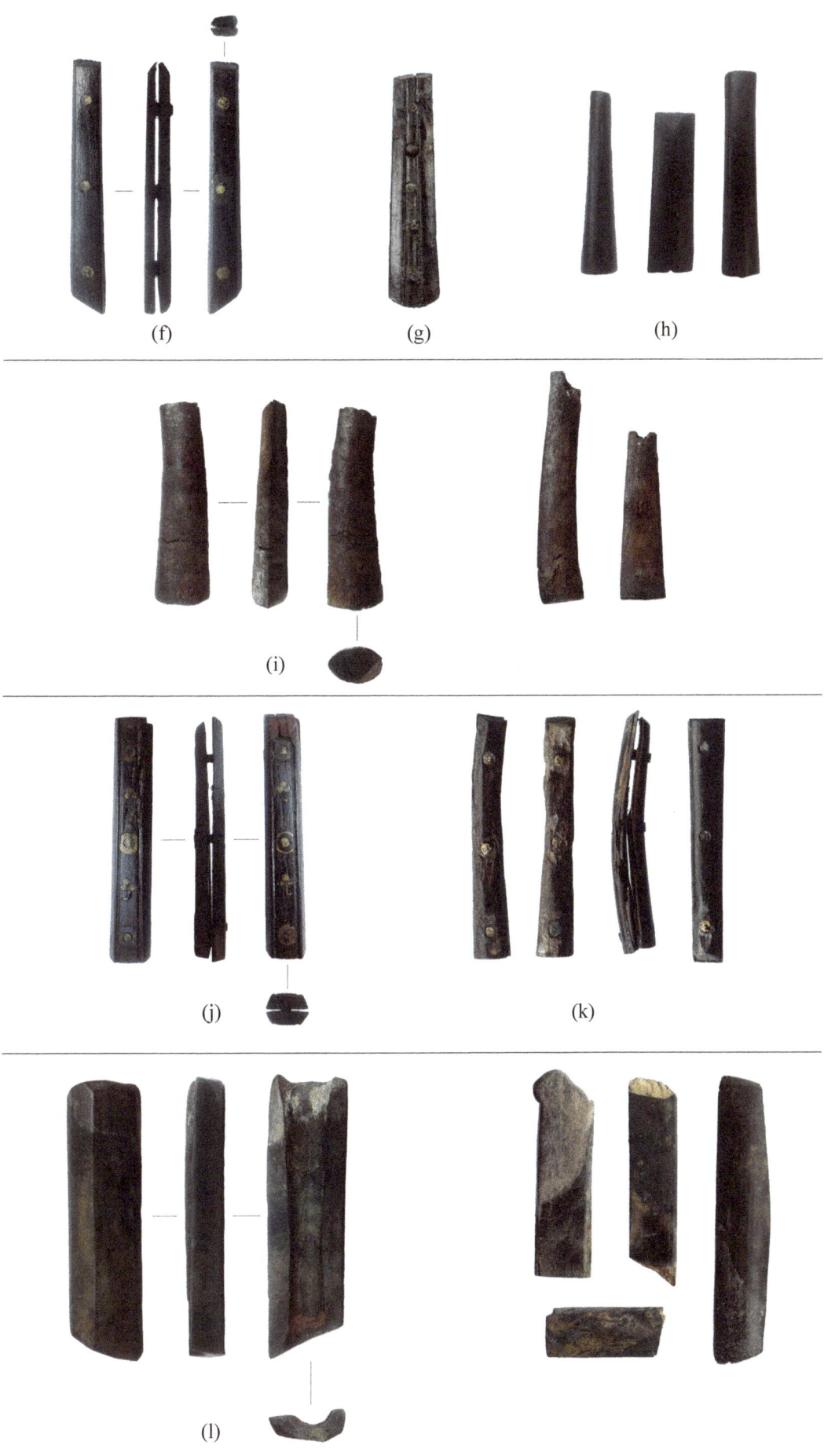

(f) (g) (h)

(i)

(j) (k)

(l)

5cm

The Zeebrugge Shipwreck

Figure 46. Different types of decorations for knife handles.

among these handles feature copper-alloy marquetry, in the shape of circles and clovers, as well as linear engravings (*Fig. 45.j*). Two objects are damaged. The others appear to be more or less complete and have a total length of 7.7-7.9cm. Their width ranges between 1.2-1.5cm and their thickness between 0.4-0.5cm. Three rivets are present, in the middle of the circular marquetry.

Five other, similar handles with three rivets feature the same engravings but without marquetry. They have a length of 6.9-7.2cm, a width of 1.1-1.2cm and a width of 0.4-0.5cm.

A large group of eighteen handles is round-sectioned and feature three rivets. They also exhibit small engravings along the sides (*Fig. 45.k*). This very homogeneous group has a length of 8-8.3cm, a maximum width of 1.3cm and a thickness of 0.5-0.6cm.

Finally, eight handles made of horn have a tapered shape, and feature three or four rivets. This is a rather heterogeneous group, with lengths varying between 6.8-8.7cm, widths between 1.4-2cm and thicknesses between 0.2-0.4cm. One of these objects is peculiar since it features a decoration similar to the ones depicted in figure 46.d.

To conclude, four objects are made of worked animal bone (*Fig. 45.l*). This group is very heterogeneous, with lengths varying between 6.9-11.1cm. The largest of these objects, however, is broken into two smaller pieces. Although these objects may have been used as tools, it seems unlikely they were actual knife handles.

Making knife handles was a different craft than making knives. Often, knives were brought to the workshops of handle makers as semi-finished products. Here, the knives were finished with nicely decorated handles (Ostkamp 2013, p. 201). The presence of such a large quantity of knife handles at the Zeebrugge wreck may indicate these objects were traded as semi-finished products as well. It may just as well be possible these handles were at one point complete with knife blades, but were the only parts to survive processes of erosion and oxidation. This latter hypothesis is very plausible, especially since at least one of the handles did feature traces of a blade. According to one of the early meeting reports (P.A.B.S., F.V., "meeting report 18/05/1991") traces of paper were discovered on some of the knife handles, indicating they were probably wrapped in paper. Also, a reference is made to oil floating on the water in which the knife handles were stored, and it is put forward the paper the handles were wrapped in may have contained traces of oil. If these handles indeed were wrapped, this may be an indication they were part of the cargo. This idea is supported by the large number of handles recovered from the wreck. Another explanation, however, could be the wooden handles themselves were treated with oil. Similar handles are known from other archaeological contexts in Belgium and the Netherlands (Marquardt 1997, p. 23-24). A decoration pattern with marquetry clovers similar to some of the handles made of horn, is depicted on the painting "Self Portrait with Wife" (1496, Antwerp) by the Master of Frankfurt.

Other than complete knife handles, a large number of copper-alloy decorations for knife handles was found as well. We can distinguish two main types of decoration. A first type comprises small, brass sheets, which decorated the surface of the handle. The other decorations were meant to be applied to the end of the handle and function as a finial.

The first type of decoration is the largest group. Each decoration features two sheets with engraved images that were supposed to be applied on opposing sides of the handle. A small rivet connects the two sheets. This rivet had to protrude the actual knife handle, which was nothing more than a flat tang. The decorations from the Zeebrugge wreck depict (religious) figures, animals, floral motives or a banderol. These latter ones may bear apparent inscriptions, yet they cannot be read. This is probably because engravers used to copy letters without necessarily being literate (Marquardt 1997, p. 28). According to Ostkamp (2013, p. 201), it is common for these decorations to depict religious scenes, and often these scenes refer to the idea of transiency. Marquardt (1997, p. 28) then again argues images of the Virgin Mary occur most frequently. He also argues St Barbara was often depicted since she was the patron saint of armourers (although it appears these knives were rather used as cutlery) and St Apollonia, related to toothache, because the knife was often used as a toothpick. St Barbara, indeed, appears to be represented on some of the Zeebrugge decorations, as well as St Catherine and St John (Vandenberghe 1997, p. 89).

Among the finds we can see different groups of similarly-shaped decorations. Group A (*Fig. 46.a*) and group B (*Fig. 46.b*) both serve a similar function. They were applied towards the end of the knife handle. The decorations of group C (*Fig. 46.c*) and group D (*Fig. 46.d*) then again were applied at the other end of the handle, where the blade of the knife starts. When seen from the side, these two latter groups narrow down into a point, functioning as a smooth transition from handle to blade. The decorations from group A have a length of 1.8-2.2cm and a width of 1.6-2cm. Group B measures 2.9-3.2cm in length, and 1.2-1.5cm in width. The two other groups are smaller. Group C has a length of 0.9-1cm and a width of 0.8-1.3cm. Finally, group D has a length of 0.6-1.1cm and a width of 1.1-1.4cm.

The second type of decorations only counts five items (*Fig. 46.e*). This is a heterogeneous group featuring different decorative styles, yet all with a similar purpose. Seen from the side, these objects feature an incision that could slide over the iron tang onto which the handle was applied. The length of these objects varies from 1.4-1.7cm, their width ranges between 1.2-1.9cm and their thickness between 0.7-1.2cm.

Similar finds, generally dated to the 15th and/or 16th century, have been recovered from different archaeological contexts, yet mainly concentrated near the Scheldt estuary (Marquardt 1997, p. 30). This seems to indicate such decorations were produced in this area. In Vlissingen (the Netherlands), a decoration similar to group A was excavated and dated to 1475-1525 (Oosterbaan & Griffioen 2015, p. 203-204). Knife handles from the Mary Rose (1545) demonstrate similar decorations (Every & Richards 2005, p. 148). Close parallels for the different shapes of decoration recovered from the Zeebrugge wreck are present in the "Aad Penders" collection (Ostkamp 2013, p. 236-251), and are generally dated to 1450-1550. The type of 'finial' decoration can be found on some more complete knives recovered from different underwater contexts in Belgium and the Netherlands, dated (based on stylistic features) to the 14th-16th century (Marquardt 1997, p. 23-24).

In addition to the knife handles and knife decorations, several leather scabbards are mentioned in the inventories. According to this information, about ten such items were recovered from the wreck. They are described as "bone or wooden knife handles with leather scabbards" (MEA 1991; P.A.B.S., P.C.2, "Geschatte inventaris Herent"). None of these scabbards, however, is present in the current collection of finds. Possibly these objects were not preserved or did not survive preservation. Neither were pictures of these finds available to the author in the frame of this research.

3.6. Sewing and dress accessories

Quite a few items recovered from the Zeebrugge wreck are related to dressing or the production of clothing. In this category, we can distinguish pins, needle cases, thimbles, hook-and-eye fasteners and bells. Except for the bells, these items occur in high quantities, and it is very plausible they all were part of cargo. Although textile is not likely to survive in a context like this, apparent traces of linen were noticed as part of a concreted lump (P.A.B.S., F.V., "Report 18/05/1991).

3.6.1. Pins

Pins were found by the thousands on site, and they even impeded the excavation work to a certain extent since these sharp objects were spread all over the site. As discussed before, these objects must have been carried in one or several of the casks that were discovered on site (cf. supra). Pins are associated with dressing and the production of clothing. In the (late) medieval and early modern period they were not only used to hold fabric together during production, but it was also common to use pins for fastening clothing or veils when worn (Deagan 2002, p. 193; Egan and Pritchard 2002, p. 297). The pins recovered from the Zeebrugge wreck are made of a separate shank and pinhead. The shank is made of sharpened brass wire. The head is made separately by winding another piece of the same brass wire around a mandrel with the same diameter as the shank of the pin. Afterwards, both parts were assembled. For some pins, the head seems to have been finished by squeezing it into a ball-shape. Other heads appear to be finished more poorly (Fig. 47). Some pins vary in colour, from gold-yellowish to black. This is probably caused by the fact pins used to be tinned after they were finished, to give them a silver appearance (Deagan 2002, p. 193-194). The black objects probably still carry a tin layer, while the gold-yellowish objects may have lost this layer due to an intense preservation process. Xrf-analysis was executed for one pin and indicated clearly it was made of brass (cu 76.8%; Zn 18.7%; Fe 1.5%; Pb 1.3%). The materials and techniques for producing pins have varied very little from medieval to modern times, and the objects therefore are no good indicators for dating a site (Ibidem).

In the MAS Museum, 1729 pins are present, and their lengths vary considerably between 0.6cm and 6.4cm (Fig. 48). The exceptional small pin of 0.6cm may be the consequence of erosion processes, as pins from about 2cm occur more regularly. When we plot the lengths in a histogram (Fig. 49), we can see four peaks and the peaks increase according to size. A first peak rises for pins with a length of about 3cm, followed by a larger peak for objects of about 4.4cm and even more objects of about 5.3cm. Most pins, however, seem to have a length of about 5.7-6cm. The different peaks may indicate certain standard lengths were approached. Although pins in general appear in considerably varying sizes, their length may indicate their use to a certain extent. While the smaller objects can be linked to tailoring, the larger pins were rather used to fasten clothing when worn (Ibidem).

One larger object, with a similar pin-shape, was found as well (Fig. 50). It is considerably larger than the previously discussed pins, with a length of 9.4cm and a width of 0.8cm (at the head). Shank and head are made out of one piece. The object is composed of lead (81.2%) and, to a less degree, tin (14.4%). It is unlikely this pin was used in relation to clothing in the way the previously discussed pins were. A possible function could have been a hairpin.

3.6.2. Thimbles

About 27 thimbles were recovered from the Zeebrugge wreck. While some of them are severely damaged, others are in excellent condition. A few of the thimbles are caught inside other thimbles and could not be loosened, and one them is stuck in the socket of a candlestick. Other than those, all thimbles were studied. We can distinguish two types among the thimbles. Type 1 represents thimbles with a single engraved line above the rim. Above this line a pattern of hand-punched indentations starts spiralling

Finds from the Zeebrugge wreck

Figure 47. Two different types of pin heads. It appears some pin heads were finished more poorly.

Figure 48. Pins occuring in many different lengths.

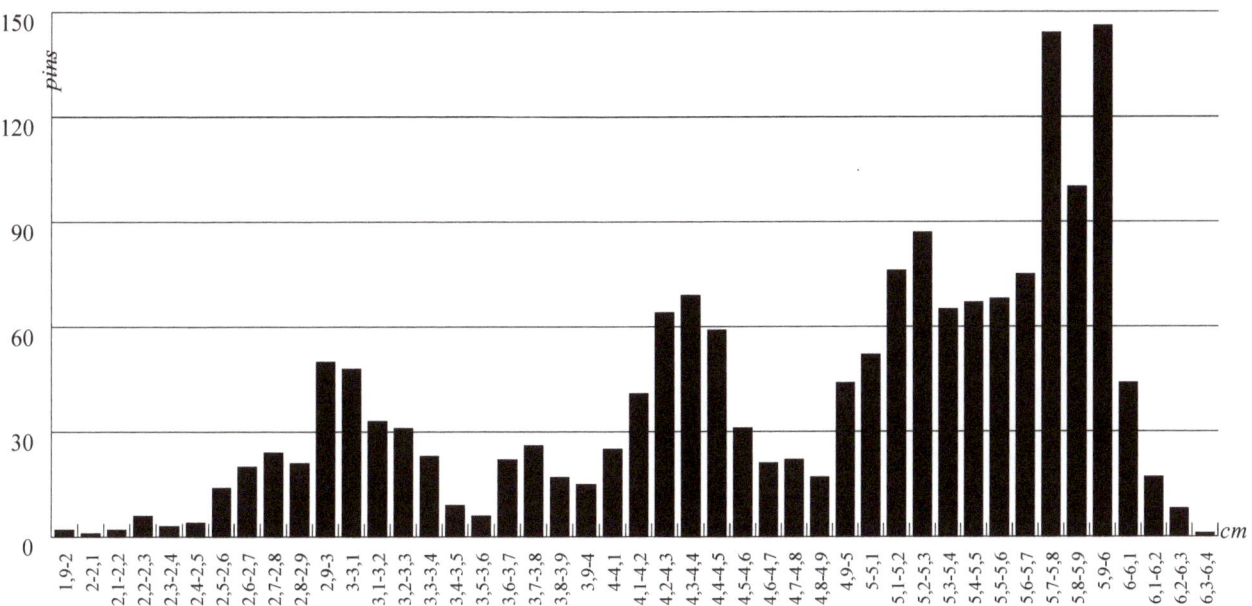

Figure 49. Histogram showing the dispersal of pin lengths.

Figure 50. One large 'pin', made of lead.

57

up along the body of the thimble, up to the middle of the domed top (*Fig. 51.a*). Type 2 is similar to type 1, also with a single engraved line above the rim and a domed top, but instead of punched pits the pattern is made of engraved, radiating lines, spiralling up to the middle of the top (*Fig. 51.b*). The thimbles were likely made by hammering a sheet of metal, as depicted in the book of trades (*Das Ständebuch*, 1568) by Jost Amman. Here, one can see how the indentations were manually added too.

The collection of thimbles comprises fifteen type 1 thimbles and twelve type 2 thimbles. Both types occur in different sizes. For type 1, the length is 1.6-2cm and the maximum width is 1.7-2cm. The width at the top is 1.2-1.6cm. Type 2 has a length of 1.6-1.9cm and a maximum width of 1.5-1.9cm. The width at the domed top is 1.1-1.5cm. The sides of the thimbles are less than 0.1cm thick. The actual thickness varies due to erosion.

To determine the alloy for both types, xrf-analysis was executed for two pieces of each type. For both types the main elements are copper and zinc. Other present elements never reach 1% of the normalized total concentrations. Yet, there are some clear differences among the types. First of all, the relative concentration of the present elements is considerably different for each type. When we only consider the proportions of the main elements, the copper-zinc concentration for the type 1 thimbles is about 95%-5%, while this is 83%-17% for the type 2 thimbles. If we bring the trace elements into consideration, cadmium (0.9%), lead (0.8%) and iron (0.4%) have the highest concentration for type 1. This is different for type 2, where traces of hafnium (0.6%) and tin (0.1-0.6%) have a higher concentration than iron. The elements hafnium and tin are not present in the type 1 samples. This may indicate the type 1 and type 2 thimbles have a different origin and could have been produced in different workshops.

It is not uncommon to find thimbles on archaeological sites, and several such finds have been discussed in archaeological literature (e.g. Egan 2005, Gardiner 2005). Dating often seems to be based upon contextual evidence, rather than on typological features. Beaudry (2006, after Holmes *n.d.*, p. 100) argues context indeed is the most reliable way to date thimbles, but nevertheless proposes a chronological overview for thimbles and thimble rings, based upon some of the thimbles attributes. Spiralling indentations, however, can be associated with different production centres (Nuremberg, Netherlands, Sweden, England) over a long period of time (ca. 1550-1730) (*Idem*, p. 102-103). Unfortunately, Beaudry's overview is rather general and does not provide visual data. Egan (2005, p. 131-132) presents some thimbles with similar characteristics to both types of the Zeebrugge wreck (for type 1: n° 527, 529; for type 2: n° 626). These finds are dated, based on context, to 1530-1550. A thimble similar to type 2 is discussed by Bartels (1999, p. 305, 1063: n° 223). This object, also made of copper and zinc and corresponding in size to the type 2 thimbles, was excavated in Dordrecht and is dated to 1525-1575.

3.6.3. Needle cases

Four decorated containers, identified as needle-cases, have been recovered from the wreck as well (*Fig. 52*). They all present a similar design and they have different lengths. The objects are hexagonal-sectioned containers with a separate cap. The container features a double rib at the bottom as well as in the middle of the body. On top, a thin edge protrudes from the container, on to which the cap fits. Between the ribs and the protruding edge, the surface of the body is decorated with linear engravings. On opposed sides, between the engraved decorations, a total of four small tubes are added to the container. These may have been used to fit a wire through, so the object could easily be carried. Also, it could be connected to its cap this way, which feature two similar tubes.

The cap features a similar design. At the bottom, where it features an opening to slide over the container, the object is double ribbed. The top features triple ribs and the most upper rib features intersections. Above these ribs the cap is domed with a small decoration on top. Between the ribs at the bottom and on top, engraved decorations similar to the ones on the container are present. On opposed sides, between these decorations, two small tubes are attached to the cap.

Although all four objects look very similar, they have different sizes. Only two objects are more or less complete and feature a container and cap. One incomplete object looks very similar to the complete objects, yet it is a solid piece without bottom. This seems to indicate we are dealing with, compared to the complete pieces, a very long cap. The fourth object is damaged on both ends, rendering it more difficult to interpret. Possibly this was part of a container.

The complete objects have a length of 10.26-12cm. They have a width of 2.1-2.3cm (including the tubes) and a thickness of 1.3-1.8cm. The caps have a separate length of 4.9-5.3cm while the containers without cap have a length of 6.8-8.5cm. The 'long cap' has a length of 11.7cm and the damaged object has a length of 10cm. Both the 'long cap' and damaged object show evidence that tubes were once attached to these objects. Xrf-analysis of one object indicates it was made of brass (Cu 81.7%; Zn 16%).

Since needlework was an acclaimed female accomplishment, needle cases were not only carried around for reasons of convenience, but also as a status symbol (Egan 2002, p. 384). Most needle cases encountered in archaeological contexts are made of bone, wood, or ivory (Deagan 2002, p. 196). This indicates the nicely decorated brass objects we are dealing with may well have been exceptional objects for the high-class society. Although no exact parallels could be found for this object, several

Finds from the Zeebrugge wreck

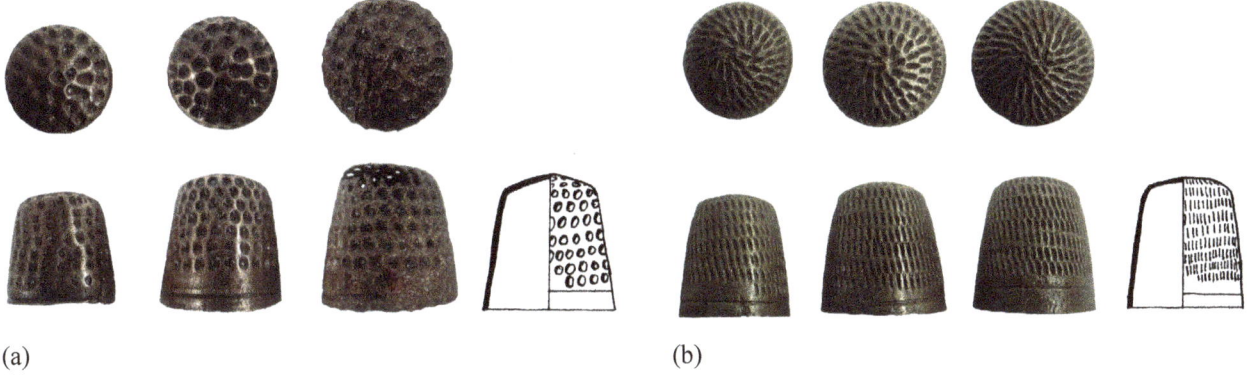

(a) (b)

Figure 51. Different types of thimbles.

2cm

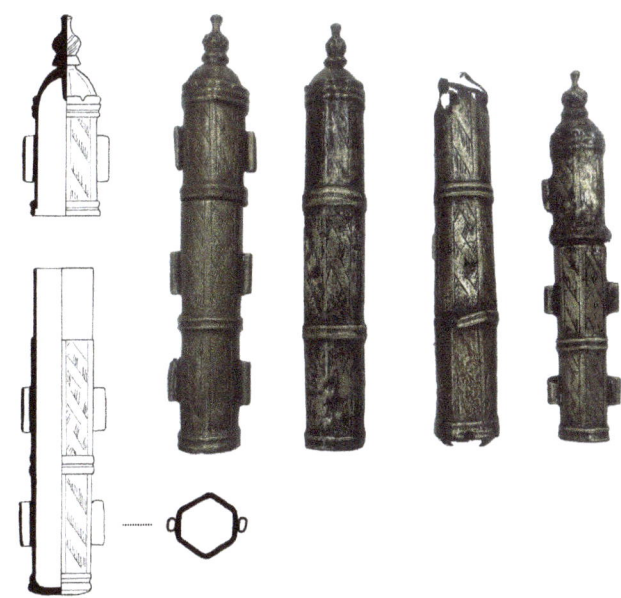

Figure 52. Needle cases from the Zeebrugge wreck.

5cm

(a) 5cm (b) 2cm

Figure 53. Hook-and-eye fasteners assembled around a metal wire (a) and individual elements of fasteners.

Figure 54. Different sized rumbler bells.

5cm

59

examples are known of needle cases featuring small tubes or loops to carry them around together with the cap (e.g. *Ibidem*; Egan 2002, p. 384-385). Although not a similar object, a close parallel for the decoration on top of the caps appears at the end of a spoon excavated in Vlissingen (the Netherlands), dating to 1500-1550 (Oosterbaan & Griffioen 2015, p. 204-205).

3.6.4. Hook-and-eye fasteners

Next in the dress accessories category are the so-called hook-and-eye fasteners. They have been recovered from the wreck in large quantities and in different sizes, grouped together on individual, circle-shaped metal wires (*Fig. 53.a*). In the MAS Museum, 32 of such circles are present. Each circle contains easily over 100 items. Some loose finds were present as well (*Fig. 53.b*). A hook and an eye were used together to fasten different clothing elements. They have been used for many centuries and are therefore difficult to date (Deagan 2002, p. 176).

3.6.5. Bells

The final objects to discuss in this category are two small rumbler bells (*Fig. 54*). These bells, made of two separate hemispheres soldered together, contain a small metal 'pea'. One of the two hemispheres is fully closed, while the other features a dumbell-shaped aperture. Contrary to most contemporaneous objects, these bells do not feature a loop to carry them. The larger object measures 4x4.5cm. The smaller one measures 3x3.7cm. Rumbler bells had several applications. They could be dress accessories for children's, men's, and/or women's clothing, or perhaps attached to rattles or used as amulets. For animals, they could be attached to the collars of pets or horses, or used as hawk bells for falconry (Egan 2002, p. 336-337; Deagan 2002, p. 139-141). It is known the bells produced in the Low Countries at the end of the 15th century were exported overseas. Among others Columbus did refer to "Hawk bells from Flanders" and an English treatise of 1496 does refer to "the excellence and low cost of Dutch hawk bells" (Deagan 2002, p. 140). A woodcut print from *Das Standebuch* by Jost Amman (1568) indicates the specialized production of rumbler bells in (Southern) Germany too. Although no xrf-analysis was executed for these objects, it appears both bells are made of copper-alloy, just like many other contemporaneous bells (Egan 2002, p. 337). Although only two bells were present in the MAS collection, at least one more bell is mentioned in several inventories.

3.7. Religious objects

According to Vandenberghe (2006, p. 19) "hundreds of religious and devotional objects" are present among the finds from the Zeebrugge wreck. The present collection in the MAS Museum only approaches this number if we include the assemblage of candlesticks in this category. Parallels for some of the Zeebrugge candlesticks have been recovered from specific religious archaeological contexts indeed, yet based upon just the collection it is hard to ascribe an exclusive religious or devotional function to these objects. Therefore, and because of the large quantity of candlesticks recovered from the Zeebrugge wreck, we will discuss these objects in a seperate section. Although not in such high numbers, there are still some objects among the recovered artefacts with a clear primary religious or devotional function. Among these objects are parts of a monstrance, a devotional pendant and a mould to produce a similar pendant.

3.7.1. Monstrance

A monstrance is a religious object used to display and protect the consecrated host that represents the body of Christ. It was only used certain times a year, when it was carried around in processions (McCune Bruhn 2006, p. 1-2). It has been argued monstrances were recovered from the Zeebrugge wreck (Vandenberghe 2006, p. 19), or that at least parts of a monstrance were present among the finds (Vandenberghe 1997, p. 89). Indeed, some damaged objects in the collection may have belonged to a monstrance. In the MAS Museum, the author recorded five items that possibly originate from such an object. It seems all these fragmentary pieces may have belonged to at least two different monstrances.

Among the objects we can identify a six-lobed foot with a flat projecting edge, showing what appear to be four tally marks on one side (width 10.4cm; height 2.6cm; *fig. 55.a*), a circular-shaped object with protruding points on the rim and traces of what may have been a hinge (width 6.2cm; height 2.8cm; *fig. 55.b*), and a hexagonal, trumpet-shaped object with a flared, open end (width 4.5cm; length 8.8cm; *fig. 55.c*). The last two objects are hexagonal-sectioned bars with flaring ends on both sides. For both objects, one end is closed and the other end is damaged. Three riveting points are visible on the closed end. In the middle of both objects a knop or "*nodus*" is present (width 4.7cm; length 15.2cm; *fig. 55.d* / width 4.6cm; length 14.8cm; *fig. 55.e*).

The element-composition of these objects is relatively similar and supports the idea of a similar origin. Main elements are copper (82.1-84.6%), zinc (10.3-13%) and a small portion of lead (1.2-2.6%). The lobed foot and the object with a knop, however, both show relatively large traces of hafnium (1.2-1.6%), while no traces of this element are present for the other objects.[32]

Three of the objects we discussed can be recognised in a monstrance from the collection of the Dutch Rijksmuseum (*Fig. 56*). First of all, we can see a very similar six-lobed foot. The circular object corresponds to the upper and lower frames that support the glass cylinder (*i.e.* the expositorium)

---

[32] The apparent presence of Hafnium can possibly be explained as an error. This may occur when the portable xrf instrument is not well placed and noise is created.

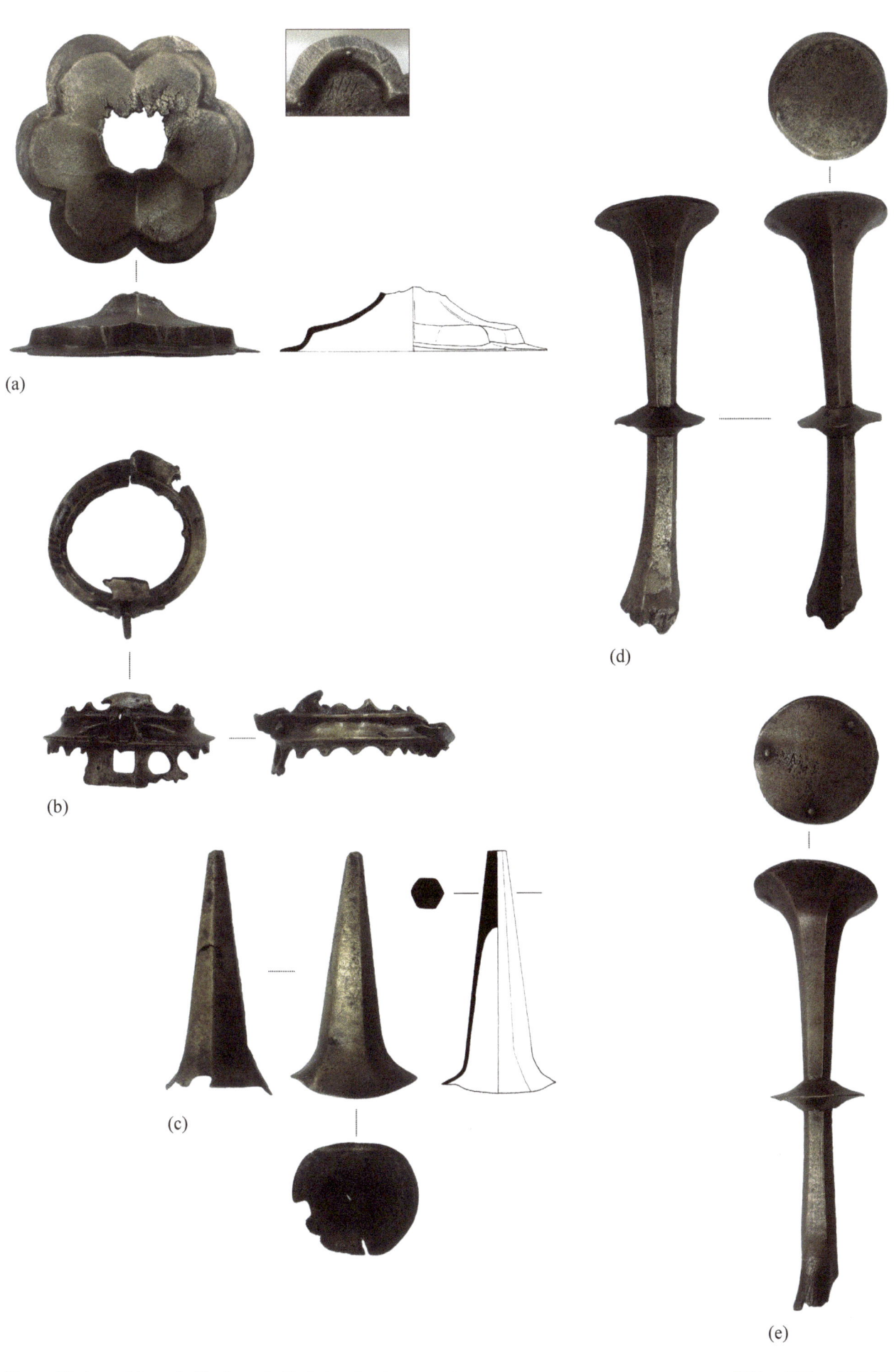

Figure 55. Assemblage of objects probably belonging to a monstrance.

5cm

Figure 56. 16th century monstrance of probably (South) German origin (Rijsmuseum, Amsterdam).

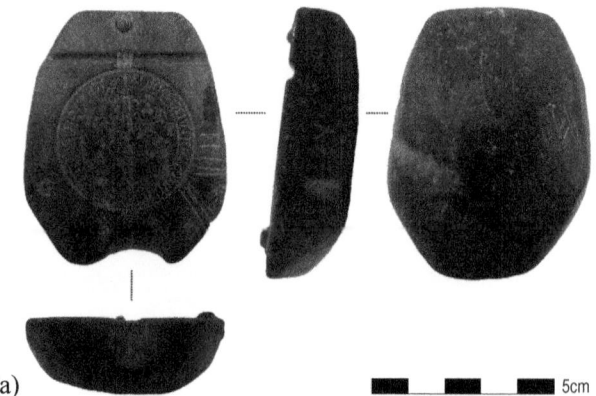

Figure 57. Stone carved mould for devotional medallion (a) with detail of the medallion's image (b).

in which the host was placed. The frames are decorated with a pattern of so-called "*Kreuzblumen*", a specific type of finial. Although this cross-shaped decoration is not present on the circular object, the protruding pattern may indicate that this object had a similar decorative pattern in the past. The trumpet-shaped object corresponds to the hexagonal spire at the top of the monstrance. Although the two hexagonal-sectioned bars cannot be recognised in the Rijksmuseum's monstrance, it has been suggested by experts from the *Centre for Religious Art and Culture* (Personal information) that each bar could well be a monstrance's stem. In that case the expositorium would be attached to the closed end of the bar. The broken end would originally have been connected to the foot. If this interpretation is correct, this would mean at least two, and possibly even more, monstances were present on board, likely as part of the ship's cargo.

Just like the objects discussed here, the monstrance in the Rijksmuseum is also made of brass. The foot is slightly bigger, with a width of 13cm. It is dated to ca. 1550 and was probably produced in the Rhineland (Rijksmuseum (no date)). Several cities in the Rhineland, such as Cologne, are known for the production of monstrances in the late medieval or early modern period (McCune Bruhn 2006, p. 48). According to Baumgärtel (1983, p. 40), however, this specific monstrance from the Rijksmuseum is characteristic for Nuremberg. He argues this type was often produced for export rather than local use. Unfortunately, he does not specify the reasons for which he believes this object was produced in Nuremberg.

3.7.2. Devotional medal and mould

A unique piece in the Zeebrugge collection is a stone-carved mould for casting a medallion. It is one of the only non-metal objects still present in the collection. Only one half of the mould was found. The mould is carved in a greyish natural stone (length 6.4cm; width 5.1cm; thickness 1.9cm; *fig. 57.a*). The side with the engraving is flat, while the opposed side is rounded. The diameter of a medallion cast in this mould would be 3.5cm. The stone has a funnel-shaped opening underneath the engraving, to cast the metal. On top of the medallion, a little eye is engraved to wear the medallion as a pendant. The eye crosses a small gully that runs horizontally along the engraved medal. Three small points protrude from the flat surface, to fit this part of the mould to its missing counter part.

When we take a closer look at the mirrored image of the engraving, we can get an idea of what the actual medallion would have looked like (*Fig. 57.b*[33]). We can see a legend surrounding the actual image. When we transcribe this text, it says: "ASPICE QUI TRANSIS QU(I)A MIHI CAUSA DOL(O)R". This Latin phrase can be translated as: "Look, you who passes, for you are the cause of my sorrows". This text, drawn from the biblical book of Lamentations (1:12), is a common inscription on images since the Middle Ages and is meant to provoke compassion (Campbell & Koering 2014, p. 47). In the image itself we can recognise several objects related to the passion of the Christ; the so-called "Arma Christi". Among them are a ladder, dice, Longinus' lance, nails, etc. The figure in the middle of the medallion, next to the ladder, may well be Christ, yet the image is unclear. Nevertheless, it is clear the image refers to Christ as the Man of Sorrows, and thus relates to the surrounding text. A medallion with a similar scene and text was excavated in Brussels and is discussed by Smolderen (2009, p. 14, 25, figure 3) in the context of late 15th century or early 16th century medals. An actual date for this parallel is not given. According to Vandenberghe (1997, p. 89), however, this mould does not just depict the Man of Sorrows, but it shows the mass of Saint Gregory. In this story, dating to the 7th century, the Man of Sorrows appears before the altar of Pope Gregory I. This image was popularised in 14th century Rome, and was spread over Europe by Pilgrims in the late medieval period (Rubin 1991, p. 122, 308-310). The medallion may well indeed depict this scene, since some kneeling figures appear to be present in the lower part of the image. Yet, it is hard to tell based on this image.

An actual medallion with a similar scene of Saint Gregory's mass, however, was recovered from the wreck as well. This medal is not present in the MAS Museum, yet it has been discussed and depicted in earlier publications (Vandenberghe 1997, p. 89, picture p. 88[34]; 2006, p. 19). The medal was made of pewter. On one side it illustrates the mass of Saint Gregory, on the other side it depicts Our Lady on the crescent moon. In the picture we can see the medallion is provided with an eye on top so it could be worn as a pendant. The medallion appears to be bigger than the carved mould discussed above. Unfortunately we were not able to locate this object for further study.

3.7.3. Holy water fonts?

Furthermore Vandenberghe (2006, p. 19) also mentions the finds of several fragments belonging to holy water fonts. Such items could not be identified by the author. A "carved stone" (75x23x10cm) was recovered from the site, but there is no indication this was a holy water font (MEA 1991; P.A.B.S. D.R., "30/03/1991"). In the past, transportable holy water pails have been used as well (Malfait & Malfait, 2003). These pails were made of metal and could have similar shapes as some of the mortars discovered on site. Yet, such pails were worn by means of a support bracket, a feature not present on these mortars. Two individual support brackets were recovered from the site as well, yet there is no clear indication they should be linked to a holy water pail. These items will be discussed later on in the category "other finds".

3.8. Candlesticks

Probably the most conspicuous assemblage among the finds is the huge collection of candlesticks and candlestick parts recovered from the wreck. No less than 292 items were recorded by the author in this regard. Later we would find out that at the time of our research a small number of candlesticks was absent because they were given in loan for temporary exhibitions. Also, one candlestick is in the presence of Barts Schiltz. This item was donated to him by the members of *vzw Maritieme Archeologie* as it was the candlestick that was entangled in the net that lead to the discovery of the Zeebrugge wreck (*cfr. supra*). Furthermore, two candlesticks were initially reported to be stolen, yet the official police report does not mention these candlesticks anymore. This means not all candlesticks are included in our research, yet with 292 recorded items we were able to study most of them and to achieve a representative image of the collection of candlesticks recovered from the Zeebrugge wreck. All recorded items are part of socket candleholders. They are either complete candlesticks, made of a separately casted base and stem attached to one another, or pieces of incomplete candlesticks. Among the pieces we could identify complete stems and bases unattached to one another, as well as damaged bits and pieces.

The collection of candlesticks is not just a striking assembly among the finds from the Zeebrugge wreck; it also seems to be a unique archaeological assembly in general. To our knowledge no candlestick collection of this size has ever been excavated in the past. Generally speaking, copper-alloy finds are less common in "land" archaeology, since damaged objects could be remelted and recycled into new ones. Nevertheless, metal candlesticks have been discovered on land in good condition (e.g. Pieters ET AL. 2013, p. 495). Larger assemblies of candlesticks, however, are more likely to be found in underwater archaeology, for example as part of a ship's cargo. This is the case for the Punta Cana Pewter wreck, where tens of (pieces of) candlesticks were recovered (Seliger and Pritchett III 2011a, 2011b, 2011c; ARS Anchor Research & Salvage Inc. 2012a, 2012b). The largest assembly of candlesticks on board an identified shipwreck would be the collection from the St Anthony wreck, which sank in 1527. According to documentary sources this ship would have

---

[33] This image was created by digitally mirroring a photograph of the engraving, turning it into a grayscale image and increasing the contrast. This way the negative of the actual carved image, or what the medallion as such would look like, is more closely approached.

[34] Unfortunately this picture is a very low quality black-and-white print. On our behalf Alexis Wielemans from the Flanders Heritage Agency's library contacted the Flanders Heritage Agency's archive, which published this photo, but the original picture was not available.

carried 3200 latten candlesticks on her way from Antwerp to Lisbon. From the wreck-site, at least 92 fragments of candlesticks were recovered, and more items are possibly present in private collections (Camidge 2013, p. 6, 21, 45). Candlesticks have been recovered from other wreck-sites, but, to our knowledge, not in such high numbers. One of the Punta Cana candlesticks is shortly discussed in relation to other objects from this site by Martin Roberts (2013a, p. 13). A study of the objects recovered from the St Anthony wreck has not been published so far.[35]

The study of the Zeebrugge candlesticks proved one of the biggest challenges for this research. Not only did the large number of objects and the great variety among these objects create a challenge, but also the apparent absence of parallels for many of these objects in the available literature made an exhaustive study of the collection rather challenging. Different typological studies on the subject of candlesticks exist (e.g. Wechssler-Kuemmel 1963, Michaelis 1978, De Hondt 2003) and time/space related characteristics for candlesticks have been suggested. Yet, as a tool for dating the candlesticks from the Zeebrugge wreck, the proposed typologies are not unproblematic. First of all, many of the publications are written from a collector's viewpoint or are meant for a more general audience. Therefore, they often lack a scientific reference system, and often the origin of certain data or statements is not specified. This does not mean the available information is incorrect, but it makes it difficult to find important -and for this research in some cases essential- additional information for particular objects. Secondly, some sources used in these publications tend to be problematic for building a solid typology since they are antiquarian items without any context. When they are used within a typology, it is uncertain whether the date and/or place is attributed to the characteristics of the object, or whether the characteristics can actually be dated because of the object. Also, examples are known of practices where two damaged candlesticks are reassembled into one new object for the antiquarian market (Personal information Dumargne). This indicates caution is needed when using auction catalogues as reference for the study of these objects, yet they are a very frequent source. Finally, and this is the most problematic part, (exact) parallels for the candleholders from the Zeebrugge wreck were almost nowhere to be found in the existing literature.

Yet, despite these problems, it should be said the typological study of candlesticks still evolves and as new data pops up existing typologies can be reassessed. Finds from the Punta Cana Pewter wreck, for example, indicate the existing date-sequence for candlestick typologies may need revision (Personal information Martin Roberts), as does the evaluation of the Zeebrugge collection. More recently, academic research on the topic of candlestick typologies has been conducted by Anne-Clothilde Dumargne, who proposed an adjusted typology in the frame of her masters' dissertation "Chandeliers et pique-cierges du XIIIe au XVIIe siècle". In this study, she addresses several problems in regards to earlier typologies and available data, and she stresses the value of archaeological contributions, especially for the period 1200-1500 (Dumargne 2013, p. 47-48). Currently, Dumargne continuous her research at the Université de Versailles Saint-Quentin-en-Yvelines, in a Ph.D. project. One of the aims of this project is to determine processes of production, use and diffusion of candlesticks from this period. In the frame of this research an exhaustive xrf-study of several international collections will be executed. We contacted Dumargne in this regard, who was excited to find out about the existence of the Zeebrugge candlesticks. This collection from the Zeebrugge wreck will now be included in her on-going research, and the results of this comprehensive study will probably add significantly to our understanding of the candlesticks from the Zeebrugge wreck.

Therefore, for this research, we will not aim to fit the Zeebrugge candlesticks within the existing typologies, partly because the existing typologies may be inadequate to support the new data this collection provides, but also because the entire candlestick collection will be included in the exhaustive typological study by Durmagne. We will, however, refer to parallels to determine a relative date and preliminary context for the collection. We mainly focused on archaeological and iconographical sources to find parallels, yet because the main body of published data for candlesticks is present in auction and collector's catalogues, we had to rely on this information when other sources could not provide sufficient data.

To start the analysis of the candlesticks, we first divided the collection into different typological groups based upon characteristic features of individual items. Again, these groups do not intend to propose a defined typology for candlesticks, nor do they follow any of the existing typologies. Rather, they are a tool to create an organised overview of the many objects of this type recovered from the Zeebrugge wreck. Since many stems and bases were recovered as unassembled, separate items, we grouped them in different categories, even when assembled. We could distinguish four different kinds of bases, and fourteen different types of stems. A fifteenth group comprises the bits and pieces that are either too fragmentary or too eroded to add to one of the other groups. Some of the groups are very homogeneous, while other groups compile more heterogeneous objects with similar features. For a more profound study on the topic of candlesticks as such, a further (sub)division of some groups may be preferable. However, for the purpose of this research the proposed typology should be satisfying.

We already mentioned not all bases are provided with a stem, and not all stems are attached to a base. In some cases this is the consequence of damage, but in many other cases it concerns original, unattached objects. Although

---

[35] Some of the St Anthony ingots were briefly discussed in a contribution to an article in IJNA (Craddock and Hook 1987). A comprehensive study of the site and finds as such, however, is not available yet.

Finds from the Zeebrugge wreck

Table 4. Overview of the different types of candlestick bases recovered from the Zeebrugge wreck. Information is given about the total number of pieces, how many pieces are attached to a stem, and the stem type to which they are attached.

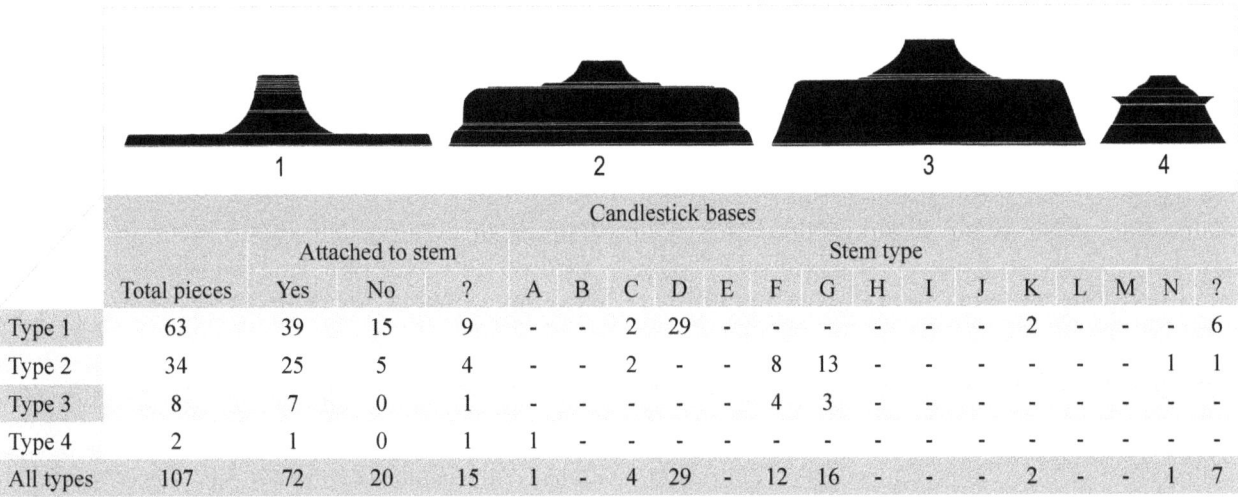

	Candlestick bases																		
	Total pieces	Attached to stem			Stem type														
		Yes	No	?	A	B	C	D	E	F	G	H	I	J	K	L	M	N	?
Type 1	63	39	15	9	-	-	2	29	-	-	-	-	-	-	2	-	-	-	6
Type 2	34	25	5	4	-	-	2	-	-	8	13	-	-	-	-	-	-	1	1
Type 3	8	7	0	1	-	-	-	-	-	4	3	-	-	-	-	-	-	-	-
Type 4	2	1	0	1	1	-	-	-	-	-	-	-	-	-	-	-	-	-	-
All types	107	72	20	15	1	-	4	29	-	12	16	-	-	-	2	-	-	1	7

Table 5. Overview of the different types of candlestick stems recovered from the Zeebrugge wreck. Information is given about the total number of pieces per type, the total number of objects to which these pieces belong, how many pieces are attached to a base, and the type of base to which they were attached. An estimation is made about the variations per type as well, yet this is a rather arbitrary and debatable contribution since all are unique handmade objects.

	Candlestick stems											
	Total pieces	Total objects		Attached to base			Base type					Number of variations
		Max.	Min.	Yes	No	?	1	2	3	4	?	
Type A	8	-	-	2	6	0	-	-	-	1	1	-
Type B	62	60	52	6	31	25	-	-	-	-	6	-
Type C	12	-	-	7	4	1	2	2	-	-	3	8?
Type D	43	-	-	32	10	1	29	-	-	-	3	3?
Type E	12	-	-	0	12	0	-	-	-	-	-	-
Type F	16	-	-	13	3	0	-	8	4	-	1	6?
Type G	18	-	-	17	1	0	-	13	3	-	1	6?
Type H	45	-	-	0	41	4	-	-	-	-	-	2
Type I	8	8	7	0	7	1	-	-	-	-	-	-
Type J	11	10	10	0	10	0	-	-	-	-	-	-
Type K	7	-	-	2	1	4	2	-	-	-	-	-
Type L	2	-	-	0	0	2	-	-	-	-	-	2
Type M	1	-	-	0	0	1	-	-	-	-	-	-
Type N	1	-	-	1	0	0	-	1	-	-	-	-
Type unknown	11	11	7	7	0	4	6	1	-	-	-	-
All types	257	254	241	87	126	43	39	25	7	1	15	27?

the stems and bases will be dealt with separately, we will discuss the relation between the objects when appropriate. An overview of the different bases is given in table 4, the different stems can be seen in table 5. The exact number of actual, original, objects is uncertain since some pieces may belong to the same object, yet not all damaged pieces could be linked to one another with certainty. The number of original stems, either attached to a base or not, varies between a minimum of 241 and a maximum of 254. The number of individual bases without stem is 35, yet 15 of these are damaged and possibly could have had a stem. This corresponds to the number of stems for which we know were once attached to an unknown base. Whether this means the 15 bases belong to the 15 stems is uncertain; they may as well originate from different objects. When we do the math, this would mean the total number of actual objects would vary between a minimum of 261 (241+20) and a maximum of 289 (254+35). Both tables also demonstrate the relation between each base and stem type. We notice some stem types tend to be related to specific base types, while other stems only occur as unattached items. We will describe all base and stem types individually, and when available discuss existing parallels or provide additional information. Afterwards, we will discuss the xrf-results for all sampled objects together.

3.8.1. Typological groups

We will now propose some typological groups for objects with clear similar characteristics. It should be said a lot of these groups are still quite heterogeneous with subtle or less subtle differences among the objects. This is due to the fact all of these objects are handmade. In the early modern period, candlesticks were made by means of lost-wax casting or sand casting; techniques that only allow one product per mould you make (Dumargne 2013, p. 8-10). The stem and base of the candlestick were cast separately and only assembled afterwards. To attach the stem to the base, the stem was given a small protrusion at the end that could penetrate the base. By hammering the protrusion from the inside of the base, it would clamp itself to the base. The assembled product was afterwards lathe-finished or finished by hand, making it a unique piece. A large quantity of the objects recovered from the Zeebrugge wreck, however, are unassembled stems. This seems to indicate that, in this case, the individual candlestick parts used to be cast and afterwards be traded as semi-finished products. At their destination, they than would be assembled to the desired base. To our knowledge, this collection appears to be the first actual evidence of this practice. From the wreck of the Dutch East Indiaman Amsterdam (1749) unattached stems and bases have been recovered too (Gawronski 1996, p. 165), yet these do not appear to be semi-finished products. In this case, the individual items were to be assembled by means of a screw system, and corresponding stems and bases were recovered. Three stem types from the Zeebrugge wreck featured a screw too, yet no corresponding bases were recovered from the site.

A common feature for the sockets of the candlesticks is the presence of apertures. For the candlesticks of the Zeebrugge wreck, all but three sockets have apertures on opposing sides. These apertures may have been used to remove wax from the bottom of the socket. Both square and circular apertures are present. According to Michaelis (1978, p. 59), square apertures should almost certainly be dated to before 1600 and sockets featuring both a square and circular opening are "even younger". Then again, according to De Hondt (2003, p. 20), square apertures were common for Gothic candlesticks, and they evolve to circular apertures in the Renaissance. Despite these conflicting statements, the Zeebrugge wreck provides sockets from one single context with square, round, both square and round and even without apertures, indicating these features must have been used contemporaneously.

To distinguish between base types and stem types, we gave every type of base a unique number (e.g. type 1) and every stem a unique letter (e.g. type A). This way, we are able to clarify what kind of object we are talking about. Also, this system allows for easy reference to the shape of a complete candlestick (e.g. a type 4A candlestick is assembled of a type 4 base and a type A stem).

Type 1

The type 1 base (*Fig. 58*) is the most common base in the Zeebrugge collection. With 63 pieces, it provides almost 60% of all recorded bases. Bases of this type are flat and discoid-shaped. They have a slightly flared skirt and feature a low conical centre. The conical centre varies in length and, in some cases, is ribbed. The width of the bases varies as well. The surface of the base often features multiple concentric circles. The type 1 base has been found as an object unassembled with any other pieces, as well as assembled to stems of type C, D, and K. For some of the type 1 bases the stem had broken off, making the type of stem unknown.

The type 1 bases vary in length between 1.7-3.7cm and in width between 13.5-19.8cm. Along the edge, the skirt measures 0.5-1.1cm. For the unassembled pieces, we were able to measure the inner diameter of the opening for the stem. This opening varies between 1.7-2cm.

Although this type of base does not seem to be a common archaeological find, it is a known type among collectors. Examples, however, often have a more pronounced conical centre and exact parallels seem to be hard to find. Such an object was sold at Christie's, described as "Franco-Flemish", and dated to the early 16th century (Christie's 2016). The stem of this Christie's candlestick is similar to the type K stem from the Zeebrugge collection. This particular combination is present among the Zeebrugge candlesticks as well.

Type 2

Type 2, with 34 pieces representing about a third of all bases, is a bell-shaped base (*Fig. 59*). It has a small, flared "step" that rises into a flattened bell-shape with conical centre. It exhibits similarities to the bell-shaped bases discussed by Michaelis (1978, p. 62-65) and Dumargne (2013, p. 42-43), yet the flattened top is a feature not present among the examples discussed by these authors.

The type 2 bases are relatively homogeneous. They have been found as unassembled objects, as well as attached to stems of type C, F, G and N. Some of the damaged bases may have been attached to an unknown stem type.

For the type 2 base, we can distinguish two main sizes. The first group, with 13 pieces, has a length of 3.2-3.8cm and a width of 14-14.4cm. For the second group, also about 13 objects, the width varies around 16-17cm and they have a length of 4-4.6cm. For the remaining objects, the width gradually increases from 17cm to 19.3cm and heights vary between 4-5.2cm. The inner diameter of the unassembled objects varies between 1.6-2cm.

Although identical objects are difficult to find, similar base types can found on auction sites (e.g. Sotheby's 2016). Known bell-shaped bases often have a more domed appearance, and may feature a dripping pan. They are mostly dated to the 17th century. According to Dumargne, the type 2 bases have a shape often associated with objects from Spain, although she presumes this shape probably originates from Flanders or the Southern Netherlands (Personal information Dumargne).

Type 3

Eight type 3 bases have been recorded (*Fig. 60*). They feature a high, slightly flared skirt and a conical centre. All types are assembled to either a type F or type G stem. For one damaged object no stem is present. The length of the type 3 bases varies between 4.5-6.4cm. They have a width of 17.2-19.3cm.

Just as for the type 2 bases, Dumargne believes this shape is often associated with Spain, but may have its origin in Flanders (Personal information Dumargne). A candlestick almost identical to this type was recovered from the Mary Rose (1545). It concerns a base similar to type 3, assembled with a stem similar to type F (Richards 2005, p. 347, fig. 8.44, candle holder 78A0065); a combination common for the Zeebrugge collection. The Mary Rose candlestick, also made of copper-alloy, stands 11cm high and has a diameter of 15.8cm. This is a little bit smaller than a very similar candlestick recovered from the Zeebrugge wreck, with a height of 11.5cm and a width of 17.1cm. The Mary Rose candlestick was considered a candlestick of "superior quality and design" compared to other candlesticks from the same wreck, and may have belonged to a senior crewmember (*Idem*, p. 346).

Type 4

Only two type 4 bases (*Fig. 61*) have been recorded and both of them are damaged. They have the shape of a flared skirt and feature a dripping pan to catch grease. One of the bases is attached to a type A stem (*Fig. 61.a*). This base has a length of 3.6cm and a width of 7cm. The other base is damaged but may have featured a stem too (*Fig. 61.b*). It has a length of 3.8cm and a width of 8.1cm. The type 4 bases seem to have a thinner surface than the other types, making them more fragile and vulnerable. This can possibly explain why only two incomplete pieces of this type have been recovered from the wreck.

A very similar candlestick was excavated in Langenzenn, Germany, and may date to the late 15th century. It features the same combination of a type 4 base with a type A stem, just like the one encountered in the Zeebrugge collection (Mende 2013, p.258, fig. 333). Because of Langenzenn's proximity to Nuremberg, it is believed this candlestick is a Nuremberg product (*Ibidem*).

Type A

The type A stems are the thinnest and probably most elegant stems in this assemblage (*Fig. 63*). With eight pieces they make about 3% of the total assemblage of stems. The round socket has four apertures. These are square and round openings on opposing sides, separated horizontally by a rib. The rims of the socket are slightly flared. The stem has an elongated cone-shaped knop, which rises into a thick discoid knop. Underneath the flared end of the stem a protrusion is present to connect the stem to a base.

We can distinguish two groups with different lengths among the type A stems. Six of the eight objects have a total length of about 12cm. The two other objects are about 11cm long. These different lengths do not seem to influence other dimensions of the candlesticks. The width of all objects varies between 2-2.5cm. The inner diameter of the socket varies between 1.5-2cm with a depth between 2.8-3.3cm. The average dimensions of the square aperture are 0.5x1.2cm, while the average diameter of the circular aperture is 0.5cm. The average protrusion is about 0.3cm long, with an average width of 0.8cm.

Two of the stems show traces of attachment to a base. For one of these, the base is still present, yet damaged. It concerns a type 4 base (*Fig. 61.a*). This is the only type of base we can relate to the type A stems. Only one parallel was found for this type of stem, excavated in Langenzenn and dated to the late 15th century (*Ibidem*).

Type B

Type B is the largest group among the candlestick stems (*Fig. 64.a*). With 62 pieces they represent almost a quarter of all recorded stems (24%). It is a very homogeneous group, with only some minor variations in length. The

The Zeebrugge Shipwreck

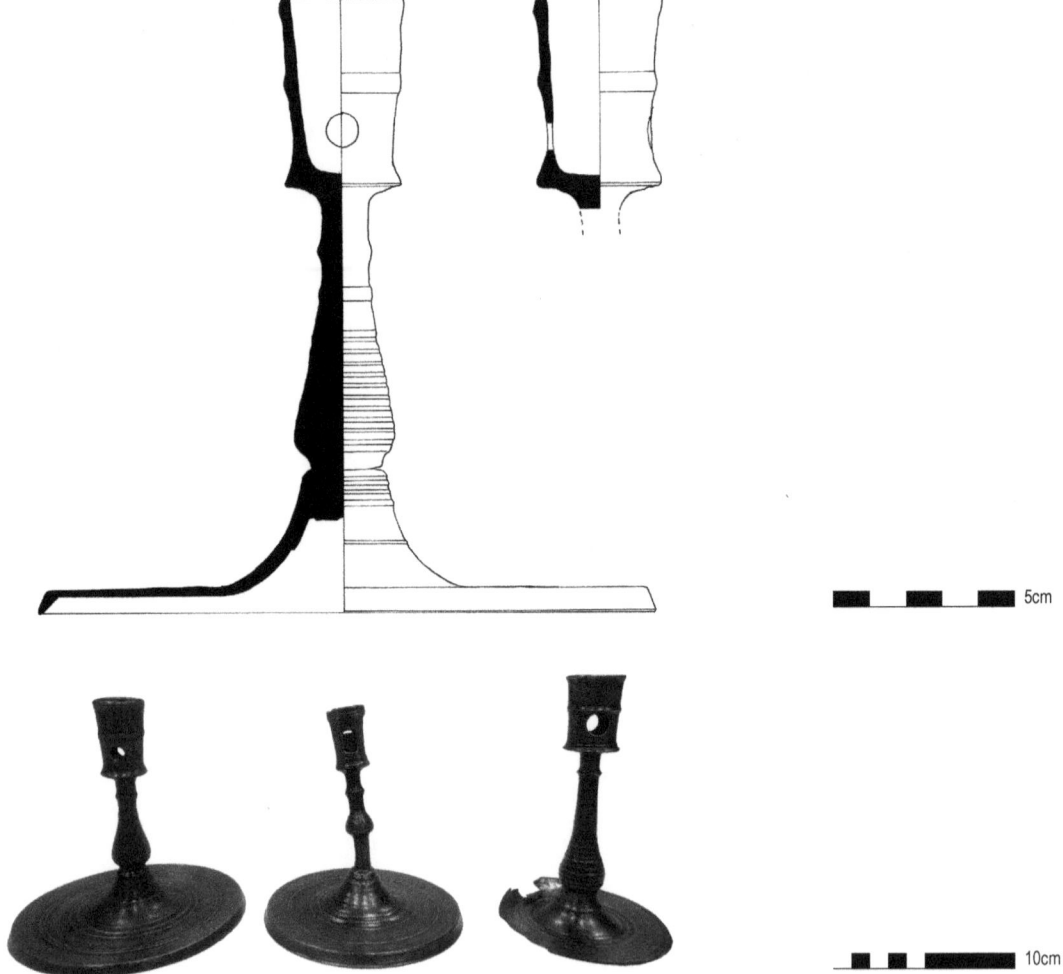

Figure 58. Type 1 bases.

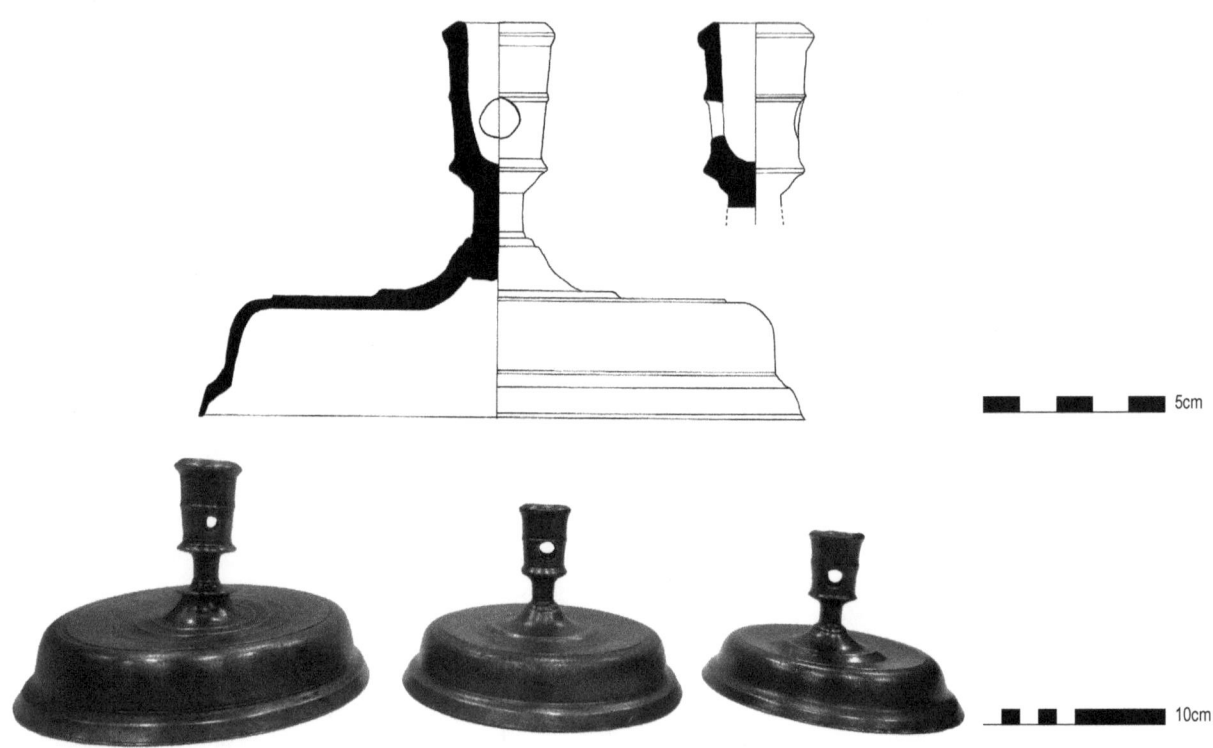

Figure 59. Type 2 bases.

Finds from the Zeebrugge wreck

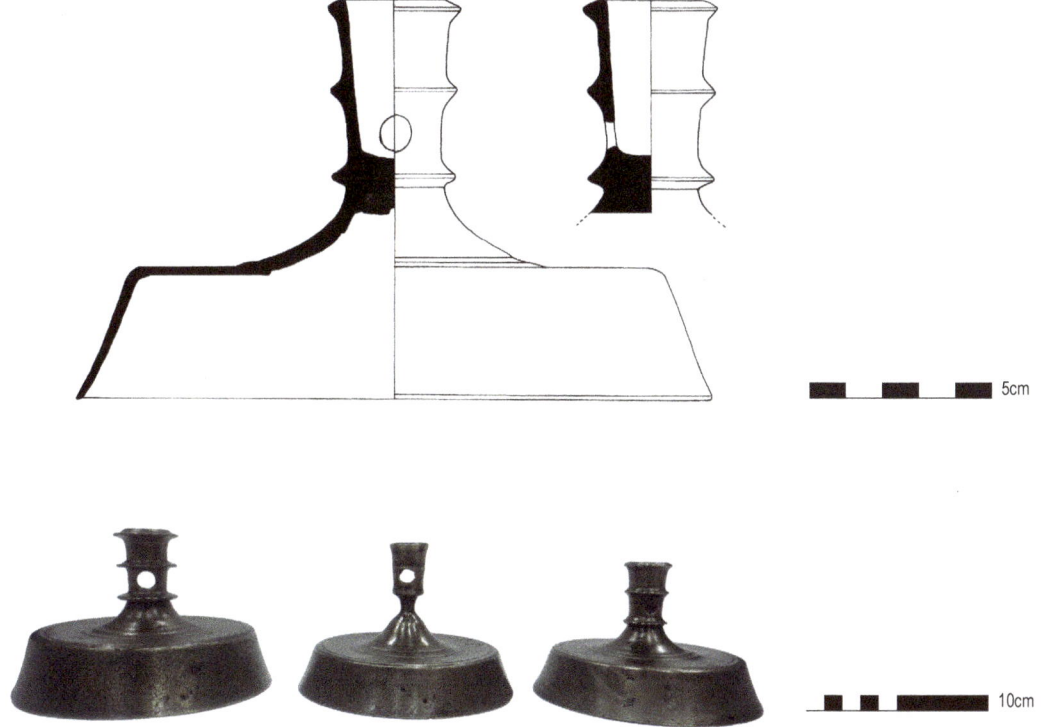

Figure 60. Type 3 bases.

(a)   (b)

Figure 61. Type 4 bases.

socket is similar to the type A socket, with four apertures (two square and two circular) on opposing sides, separated by a rib. Also the socket's rims are slightly flared. Unique for this type, however, is the acorn-shaped knop at the bottom of the stem. Above this knop, a pear-shaped knop is confined between two thick discoid knops. Here, again, a protrusion is present underneath the flared end to connect the stem to a base. A common feature for this type is the double incised line halfway up the pear-shaped knop. Despite the uniformity and high presence of this type in the collection, the particular shape of this type seems to be rather rare.

For this type, several smaller, damaged pieces, are present. We can distinguish 22 incomplete fragments which, due to stylistic characteristics, can be attributed to this type (*Fig. 64.b*). It is not probable that every fragment originates from a different stem; it is more likely that some of these bits and pieces belong together. For four pieces this is quite clear. A perfect fit between two pairs made it clear that the four pieces belonged to two complete stems. For the other pieces, however, no perfect fits could be made, yet the total number of sockets does correspond to the total number of bodies (both eight). Three pieces are more complete with the socket attached to part of the stem. One small stem part, however, could still belong to one of these three more complete pieces. Thus, considering the two "perfect fits" as two candlesticks, these 22 incomplete pieces belong to a minimum of 12 separate stems, while the maximum would be 20. The other 40 pieces are, in general, more complete objects, although in some cases the socket or lower end of the stem is damaged. In order to discuss the dimensions of this type, we only included those objects that could provide representative data. This means not all dimensions given were extracted from the same batch. Yet, because of the general uniformity of this type, this is not considered a problem.

The length of the type B stems varies between 14.4-14.9cm and their width varies between 2.4-2.8cm. The inner diameter of the socket varies between 2-2.5cm, with the majority centering around 2.2cm. The depth of the socket varies between 3.4-4.1 cm. The average dimensions of the square opening are 1.5x0.8cm, while the average diameter of the circular opening is 0.56cm. The protrusion is on average 0.9cm wide and 0.4cm long. Six stems show traces indicating they were once attached to a base. Ten other objects are missing the flared end with protrusion at the bottom of the stem. Since this part becomes more vulnerable when attached to a base, it is plausible these objects were also part of a complete candlestick. None of the type B stems can be linked to a specific type of base.

Type C

Type C is a more complex group, since it is very heterogeneous. The objects of this group are linked because of stylistic characteristics, yet they are not identical to one another, and they vary considerably in size (*Fig. 65*). The group contains 12 objects. The main feature for this group is a (partly) ribbed, pear-shaped knop halfway the stem. This knop may rise into a discoid knop or collar underneath the socket. In some cases another discoid knop is present underneath the pear-shaped knop. They all have a pronounced collar at the end of the stem, with a protrusion to attach the stem to a base. The socket is single-, double- or triple-ribbed at the rims and in the middle. When triple-ribbed, the middle rib can be more pronounced. Between the ribs in the middle and the lower rim, circular openings are pierced on opposing sides. Two objects of this type are strongly eroded and lack any ribs, yet stylistic they can be included in this group.

Figure 62 visualises the different dimensions of this type of stem. We can see the length of the different objects varies considerably. It increases gradually from 9.5-12cm. One object (*Fig. 65.a*) is considerably longer than the other objects, measuring 15.5cm. The smaller outlier is an incomplete item. The chart also brings to light other dimensions, such as the diameter of the socket or apertures, are not proportionally related to the total length of the object. The inner diameter of the socket varies between 1.9-2.8cm and the depth varies between 2.9-4.9cm. The circular apertures range from 0.6 to 1.3cm. Four type C stems are still attached to a complete base. They can be linked to base types 1 and 2. Three others are attached to part of a base, yet the types are unknown. One of the stems is missing the bottom part of the stem. The other four stems were not attached to a base. The protrusions vary between 1.3-2.2cm in width, while their lengths vary between 0.4-0.8cm.

Although, again, it is difficult to find exact parallels for this type of stem, the stem with pear-shaped knop is not uncommon. In Belgium, several museums hold similar stems in their collections, yet often connected to bases distinct from the Zeebrugge types. Some of them are dated rather broadly to between 1401-1600 (e.g. BALaT KIK-IRPA (no date), Object number 108480), while others have a smaller date range between 1451-1500 (e.g. BALaT KIK-IRPA (no date), Object number 132347).

Type D

With 43 items, type D is the third best-represented group among the stem types (*Fig. 66.a*). The type D stems are quite similar to the type C stems, also featuring a pronounced, ribbed, pear-shaped knop. However, in the case of the type D stems, this knop forms the end of the stem. A protrusion extends directly from this knop to connect the stem to a base. Towards the socket, the pear-shaped knop may rise into a collar or small discoid knop. In some rare cases there are two small knops underneath the socket, which gives the impression of an extended shaft. The sockets have, in general, slightly flared rims and a rib in the middle. A few exceptions show an additional rib near the rims, and/or triple ribs in the middle of the socket with a pronounced middle rib. All but one of the type D stems are pierced on

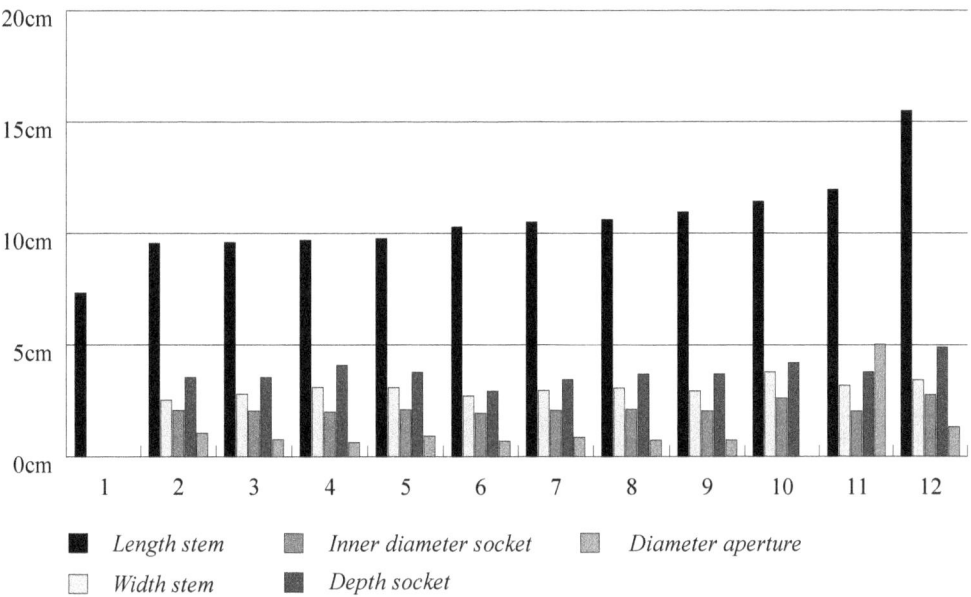

Figure. 62. Dimensions type C stem.

opposing sides in the lower part of the socket. The one exception is not pierced at all, which is a feature only three sockets exhibit in the entire collection of candlesticks. The other sockets mostly have circular apertures. Three objects, however, have wide, square openings in the lower part of the socket (*Fig. 66.b*).

Just like the type C stems, type D is a rather heterogeneous group. Lengths increase gradually, and other dimensions do not seem to be proportional to differences in stem-length. Yet, when we plot these dimensions on a chart, we can notice some uniformity for two smaller groups (*Fig. 69*). Although in general the different dimensions do not increase proportionally to the length of the stems, for these two groups all dimensions are relatively stable.

The total length for this type varies from 9.4cm to 15.2cm and the width ranges from 2.8-3.9cm. The socket's inner diameter varies between 2.1-3cm and its depth between 3.5-5cm. The circular apertures range from 0.6-1.6cm; some of these larger openings seem to be the consequence of severe erosion. The average opening of the square apertures is 1.5x1.7cm. The two uniform groups centre around lengths of 10.8cm and 11.9cm.

The majority of this group of stems is attached to a type 1 base: the only base type linked to the type D stems. Three stems were once attached to an unidentified base, and one of the stems is missing the part with protrusion. For the ten stems with measurable protrusion their average length was 1.8cm, the average width 0.7cm.

When looking for parallels, the type D stem appears to be less common than the type C stem. A candlestick with a stem similar to this type is depicted in one of the Nuremberg *hausbücher*, dated to 1528, as a product of a local craftsman (*Fig. 66.c*).

Type E

The type E group, consisting of 12 very uniform stems, is characterised by its donut-shaped knop halfway up the stem in combination with a round socket (*Fig. 67*). It is almost identical to the type J stem, which has a similar knop yet combined with a hexagonal socket. Just like types A and B, the socket of the type E stem is characterized by slightly flared rims and a rib in the middle of the socket. Four apertures are present; two square openings and two circular openings opposed to one another. Other than the knop in the middle, the shaft has a flared collar at the end. A screw protrudes from the end of the stem. This feature is different from the protrusions discussed for the earlier types, and it implies the need for a specific base, adjusted to this screwing system. No such bases, however, are present among the finds from the Zeebrugge wreck.

The length of the type E stems varies from 11 to 11.6cm. One object is a little bit smaller because of a damaged screw protrusion at the end of the stem. The width varies between 2.7-3cm. The inner diameter of the socket varies between 2.3-2.6 and the depth of the socket between 3.9-4.3cm. The square aperture has average dimensions of 0.8x1.6cm and the average diameter of the circular aperture is 0.7cm. The average length of the screw protrusion is 0.9cm, its average width is 0.8cm.

It is not entirely certain whether the shaft of the type E stems is solid or hollow. For one object, the donut-shaped knop is punctured and it demonstrates this knop is at least partly hollow. The observation, however, does not reveal to what extent the shaft is hollow.

A candlestick with similar knop is depicted on the painting "The Money Changer and his Wife" (1539) by Marinus

The Zeebrugge Shipwreck

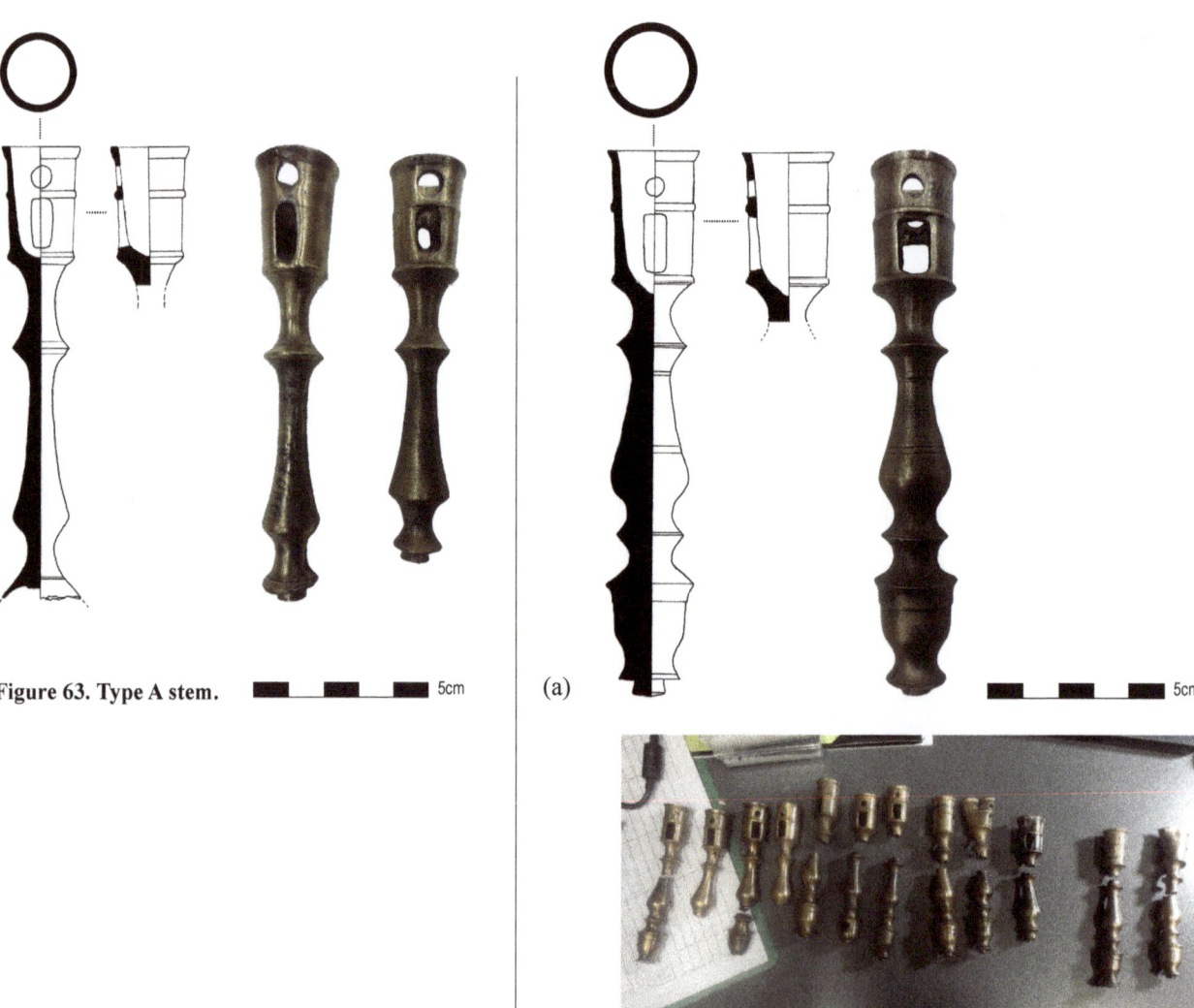

Figure 63. Type A stem. 5cm

Figure 64. Type B stem (a) and pieces of damaged type B stems (b).

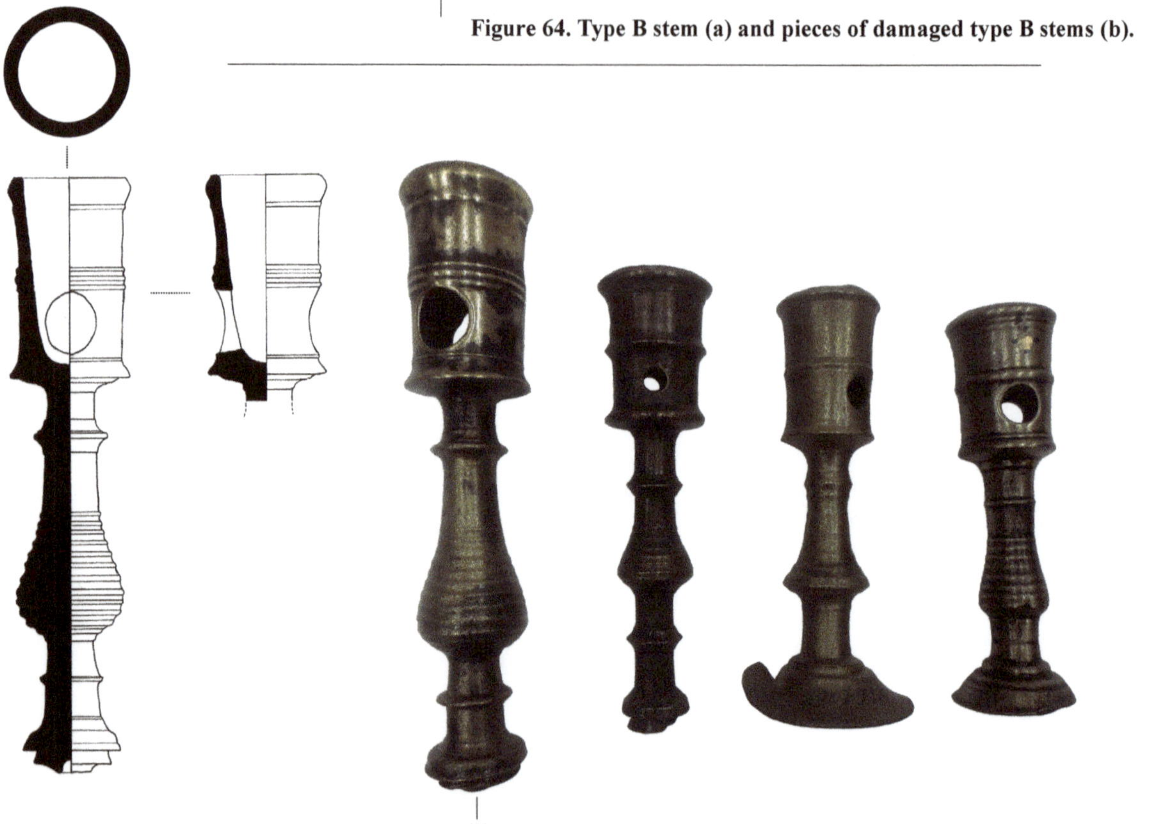

Figure 65. Type C stems. 5cm

72

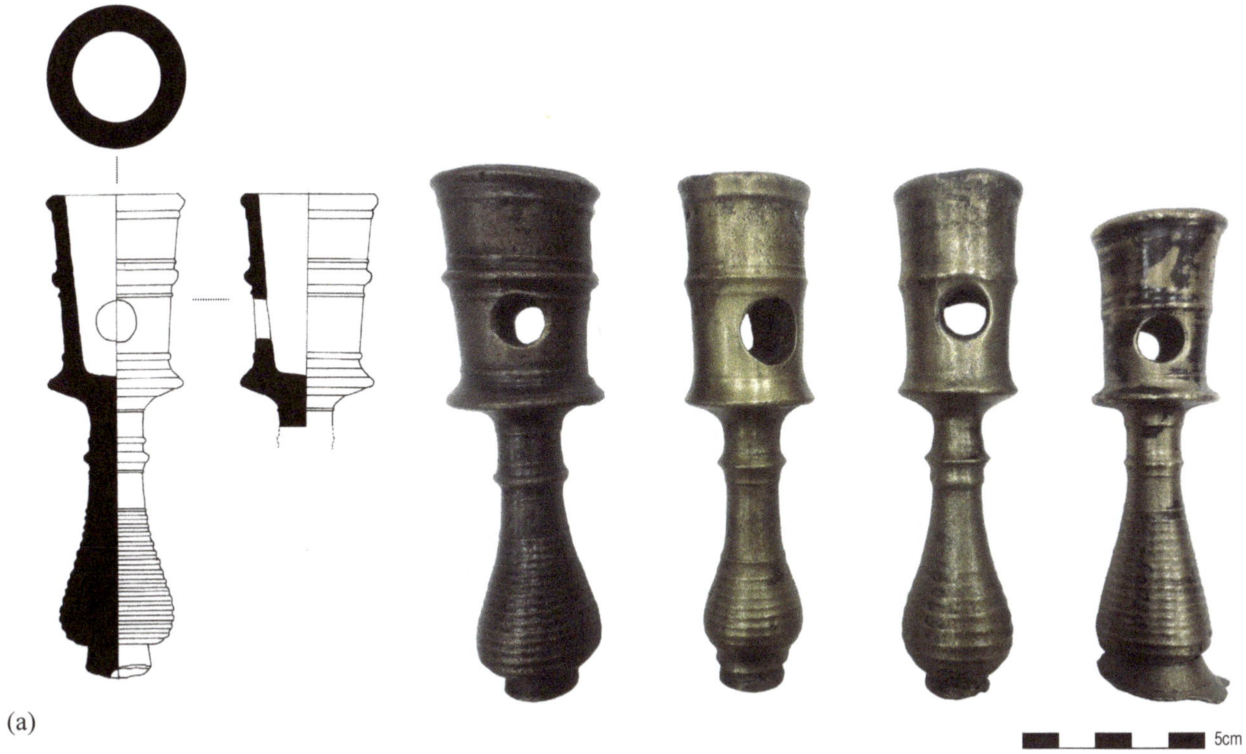

Finds from the Zeebrugge wreck

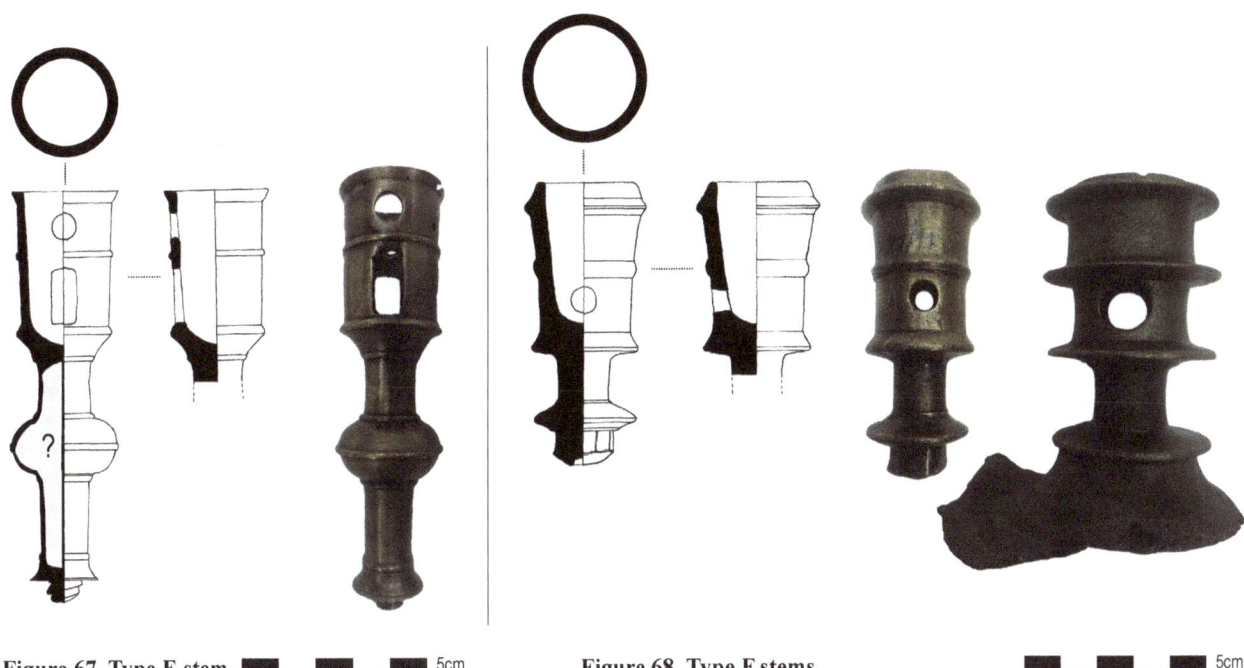

(a)

(b) (c)

Figure 66. Type D stems (a) with detail of wide, square apperture (b) and a detail of de Nuremberg *Hausbücher* (1528) (c) (Stadtbibliothek Nürnberg, Amb. 279.2° Folio 18 recto (Landauer I)).

Figure 67. Type E stem. 5cm

Figure 68. Type F stems. 5cm

73

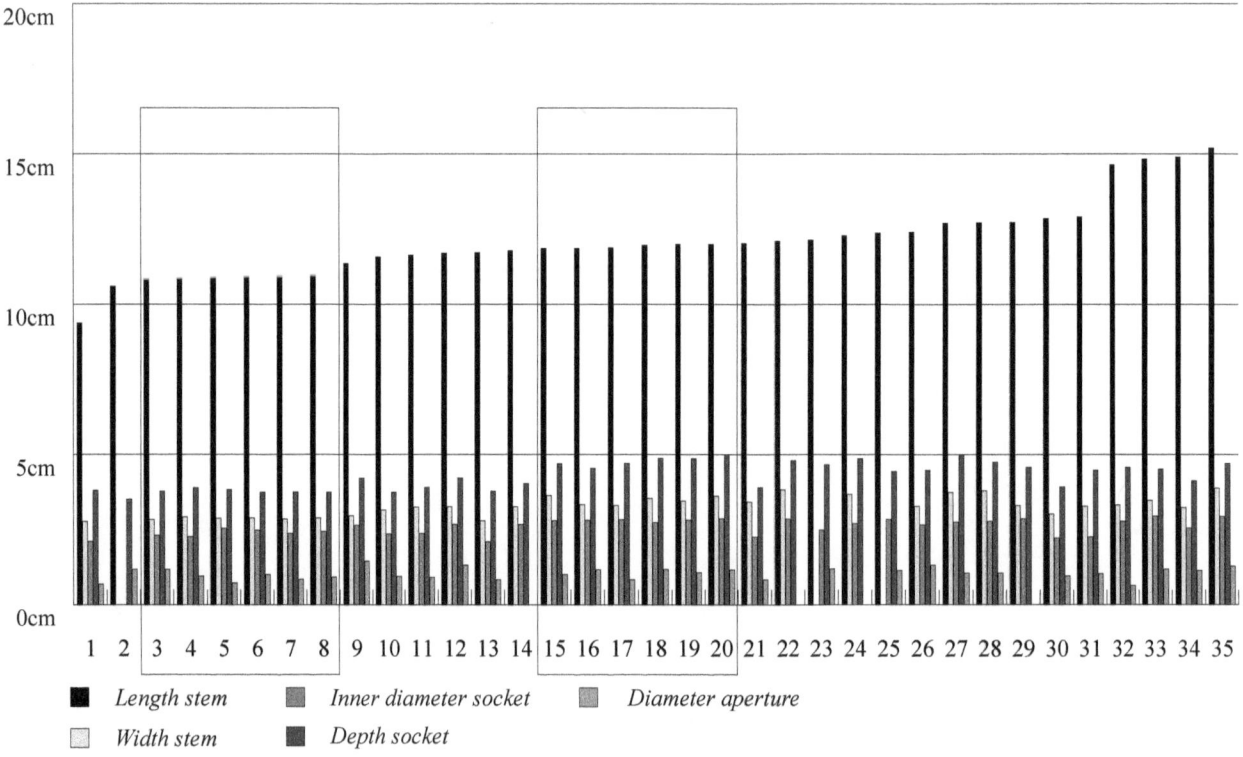

Figure 69. Dimensions type D stem.

van Reymerswaele, yet the socket here is different from the Zeebrugge types. Two very similar stems were recovered from the Villefranche 1 wreck, which was identified as the Genoese ship "Lomellina" (1516) (Architecture et Patrimoine (no date)).

Type F

The 16 type F stems form a heterogeneous group, characterized by a very short shaft (*Fig. 68*). The shaft is in general shorter than the socket and only has one discoid knop at the bottom. The size of this knop may vary in width, and in some cases could better be described as a pronounced collar. Ribs can be present at the rims of the socket, as well as in the middle of the socket. These ribs vary from small single ribs, to large discoid ribs, to multiple ribs. With the exception of one object, all items have circular apertures on opposing sides in the lower part of the socket. The one exception has no apertures at all which makes it, together with one of the type D and type G stems, unique in this regard. Underneath the discoid knop at the end of the stem, a protrusion is present.

The group is quite heterogeneous and the different items rise gradually in length (*Fig. 70*). Although there are several exceptions, we can notice a certain relation between the length and width of the stem and the depth and inner diameter of the socket, which all, to a certain extent, rise gradually.

The length of the type F stems varies between 5.6-7.5cm. Since most of these stems are attached to a base, the protrusion at the end of the stem is not included in this number. Three objects were unattached, with an average protrusion length of 0.9cm and width of 2.3cm. The total length of an unattached stem would therefore vary between 6.5 and 8.4cm. The width of the stems varies between 2.7-4.4cm. The inner diameter of the socket ranges from 1.9cm to 2.7cm and its depth varies between 3-4.6cm. The circular apertures range gradually between 0.5-1.1cm.

The majority of the type F stems are attached to a base. They are linked to type 2 bases (8x) and type 3 bases (4x). One stem was attached to an unknown base.

Similar stem types have been recovered from the wreck of the St Anthony (1527) (e.g. Camidge 2013, p. 32, find 66)[36], as well as from the Punta Cana Pewter wreck (late 1540's-early 1550's) (e.g. Seliger & Pritgett 2011a, p. 45). At the site of Puerto Real, Haiti, similar stems have been excavated in the area that was identified as the town's church. This town was founded in 1503 and destroyed by an earthquake in 1577 (Personal information Kathleen Deagan). It should be said, however, that candlestick bases recovered from these sites do not correspond to the models from the Zeebrugge wreck. An exception would be one of the candlesticks recovered from the Mary Rose, which makes a close parallel for the Zeebrugge candlesticks (*cf. supra*).

---

[36] We would like to thank Mark Dunkley and Historic England for providing the full database and additional pictures of these finds.

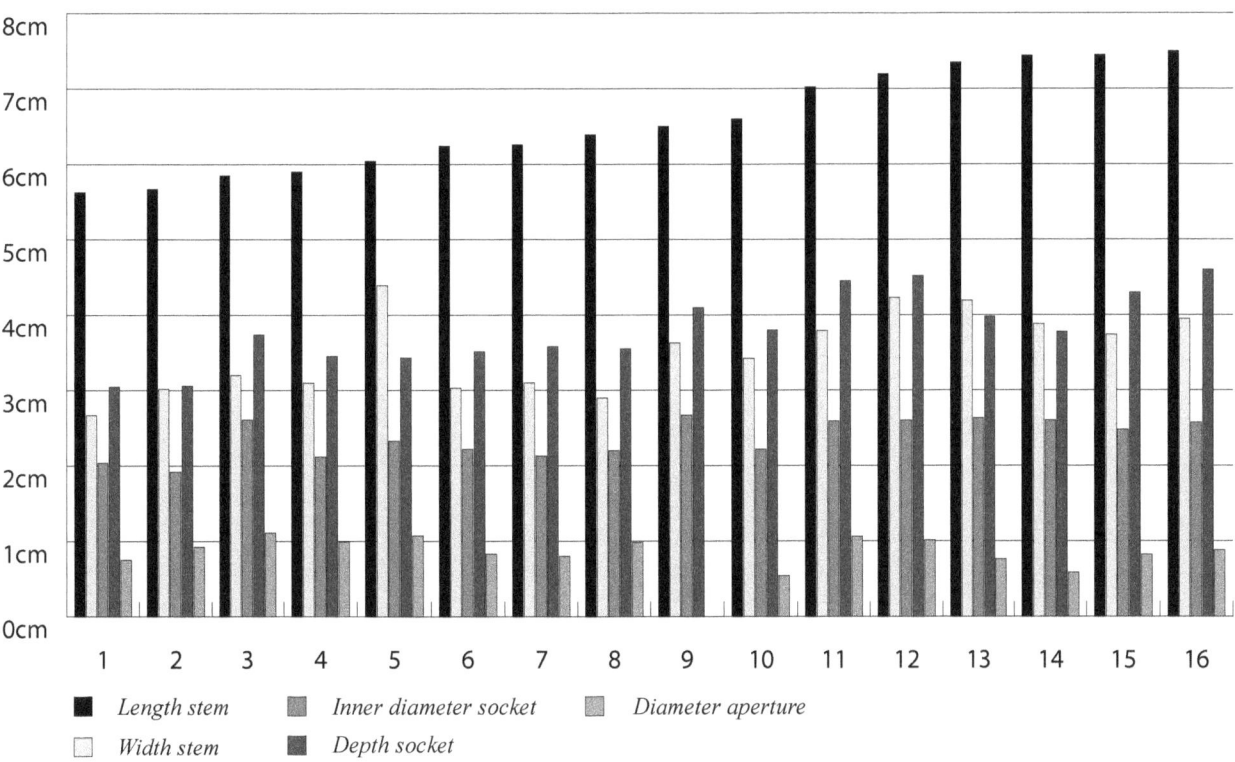

Figure 70. Dimensions type F stem.

Type G

Type G distinguishes itself from the other types by being only a socket (*Fig. 72*). There is no additional shaft. The 18 type G stems are all round sockets with ribs near the rims and, except for one item, a rib in the middle. The ribs can vary in size, from thick collars to wide and flat discs. The objects generally have two circular apertures in the lower part of the socket, yet there is one item without any apertures at all. Most stems are still attached to a complete base. We can distinguish thirteen type 2 bases and three type 3 bases. The two other stems are not attached to a complete base. At least one of them must have been attached to a base since traces of the base are still visible (*Fig. 72.b*). The other stem may have been attached too, yet we were not able to determine this conclusively (*Fig. 72.a*).

The type G group is very heterogeneous. The length of the sockets (without protrusion) ranges from 4.3cm to 6.3cm. Here, again, the other dimensions do not seem to be proportional to changes in length. This becomes very clear when we plot all dimensions on a chart (*Fig. 71*). The width of the type F sockets varies between 3-4.7cm. The inner diameter ranges between 2.2-3.1cm and their depth varies from 3.5-5.5cm. Apertures have a wide range from 0.6cm to 1.3cm. Only one protrusion could be measured, and, as indicated before, it is uncertain whether this is an actual protrusion or part of a base. Its length is 0.8cm, its width 3.3cm.

Some candlesticks from the Punta Cana Pewter wreck seem to have stems similar to the type G stems discussed here (e.g. ARS Anchor Research & Salvage Inc. 2012c, p. 8-9), yet they are attached to capstan-style bases. When looking for parallels in general, it appears sockets without shaft are often combined with this type of base. We did not find any close parallels for the type G stems in combination with the respective bases from the Zeebrugge wreck.

Type H

With 45 items type H (*Fig. 73.a*) is the second-largest typological group, representing 17.5% of all stems. The type features a lightly tapered, hexagonal socket with a double collar at the top rim and a single collar at the bottom rim. This collar evolves into a narrow, open ring-shape. Underneath the ring the object widens a bit again, and a small protrusion is present at the end. The socket has four apertures; a square aperture underneath a circular aperture on opposing sides. The 45 pieces make a very homogeneous group, with one odd exception. This exception has an octagonal socket, but other than that features all the same characteristics. None of the objects is attached to a base, nor can be linked to one of the present base types.

The length of the type H stems varies between 6.2-6.5cm. Their width varies between 2.3-2.6cm, the thickness between 2-2.3cm. The inner diameter of the socket measures 1.6-2cm, the depth of the socket measures 3.4-3.8cm. The depth of the octagonal socket is 4.3cm, deviating from the others. Its total length and width, 6.7cm and 2.2cm, may not be representative because the ring-shape is partly squeezed. For all items, the

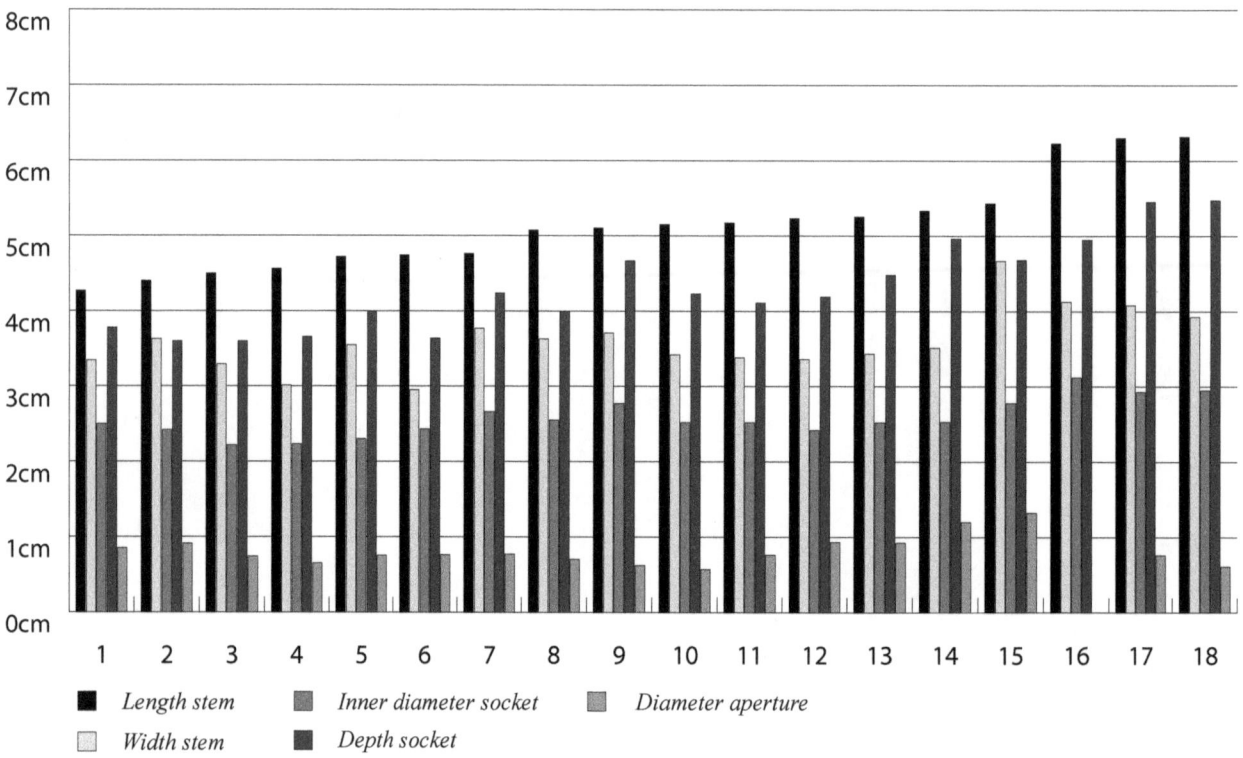

Figure 71. Dimensions type G stem.

average dimensions of the square aperture are 0.6x1.7cm while the average diameter of the circular aperture is 0.4cm.

Ring-shaped stems similar to the type H stems are depicted in a Nuremberg Hausbuch, dated to 1518 (*Fig. 73.b*). A similar object, yet with a more pronounced protrusion and without collar at the top, was excavated in England and dated to the late 15th – early 16th century based upon context finds (Egan 2005, p. 80-81), and similar objects are recorded in the online Portable Antiquities Scheme (e.g. P.A.S., finds KENT-4389B5, NLM-AF8214, WMID-4BDA01, etc.). The dimensions of these objects approach the dimensions of the type H group closely. In museums and private collections, we can find examples of this type attached to a base (Bang 1995, p. 73-74; Brownsword 2003, p. 18-20; Guildhall Museum 1903, p. 300) or as part of a chandelier (e.g. Lockner 1982). The common base type for this object seems to be a small, conical base with a collar at the lower rim and a flaring grease pan; a shape similar to the type 4 bases from the Zeebrugge wreck. In the existing literature, however, disagreement exists about the actual relation between this base and stem type. While Brownsword argues these are original dinandery products, Bang makes a good case for the stem being attached to the base at a later stage. He disclaims this type of candlestick is an original product, but rather an "ancient marriage" of two products. The huge collection of type H stems recovered from the Zeebrugge wreck may shed new light on this discussion. The fact such quantities of unattached stems were traded without base seems to indicate they were to be attached locally to a candlestick or chandelier. This means Bang's "ancient marriage" may be the original contemporary product as it was meant to be, yet not the product of one single workshop. The picture of this type in a Nuremberg *Hausbüch*, however, does indicate they could be completed in a single workshop as well. One source mentions a "fragment of a gothic chandelier" was recovered from the site as well (P.A.B.S., D.R. "Bergingsinventaris 20/07/1994"). However, such an object does not appear to be present in the MAS collection, nor is it mentioned in any of the publications or inventories. If indeed part of a chandelier was excavated, the type H sockets are almost certainly related to it.

Type I

Type I has a hexagonal socket, and is the only type with a hexagonal shaft too (*Fig. 74*). It is a homogeneous group of 8 pieces. Two pieces are incomplete and they may belong to the same object, yet they could be part of different objects as well. The hexagonal socket has collared rims and a rib in the middle. It has four apertures. Just like earlier discussed types it features two circular openings on opposing sides in the upper part of the socket and two square openings on opposing sides in the lower part of the socket. The shaft is characterized by a thick, hexagonal, collared knop in the middle. Flared collars are present underneath the socket and at the end of the stem. Just like type E, a screw protrudes from the stem to attach it to a base. None of the type I stems are attached to a base, yet for one of the stems the bottom part is missing. Although this item could have been attached to a base, this seems unlikely since no bases with such a screw system are present among the finds.

If we exclude the incomplete objects, the type I stems vary in length between 11.2-11.5cm, and they vary in width between 3-3.2cm (measured at socket). One item is a little bit smaller with a width of 2.7cm, due to erosion. The inner diameter of the socket varies between 2.2-2.3cm and its depth between 3.4-4cm. The average of the square openings is 0.8-1.4cm, the circular apertures have an average diameter of 0.7cm. All screws have a width of about 0.9cm and protrude about 1.1cm.

Similar objects seem to be difficult to find. Some identical stems are present on auction sites (e.g. piasa (2016)), where we can see the stem combined to a base similar to type 3 from the Zeebrugge wreck. According to Dumargne (2013, p. 36), this type dates to the 16th century. It would be of Flemish origin, although the type inspired workshops in the Netherlands and Germany too.

Type J

Type J is a homogeneous group, very similar to type E yet with a hexagonal socket (*Fig. 75.a*). Two of the eleven registered objects are incomplete and fit perfectly together; making the total of actual type J stems ten. The hexagonal socket is very similar to the type I sockets. They have collared rims and a rib in the middle. Two each of circular and square apertures are present on opposing sides. The round-sectioned shaft has a donut-shaped knop in the middle. Underneath the socket and at the end of the stem, flared collars are present. A screw, similar to types E and I, protrudes from the bottom of the stem. None of the type J stems is attached to a base.

The length of the type J stems varies between 11.1-11.5cm, their width varies between 2.9-3.2cm. The inner diameter of the socket measures 2.3-2.4cm, the socket's depth varies between 3.6-4.2cm with the majority having a depth of about 4cm. The average dimensions of the square aperture are 0.9x1.7cm, the average diameter of the circular aperture is 0.7cm. The screw protrudes 1-1.2cm from the stem and has a width of 0.8-1cm.

Several items similar to the type J stem have been excavated at the site of Concepción de le Vega (1494-1562), Dominican Republic. There, they have been found as individual stems or attached to a capstan-style base. They come from a religious context which was identified as the town's hospital, adjacent to the church (Kulstad 2008, p. 134). One of the stems from this site seems to be a hybrid version of types I and J, with hexagonal-sectioned shaft and donut-shaped knop (*Fig. 75.b*). This object was excavated at the town's *fortaleza* and dates to between 1520-1562. Also a type H socket was recovered from this site (Personal information Deagan).

Type K

Although type K (*Fig. 76*) is a rather homogeneous group, there are small differences in the way the objects are finished (e.g. specific shape of the knop). They are similar to the type C stems, yet with a hexagonal socket. The hexagonal socket features strongly pronounced collared rims, and two square apertures opposed to one another. In the middle of the shaft, this type features a ribbed, slender, pear-shaped knop that rises into another small knop. At the bottom of the stem a thick collar is present. Underneath this collar a protrusion is present to attach the stem to a base. Two of the stems are attached to a type 1 base. Three objects are incomplete and may have been attached to a base. Two other stems are nearly complete, yet for one of them the protrusion partly broke off, which may be an indication this stem was once attached to a base too.

The length of the type K stems varies between 11.5-12.6cm, their width varies between 3.5-4cm. The inner diameter of the socket varies between 2-2.7cm, the depth of the socket measures 3.9-4.1cm. For one of the objects a thimble is stuck inside the socket. The average dimensions of the square apertures are 0.9x1.6cm. The only complete protrusion has a length of 0.8cm and a width of 1.8cm.

A candlestick similar to this type was sold by Christie's (*cf. supra*) and was described as Franco-Flemish and dated to the early 16th century. Just like the Zeebrugge candlesticks, it is combined to a base similar to type 1, yet with a more articulated dome. We could not find any parallels from more secure contexts for this type.

Type L

Only two type L stems have been recovered from the Zeebrugge wreck (*Fig. 77*). Although these two objects are not identical, they show similar characteristic features. They have hexagonal sockets similar to type K, with strongly pronounced collared rims, and square apertures on opposing sides. Their shafts feature two thick, discoid knops. In both cases, the lower knop is more pronounced and features a rib along its middle. Both objects are lacking a clear protrusion as encountered for the other stem types. However, since there are no clear traces of damage, it is possible the type L stems could have been mounted on a base just like this. They cannot be linked to a specific type of base within the collection, and we did not find any clear parallels for this type either.

The dimensions of both stems are very similar. Object A (*Fig. 77.a*) has a length of 11.1cm and a width of 4cm. The inner diameter of the socket measures 2.4cm and its depth 4.1cm. The apertures measure 0.9x1.8 cm.

Object B (*Fig. 77.b*) has a total length of 11.2cm and a width of 3.9cm. The socket's inner diameter measures 2.1cm and its depth 4cm. The aperture deviates a bit from object A, with a width and length of 0.8x1.4cm.

The Zeebrugge Shipwreck

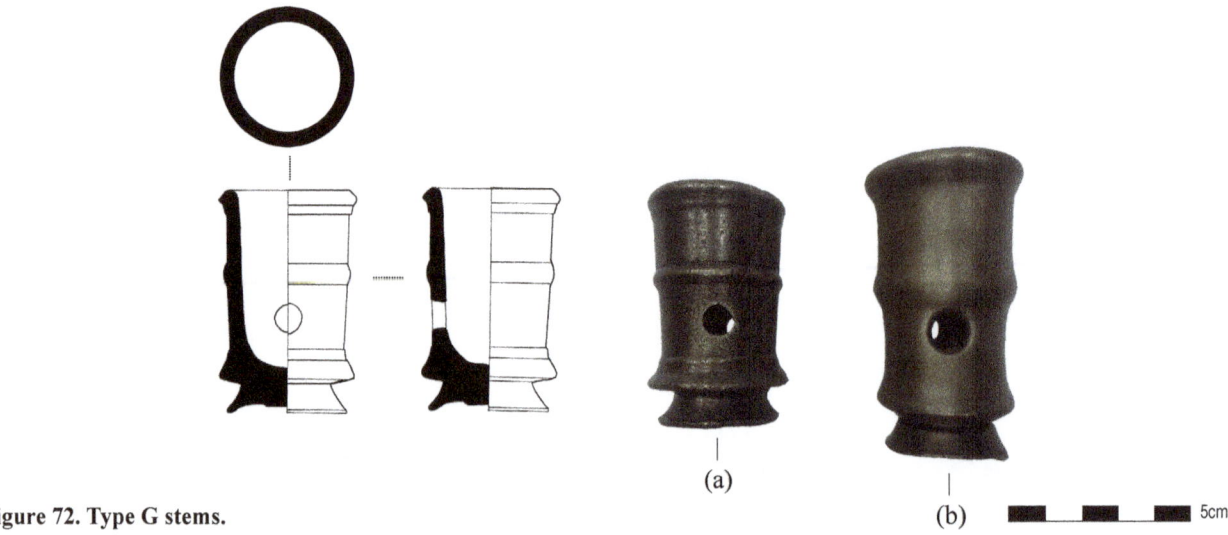

Figure 72. Type G stems.

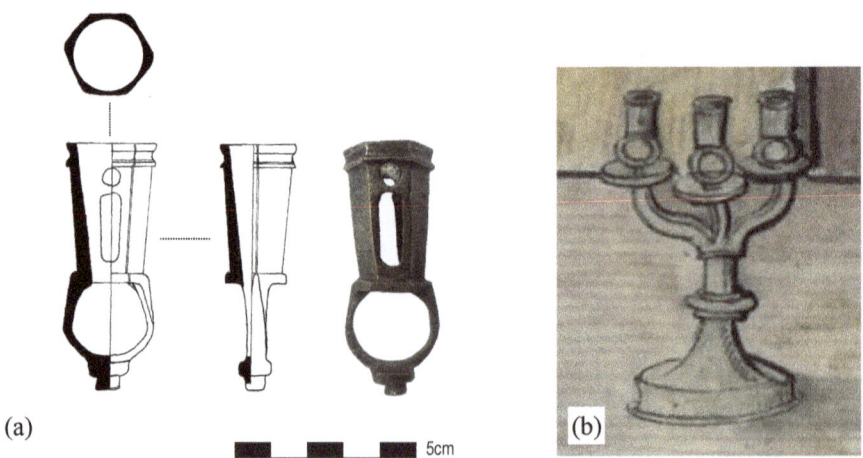

Figure 73. Type H stem (a) and similar stem types from Nuremberg (b) (Stadtbibliothek Nürnberg, Amb. 279.2° Folio 9 recto (Landauer I)).

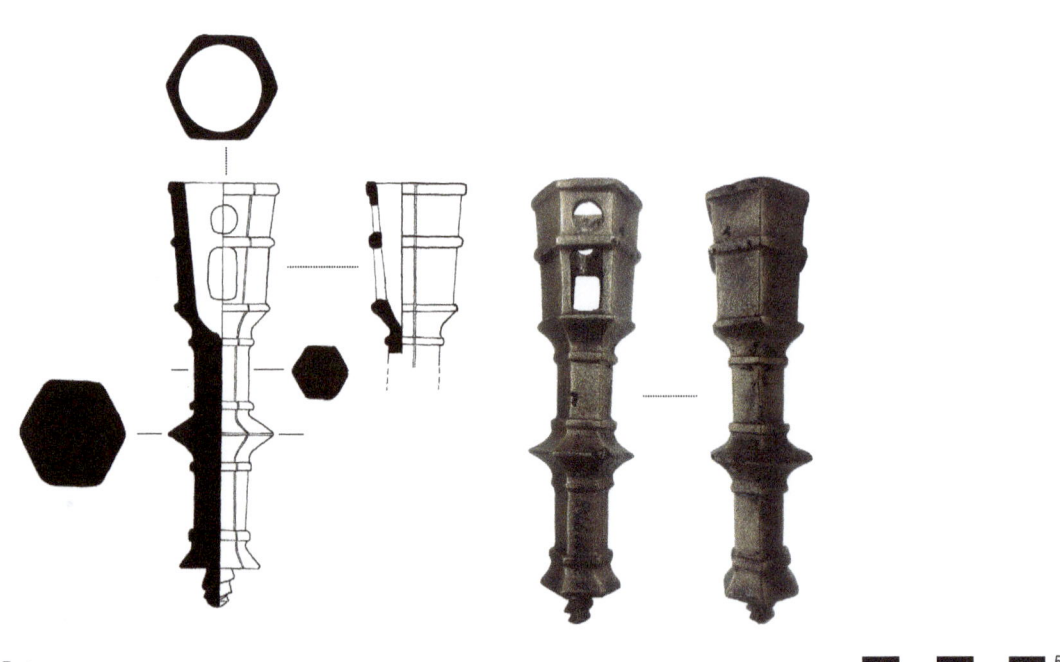

Figure 74. Type I stem.

Finds from the Zeebrugge wreck

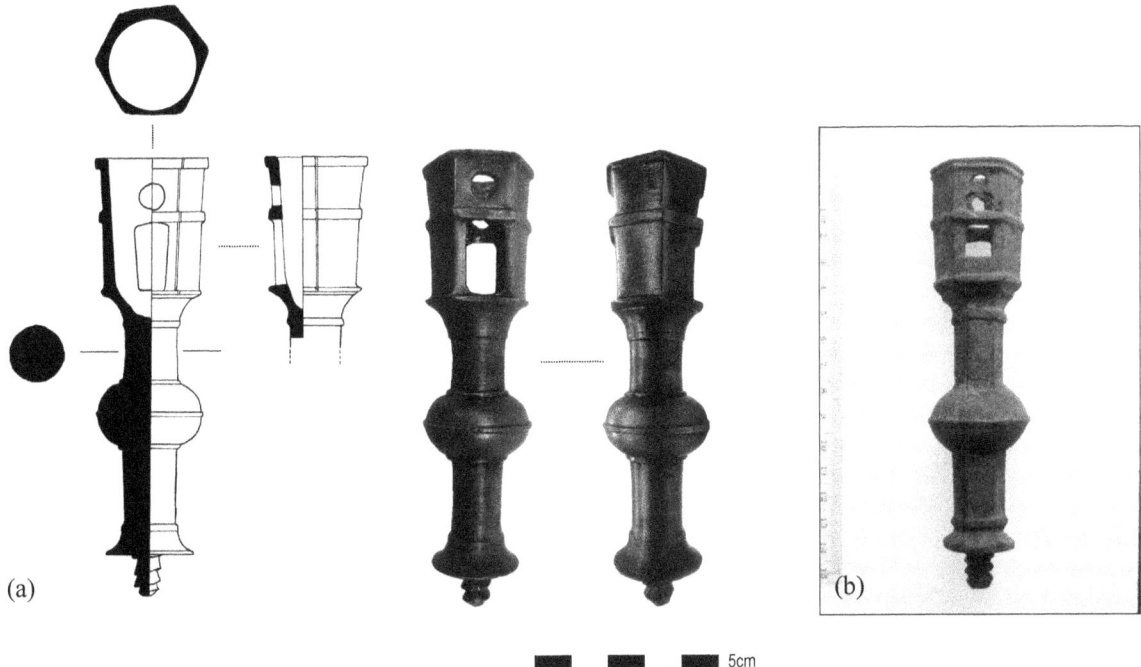

Figure 75. Type J stem (a) and a similar stem from the early 16th century (b), excavated at the site of Concepción de la Vega (Dominican Republic), featuring elements from both the type I and J stems from the Zeebrugge wreck (Florida Museum of Natural History, University of Florida).

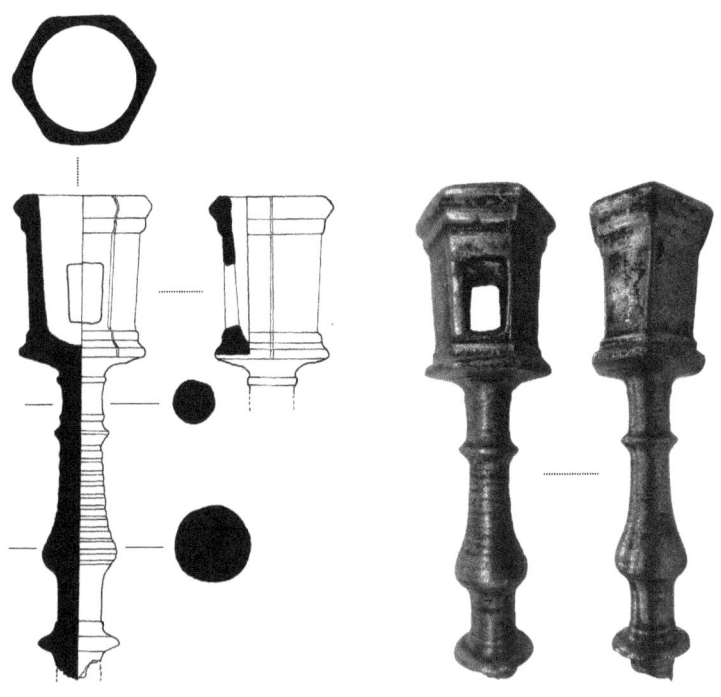

Figure 76. Type K stem.

Type M

There is only one object classified as a type M stem. It distinguishes itself from the other stems because of its floral decoration; an oddity for this collection (*Fig. 78.a*). The incomplete stem has a hexagonal socket. The socket features double ribs at the upper rim and lower rim, and in the middle. It also is the only stem that has six apertures in the socket. It features a rectangular, oval, and circular opening on opposed sides. The shaft's section features six lobes. These lobes seem to rise into flared leaves, evoking a flower's calyx from which the socket sprouts. Underneath this floral decoration the shaft, now round-sectioned, continues, yet this part broke off. It is the only stem type for which we can conclusively say it is hollow on the inside.

The incomplete stem has a total length of 10.1cm and a width of 3.8cm. The inner diameter of the socket measures 2.7cm and has a depth of 5.6cm. The square aperture measures 0.8x1.4cm, the oval aperture 0.7 cm and the circular aperture 0.6cm.

The closest parallels we could find for the type M stem are two candlestick stems excavated in Concepción de la Vega. These stems are not identical, yet they feature similar floral characteristics (*Fig. 78.b*). Just like the other candlesticks from Concepción de la Vega (*cf.* type J), they should be to dated in the first half of the 16th century.

Type N

The type N stem is the last type to discuss. There is only one stem of this type, and it is strongly eroded (*Fig. 79*). Therefore, not all features are clearly visible, yet it is clear this stem could not be included in any other group. The socket narrows down a little in the middle, and features circular apertures on opposed sides. Ribs or collars may have been present, but because of erosion this is uncertain. What distinguishes this type from the rest is its relatively short stem with a single knot in the middle. At the end of the stem a flared collar is present. The stem is attached to a type 2 base.

The length of the stem is about 8cm long and has a width of 2.7cm. The inner diameter of the socket measures 2.1cm and has a depth of 3.3cm. The apertures measure 1.2cm. The base has a width of 16.3cm and the total length of the candlestick is about 12cm.

3.8.2. *pXRF-analysis*

As discussed in the introduction, the main goal of the pXRF-analyses in this research is to execute a qualitative analysis to identify the elements present in the samples. Because of the significant number of candlesticks, however, a semi-quantitative analysis was executed for these objects as well, comparing the relative concentrations of the different samples within the collection. All together, 55 samples were measured for the candlestick collection, consisting of 38 stem samples and 17 base samples. For all samples, peaks were present for the same elements (*Fig. 80*), being mainly copper (Cu), but also zinc (Zn) and to a lesser extent lead (Pb). The copper alloy used for these candlesticks can thus be identified as brass, yet we find considerable traces of lead too. Just like tin, lead was often added to improve the fluidity of brass when molten (Goodall 1981, p. 63), although it is also possible lead was just added to cut costs.

The main elements, copper and lead, relate to one another between 75%-25% and 90%-10% regardless of the other elements. When we include the element lead, however, the proportions of these three elements fluctuate much stronger since the relative lead concentration knows a lot of variation within the sampled batch (0.4%-18.8% in the total spectrum). In some cases, the lead percentage approaches or even surpasses the zinc percentage. This is the case for some of the type C, F, G, L and N stems. Other than copper, zinc and lead, traces of several other elements were encountered, mainly iron (Fe) and cadmium (Ca), although in some rare cases tin (Sn) or even hafnium (Hf) was present.

We plotted the concentration for the most common elements per object and grouped typologically (*Fig. 81-82*). Every bar of the chart gives the normalized results of an individual measurement for one object. This way, we can compare the relative element concentrations per item and per typological group. Although the main elements are similar for all typological groups, we can see differences in concentration for different typological groups. Also, we can notice more homogeneous typological groups seem to present more homogeneous concentrations and vice versa. Whether these variations should be interpreted as different batches of production from one workshop, or batches from different workshops, is uncertain. Possibly a closer examination of trace elements and comparative data could answer this question. The analysis of the present data as such, however, is not extensive enough to answer such a question. The most frequent trace elements are not uncommon (e.g. Fe, Cd, Sn), yet the relatively large presence of hafnium may raise questions. Especially intriguing is the fact that in some cases this element is present up to 3%, while for many other objects it is absent. The presence of hafnium can possibly be explained as noise, due to the conservation process of these objects, or caused during the measurements. Further and more exhaustive xrf-analysis of the objects, as will happen in the frame of Dumargne's research, may clarify the presence of this element.

Finds from the Zeebrugge wreck

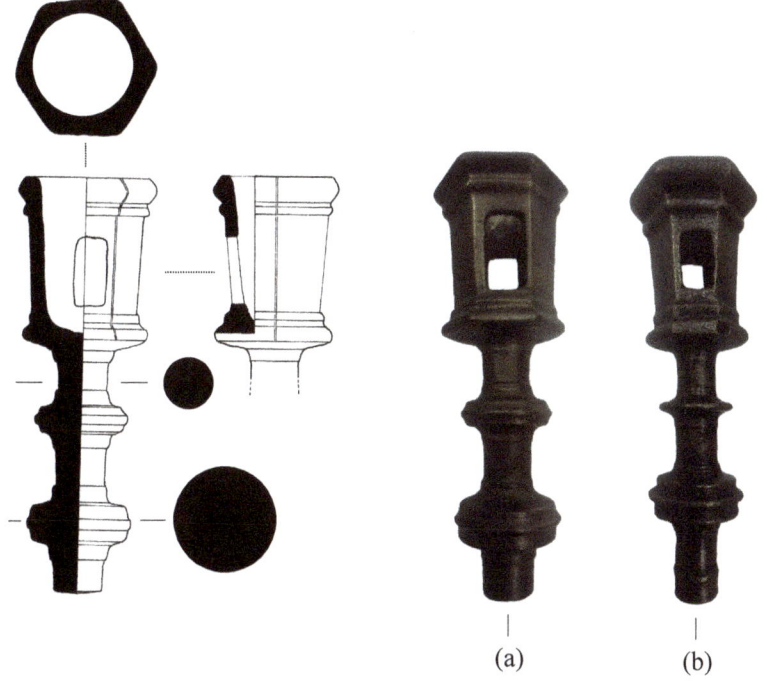

Figure 77. Type L stems.

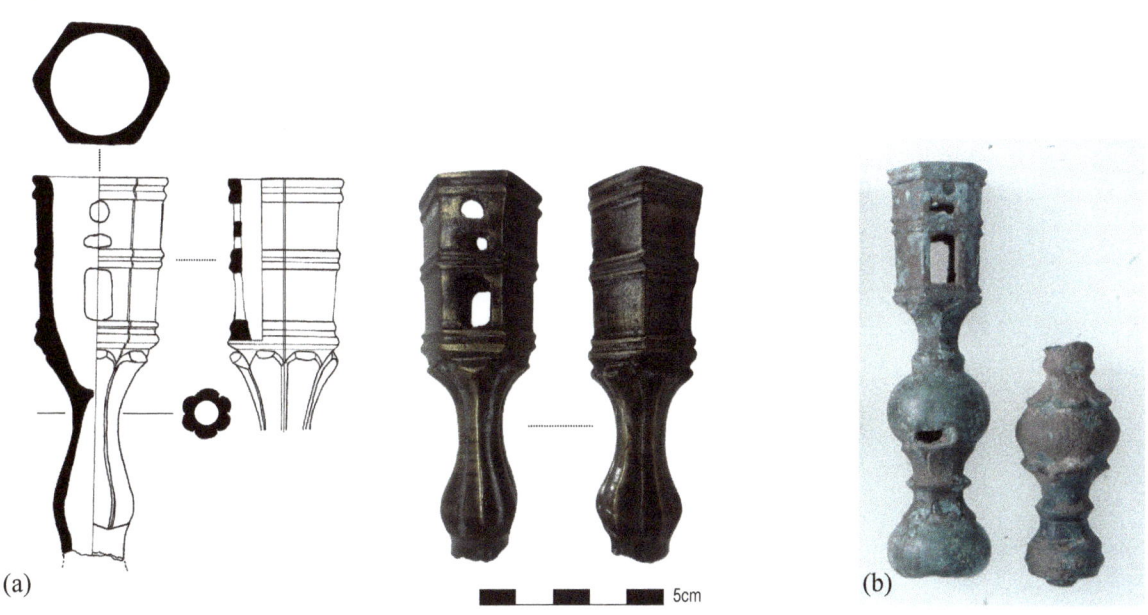

Figure 78. Type M stem (a) and a stem excavated at the site of Concepción de la Vega (Dominican Republic), featuring similar characteristics, yet it is not identical (b) (Florida Museum of Natural History, University of Florida).

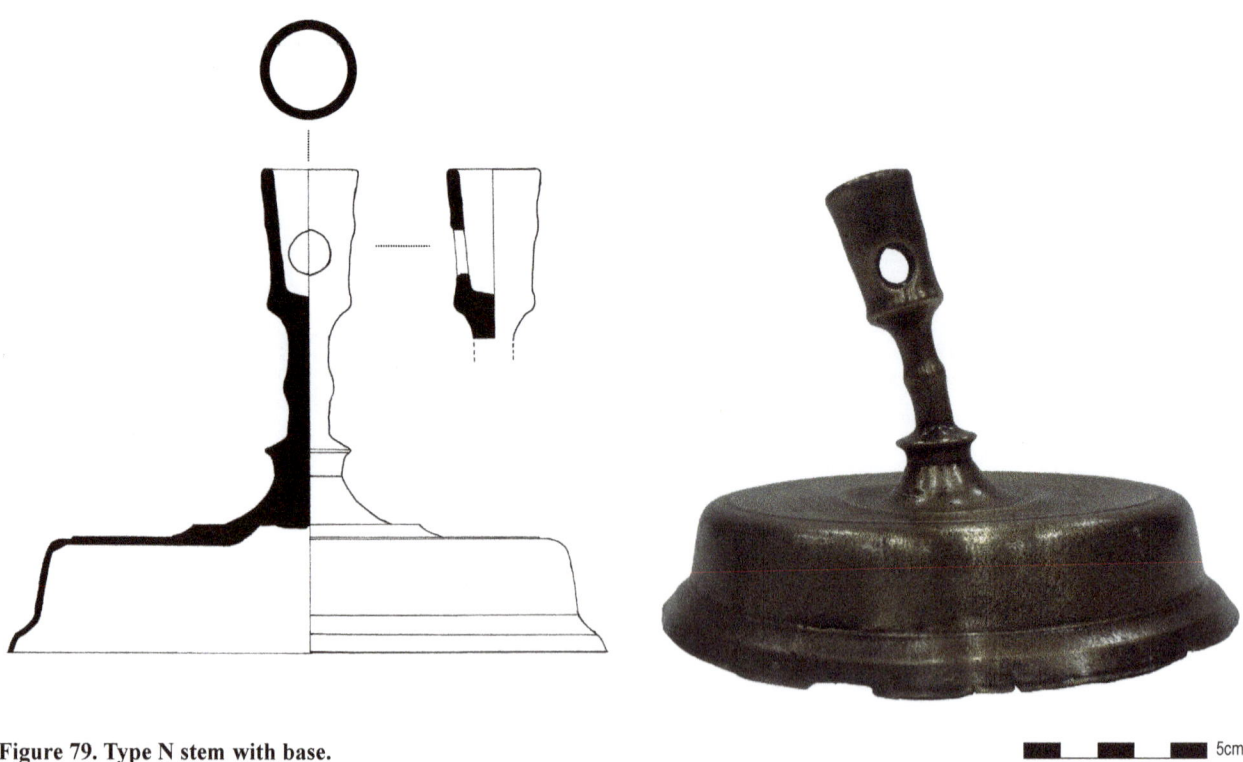

Figure 79. Type N stem with base.

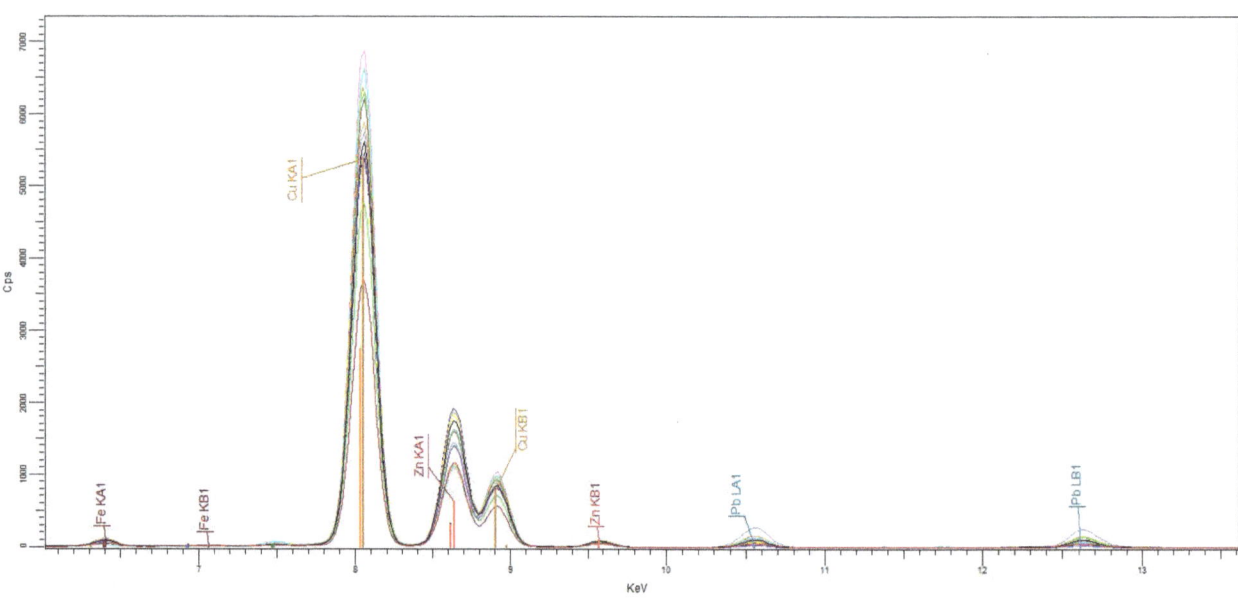

Figure 80. Normalized spectra for all candlestick samples. We can see consistent peaks for the same elements (©Flanders Heritage Agency, image: Leentje Linders).

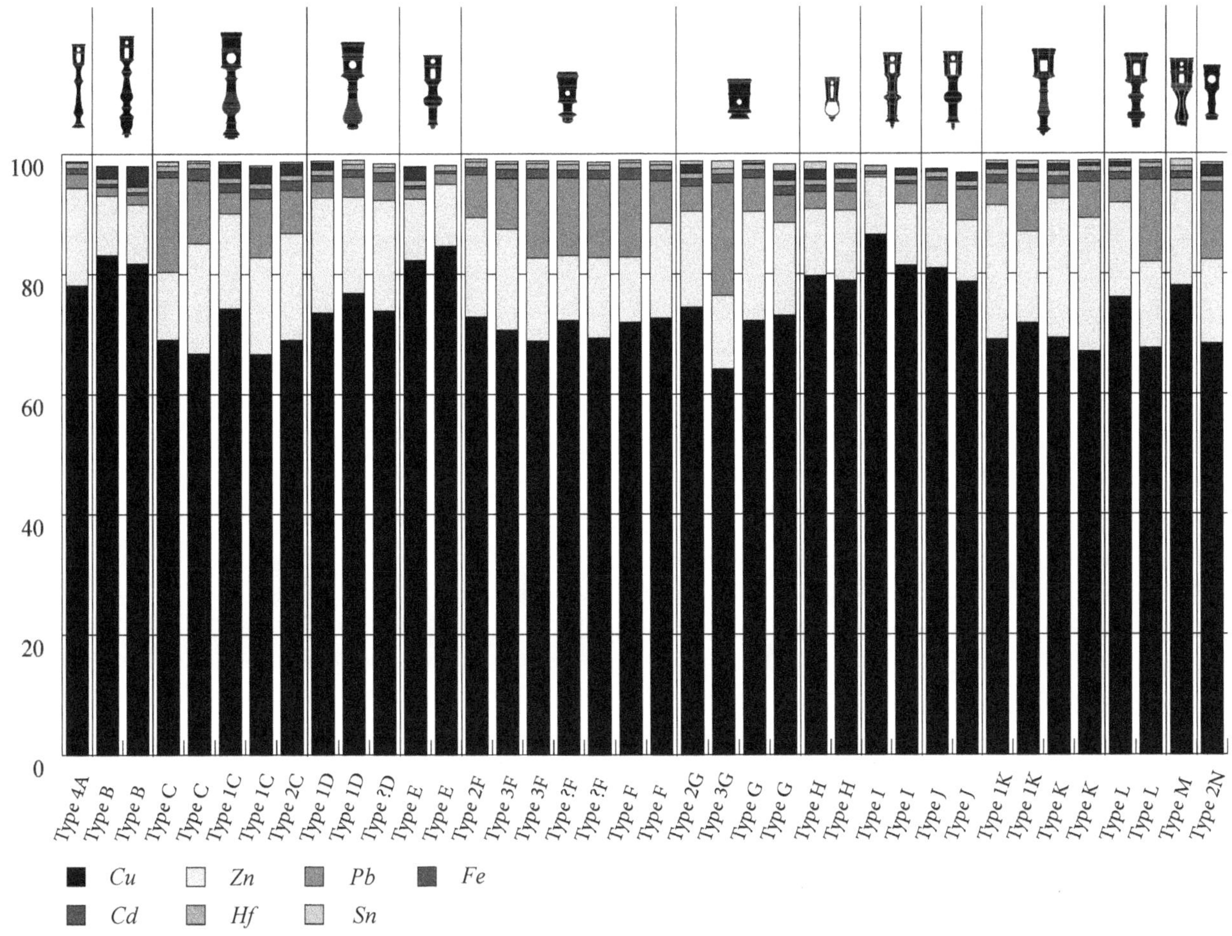

Finds from the Zeebrugge wreck

Figure 81. Overview of main elements of all sampled stems, grouped per type.

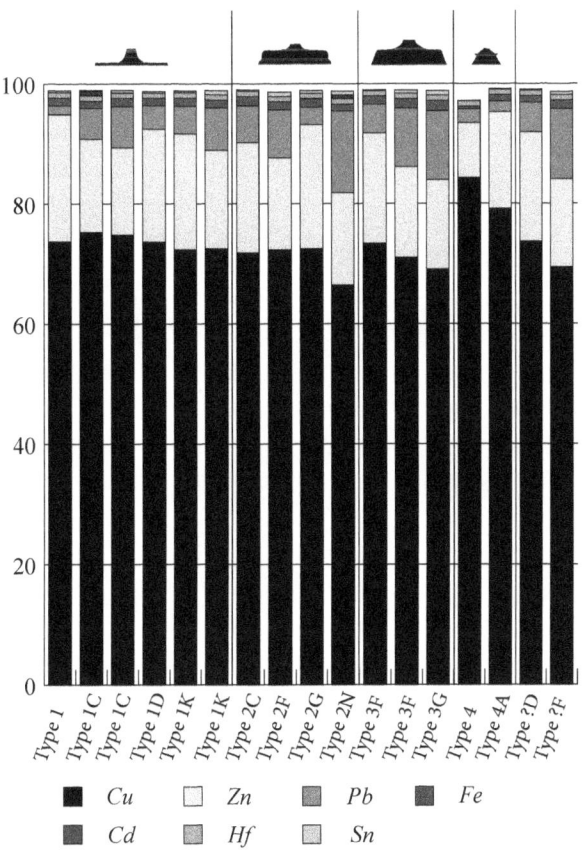

Figure 82. Overview of main elements of all sampled bases, grouped per type.

3.9. Weaponry

A large quantity of stone and iron round shot was found on site, as well as several pieces of ordnance. Traces of a musket were recovered, and one part of a mould to cast musket shot was found too. Unfortunately, only a large quantity of iron shot and the mould are actually present in the current collection of finds in the MAS Museum. One of the cannon, a wrought iron bombard, is preserved and is currently located in the headquarters of the Zeebrugge port authorities. The other cannon, the stone shot, and the musket parts appear to have been destroyed or lost over time. However, by means of the available information we will discuss these objects as comprehensively as possible.

3.9.1. Mould for musket shot

One part of a two-piece copper-alloy mould, to cast musket shot, was recovered from the site (*Fig. 83*). The square-shaped object (2.2 x 2.2cm) features a rectangular 'handle' on the back. The complete thickness of the mould is 1.5cm. The thickness without the handle is 0.9cm. The opposed side features a hollow hemisphere to cast half a shot. The hemisphere has a depth of 0.7cm and a diameter of 1.5cm. Two perforations, with a depth of 0.5cm, are present on opposite corners to fit this half of the mould to the other (missing) part. Half of a funnel-shaped opening is present to pour the fluid metal in the mould. The mould is made of copper (92.5%) with traces of iron (1.7%), tin (1.7%) and lead (1.1%).

Shot casted with this mould would have had an approximate diameter of 1.4-1.5cm. At least one bullet with these proportions was recovered from the site (*cf. infra*). Since only one shot mould was recovered from the wreck, and musket shot was recovered from the wreck as well, it seems likely this object was brought for use on board, rather than as part of a cargo.

Shot moulds have been found on other wrecks too, such as the Molasses Reef Wreck (early 16th century), the Lomellina (1516), and the Mary Rose (1545) (Keith ET AL. 1984, p. 55; Guérout ET AL. 1989, p. 115; Rule 1973, p. 386-387). Although the latter two are made of stone, there certainly are resemblances in design with the Zeebrugge mould.

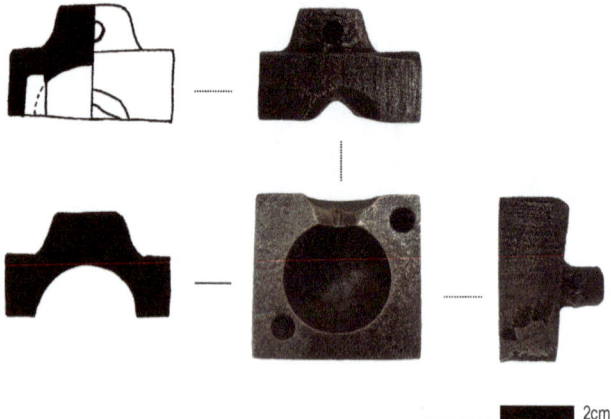

Figure 83. One part of a mould for casting musket shot.

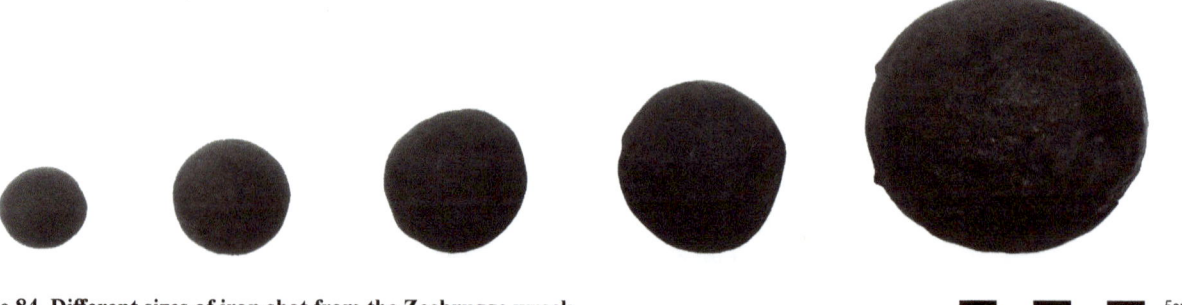

Figure 84. Different sizes of iron shot from the Zeebrugge wreck.

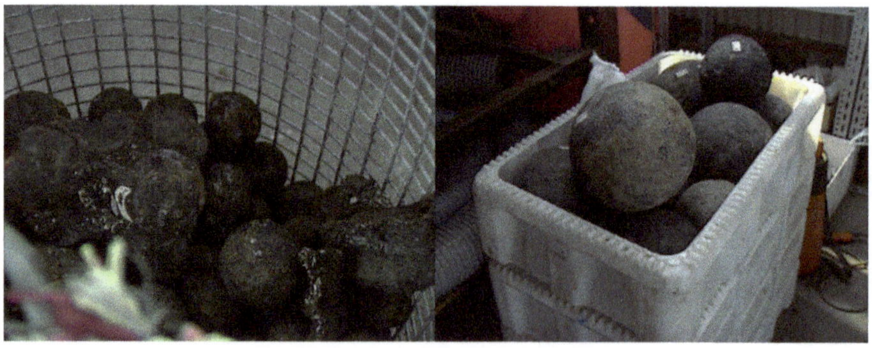

Figure 85. A basket filled with iron shot and a container filled with stone shot (©VRT).

Figure 86. One of two stone shot owned by Bart Schiltz.

3.9.2. Round shot

A large quantity of round shot was present on site. Both stone shot and lead-coated iron shot were found in many different sizes (*Fig. 84*). Although during excavation all shot was stored together according to material type (*Fig. 85*), at one point the collection of stone shot was thrown away accidentally (Personal information Bart Schiltz). Currently, the collection in the MAS Museum exhibits 188 pieces of iron shot, and two stone shot are still in possession of Bart Schiltz (*Fig. 86*).

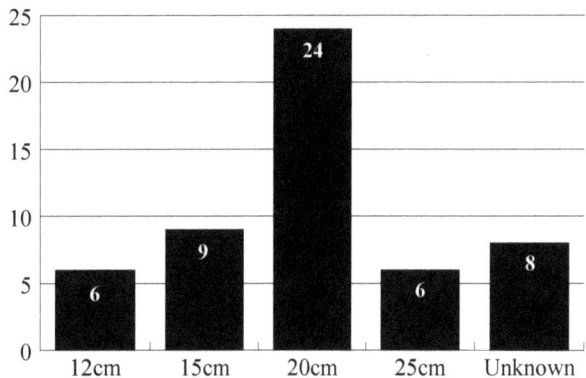

Figure 87. Number of stone shot per recorded size.

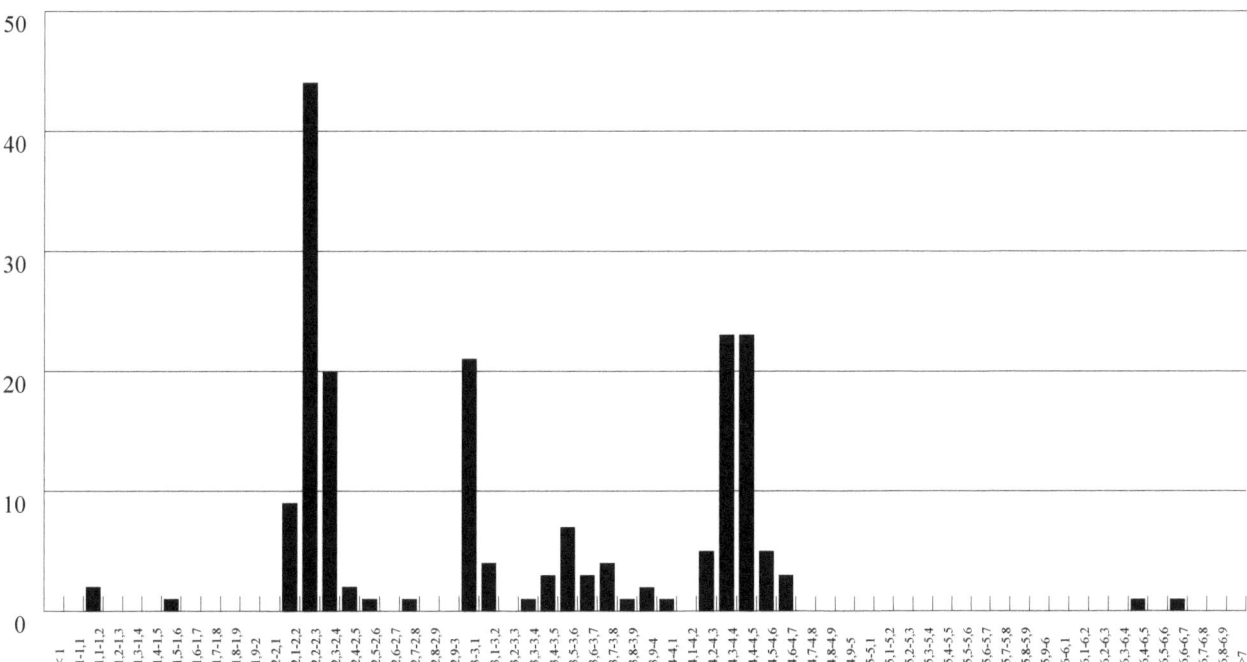

Figure 88. Histogram showing the dispersal of diameter size for the recorded iron shot.

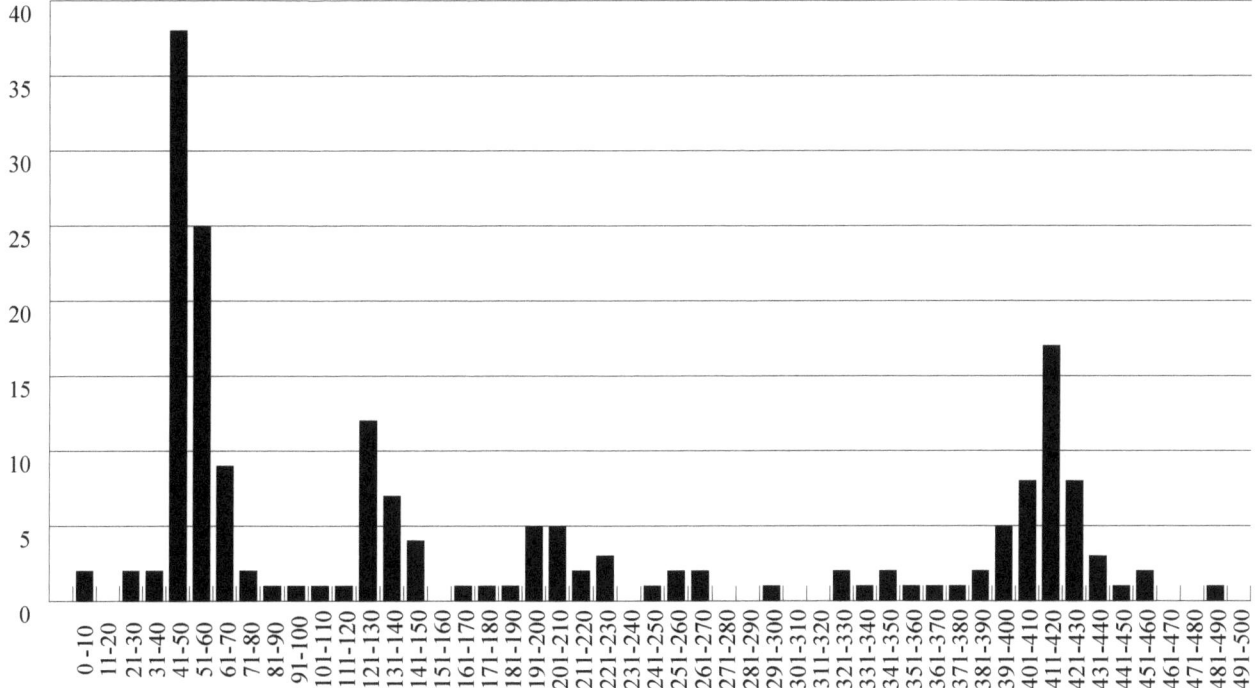

Figure 89. Histogram showing the dispersal of weight for the recorded iron shot.

When we look at the finds list from 1991, we see most shot is referred to by material type, and for quite a few stone shot the diameter is given. We can count a total of 51 stone shot. However, one item refers to an unspecified number of multiple stone shot. For five round shot the material is not specified, yet for two of these objects the diameter is given. These diameters (15cm and 20cm) correspond to the stone shot rather than the iron shot, which, for the Zeebrugge wreck, is generally smaller. This indicates over 53 stone shot were recovered from the site. However, when we look at the total of iron shot (or musket shot) mentioned in these registers, only 33 finds occur, while 188 objects are present in the MAS Museum. This indicates the actual number of excavated stone shot may be much higher. Bart Schiltz informed us tens of stone shot were recovered while a part of stone shot was left *in situ* too.

Among the registered diameters for stone shot, we can distinguish four sizes (*Fig. 87*). The most frequent diameter is 20cm (24x), followed by 15cm (9x) and 12 and 25cm (both 6x). The size of the other stone shot is not specified. Also, two half parts of (probably) stone shot are mentioned in the 1991 register.

All iron shot present in the MAS Museum was measured and weighed. Since some of the shot suffered from severe corrosion, weight and size do not always correspond. Diameter for all 188 iron shot varies between 1.2 and 6.6cm. When we plot this in a histogram, we can see three clear peaks (*Fig. 88*). Most iron shot has a diameter of 2.1-2.4cm. The next largest group has a diameter of 4.3-4.5cm. The third peak represents shot with a diameter of 3-3.1cm. Two shot have a diameter of about 6.5cm, while only three other objects have a diameter less than 2cm. However, in the 1991 register at least 10 musket shot are mentioned.

Table 6. Relative elemente concentration small shot

Shot type	Elements
Iron shot (1cm diameter)	Pb (85.8%), Sn (6.7%), Fe (4%)
Iron shot (1cm diameter)	Pb (91.7%), Sn (3.1%), As (1%)
Iron shot (2cm diameter)	Pb (89.2%), As (3.5%), Fe (3.2%),
Iron shot (2cm diameter)	Pb (92%), Fe (2.7%), As (1%)

Figure 90. Damaged shot and shot concreted together (left) (©VRT) and a peculiar aperture (right). Are these possible indicators for a use as bar shot?

Figure 91. Shot featuring 'crossed ribs'. 2cm

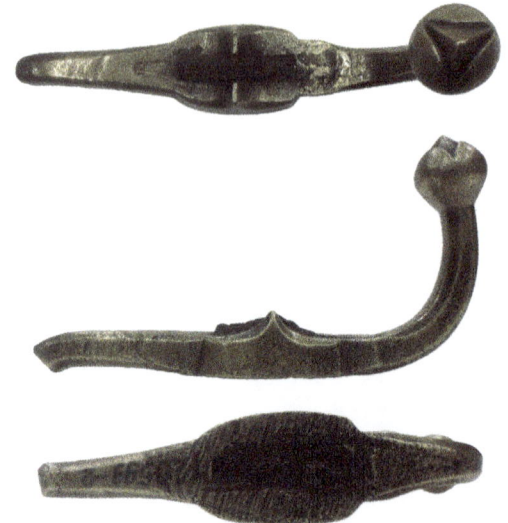

Figure 92. A dagger's guard? 2cm

The weight of the iron shot varies between 9 and 981g. When we plot all measured weights in a histogram we can see the same three peaks again, albeit less pronounced (*Fig. 89*). Most iron shot has a weight of 40-60g. The next largest group weighs around 410-420g. Finally a relatively small peak appears around 120-130g. The two larger shot of about 6.5cm fall outside this histogram. Their weights, 668g and 981g, do differ quite a bit due to corrosion. In the 1991 register, two iron shot are specified to be an eight-pounder and a twelve-pounder. These objects do not seem to appear in the MAS collection. One inventory (P.A.B.S., F.C.2, "Geschatte inventaris Herent") mentions the presence of an estimated 160 canister shot. It is indeed very well possible at least part of the iron shot was used for canister shot or grapeshot, however, to our knowledge no traces of actual canisters were encountered during excavation. Since the data related to ordnance from this wreck is rather scarce, we cannot link all different sizes of shot to a specific gun or cannon either.

Most iron shot is at least partly damaged, featuring cracks and corrosion. Some of the iron shot also appears to be partly hollow, while the shell is better preserved. This oddity made us wonder whether the shot could have been coated with lead. The lead coating of iron shot has been attested on several wrecks, such as the Lomellina (1516), where stone shot was also present, or the Portuguese wreck discovered off the coast of Boudeuse Cay (mid-16th century) (Guérout ET AL. 1989, p. 115; Blake & Green 1986, p. 10-11). Although we only performed xrf-analysis for some of the smaller objects, the results indicate clearly these objects were either made of lead, or otherwise at least are wrapped in lead (*Table 6*). Furthermore, some shot features large apertures (*Fig. 90*). At first we believed these openings or gaps were the consequence of taphonomic processes. Similar finds recovered from the Boudeuse Cay wreck, however, tell us these objects could also have been part of bar shot. Although the shot may need further examination in this regard, this seems a very plausible explanation for the presence of some of the apertures. Finally, some shot features crossed 'ribs' (*Fig. 91*). A possible explanation could be these ribs are traces of the casting process. However, since the bullets were casted with a mould existing of two hemispheres, this would only explain one rib. We could not find any parallels for this particular feature either. For now, it is unclear what the cause of these ribs may be.

3.9.3. Ordnance and other weapons

Only very little information is available in relation to actual weaponry. In the 1991 register, remains of a musket are mentioned. These remains would have been two small copper sheets, in bad condition. However, no further information on these finds is available. A decorated handle belonging to a "large dagger or small sabre" was found too (P.A.B.S., D.R., "week 11"). This could well be the object depicted in figure 92, which we believe is a dagger's guard. The object is damaged at its lower end and features a knop at the top. It has a length of 9.1cm, a height of 4.5cm and a width of 2cm. Seen from the top, it widens in the middle, where it also features a square aperture (2.4x0.6cm). This opening is filled with what appears to be timber, possibly these are remains of a former handle.

The main weaponry on board the Zeebrugge wreck appears to be heavy ordnance, yet, in this regard only limited and rather vague data is available. Only one cannon, a bombard, is known with certainty to still exist. The conservation of this object is briefly discussed by Van Dromme (2006, p. 21). Although Van Dromme refers to this cannon as a "cast-iron bombard", observation demonstrates this is rather a wrought iron gun. Vandenberghe (2006, p. 19; 2007, p. 60) mentions a total of "four iron cannon" were found, "of which one with an intact carriage was lifted and preserved". Parmentier (2000, p. 236) refers to "four large sea ordnances" and specifies these were "breech-loading guns in wrought iron and shaped like tubs". Schiltz (Personal information) informed us a bombard was preserved, while the other ordnance were three breech-loaders. According to Schiltz, one of these three guns was accidentally destroyed during treatment and scrapped afterwards (*cf. supra*). Another incomplete gun was also scrapped for reasons unknown. A third gun may have stayed *in situ*.

The information we retrieve from the dive reports, however, deviates from the statements above. In 1991, at least three cannon were recovered from the site. The first cannon was recovered 21/07/1991, and, in the 1991 finds register, is referred to as 'ordnance – mortar (200kg)'. We believe this weight is an estimation based upon the size of the lifting bag used for recovering this find rather than a precise measurement. The dive report for this date does not mention a cannon, but refers to a 'heavy, iron melting pot with rings and a heavy cover'. However, such an object is not present in the MAS Museum and is not mentioned in any inventory or publication either. A sketch, present in Schiltz' archive (P.A.B.S., F.C.1, "sketch bombard") and accompanied by a similar description, refers to a bombard instead of a melting pot (*Fig. 93*). On 03/08/1991, another bombard was recovered from the site. The object could not be lifted with a 250kg lifting bag thus must be heavier. The object is described as "a bombard of a different type, relatively well-preserved" (P.A.B.S., D.R., "03/08/1991"). In the official register for that year this find is mentioned as "bombard with stamps" (MEA 1991). The preserved bombard features vague images that appear to be carvings rather than stamps. It is unclear whether this is the "bombard with stamps" referred to.

The same day, one of the three cannon represented on the site plan (*Fig. 15*) was lifted too. Up to this point, the excavation team did not know these three objects were cannon. The positive identification of this object led to the conclusion the two other objects had to be cannon too. The lifted cannon, the smallest and most southern of those depicted on the site plan, lay in a wooden carriage and was fastened with rope, which at some places was well preserved (P.A.B.S., D.R. "week 7"). According to the 1991 register this was a twelve-pounder cannon.

However, with three cannon recovered and two cannon *in situ*, the Zeebrugge wreck appears to have carried more than the four cannon referred to in most publications. Furthermore, another cannon was detected on 30/08/1991, east of the three cannon on the site plan (in frame IA8-IB8). In the 1994 field season, a cannon with carriage was lifted on 28/06/1994, and another three cannon were lifted on 10/10/1994. The information in these latter reports is very limited and does not provide any further details about the finds. A dive report from some weeks earlier, however, refers to the presence of an unspecified cannon, a muzzleloader and a 'large cannon with carriage' on site (P.A.B.S., D.R., "22/09/1994").

We know some objects were stored in the Brittannia dock for temporary preservation and were lifted again for conservation afterwards (*cf. supra*). However, the bombard was only recovered from this dock in the year 2000, and the reports for the above-mentioned dates refer specifically to the Zeebrugge wreck as work location. This indicates at least seven cannon, of generally very different type, were recovered from the Zeebrugge wreck. Among the finds would have been (guns interpreted as) a mortar, a bombard, a twelve-pounder, breech-loading cannon, a muzzleloader and other unspecified cannon of different sizes. At least three of these cannon would have been assembled onto carriages. If this information is correct, this means the Zeebrugge wreck was a rather heavily armed ship, with different types of guns and shot.

The actual archaeological data related to these finds, however, is very scarce. The drawing of the first recovered bombard or mortar (*Fig. 93*) is an interpretation rather than an accurate representation of the object. When recovered, one of two handles was missing. The other handle was about 60% corroded away. According to the brief description of this object some kind of cover was present, featuring an aperture (on the drawing, the cover would be the protrusion on the right side of the object).[37] Without cover, the object has a length of 68cm. The tube narrows down a little. The larger end has a width of 30cm, the smaller end has a width of 26cm. The end of the cover has a width of 12cm. No further information is available for this object. The presence of two rings on top of ordnance has been attested on other wrecks too. An example of a different type of gun with this similar feature was found on the Lomellina (1516). There, the gun was mounted on a wooden carriage (Guérout ET AL. 1989, p. 101-104).

Schiltz did provide some visual data for the largest of the three cannon we see on the site plan, located at point A. Photographs taken shortly after excavation show the strong concretion. We can see part of the wooden carriage as well as a wooden rammer sticking out of the barrel (*Fig. 94*). An archaeological drawing[38] of this gun (*Fig. 95.a*) shows this was a wrought iron breech loader, featuring the typical reinforcement hoops for this type of gun. On top of the gun, one handle is present, probably used for lifting the loading chamber. According to Schiltz, its length was about 275cm. Also the structure of the carriage is depicted (*Fig. 95.b*). It appears the carriage was made of a solid piece of wood. According to the drawing, it appears metal straps were applied to the upper edges of the carriage along the breech chamber. A gully to fit the cannon and an opening towards the end to fit the guns chamber appear to have been carefully trenched. The gun was attached to the carriage by means of rope, at three different places. The edges of the carriage are bevelled where rope was present.

The only preserved cannon is the aforementioned bombard (*Fig. 96*), which we were able to study *in situ* at the headquarters of the Port of Zeebrugge. The wrought-iron gun has an overall length of 115cm. The muzzle's face has a diameter of 38cm. At this section, the bore has a diameter of 29cm. It was difficult to get accurate measurements of the diameter of the bore near the chamber, but it appears that the diameter is slightly smaller here, measuring approximately 23cm. The bore has a length of 63cm. The chamber has a length of about 43.5cm and a diameter of 9cm. While the chase is circular in cross-section, the reinforce is octagonal in cross-section. The width/thickness of the reinforce is approximately 22cm. Based upon carvings near the vent of the gun (*Fig. 96.a*), this may well be the "bombard with stamps" referred to in the 1991 register, which was described as weighing over 250kg. Since chisels were used to remove concretion from the gun, these carvings may just as well be a consequence of the removal process. Nonetheless, it is notable that the carvings appear only in the specific area near the vent. Although it is unclear what the carvings depict, we can distinguish six X's underneath what appears to be an angle with a cross on top. Possibly this is a rudimentary depiction of a church roof.

According to ordnance expert Rudolf Roth (Personal information) this gun should more correctly be called a bombardelle, the calibre of bombard used for sieges but also suitable as part of a ship's armament. He informed us that this specific design goes back approximately to the 14th century. The size of the Zeebrugge bombardelle, however, was common around 1450 and was used well into the 16th century. Based upon the measurements of the gun, Roth argues that the gun was very likely manufactured in the city of Liege, a famous gun-producing centre in today's Belgium. Liege's coat of arms features a so-called 'perron', *i.e.* a stone column with a *globus cruciger* on top. Although

---

[37] The description refers to photos of this object. These were not available to the author, yet they could certainly contribute to the interpretation of this object.

[38] These drawings, provided by Bart Schiltz, did not feature an actual scale. According to Schiltz, however, this gun had a length of 275cm.

Finds from the Zeebrugge wreck

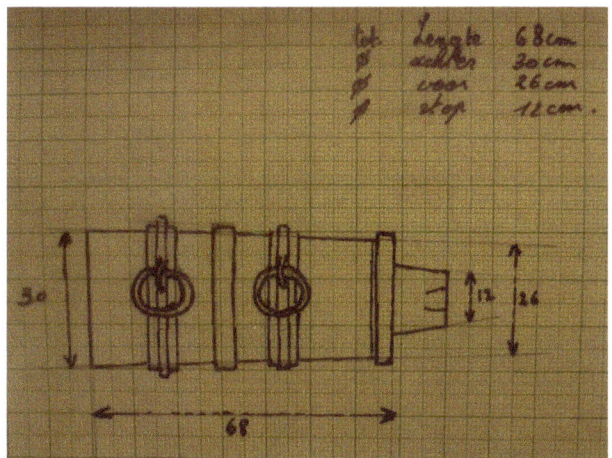

Figure 93. Sketch of first recovered cannon (P.A.B.S., F.C.T., "schets bombarde").

Figure 94. Wrought iron breech loader, shortly after excavation (images provided by Bart Schiltz).

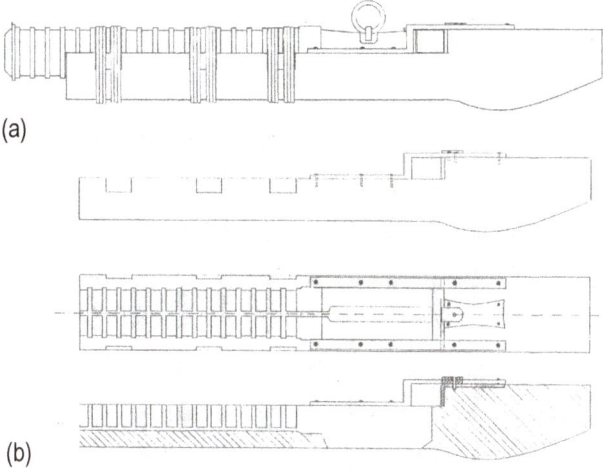

Figure 95. Drawings of the wrought iron breech loader and carriage. According to Schiltz the actual length is about 275cm (images provided by Bart Schiltz).

the bombardelle was very likely produced in Liege, it may at this point be a bit too farfetched to associate the cross-like carving on the gun with the city's perron.

The carriage on which the bombardelle is mounted is made of a solid piece of wood, identified as oak (Van Dromme 2006, p. 21; Vandenberghe 1997, p. 89). The ropes, to hold the gun in place, were still intact when excavated yet not preserved now. Van Dromme mentions no wheels were present here. Finds from the Lomellina demonstrate a gully could be provided in the bottom of the carriage, to add wheels under the gun. such a gully seems not to be present here either.

Carriages similar to the ones recovered from the Zeebrugge wreck are known from early 16th century wrecks such as the Lomellina (1516), the Cattewater wreck (ca. 1530), and the Mary Rose (1545) (Guérout ET AL. 1989, p. 101-111; Redknap 1984, p. 49-62; Hildred 2009, p. 130). For the Cattewater wreck, however, the wrought iron gun was fixed to the carriage by means of iron straps, while the guns from the Lomellina and the Mary Rose were probably fixed with rope, in a similar manner the Zeebrugge ordnance was fastened. Traces of metal reinforcements similar to the one on figure 95 were attested on one of the Lomellina guns, as well as on the Cattewater guns. Based on the limited evidence, it appears all guns from the Zeebrugge wreck were wrought iron cannon. On the Mary Rose, cast iron guns were recovered together with wrought iron guns and they have been referred to as "the earliest securely dated examples of cast-iron used to form guns" (Hildred 2009, p. 291). The combination of wrought iron and cast iron cannon on a single wreck has been attested for later wrecks too, such as on the Western Ledge Reef wreck (late 16th century) (Watts 1993, p. 115). The parallels with ordnance from early 16th century wrecks, and the appearance of cast iron cannon from the mid-16th century onwards, seems to encourage the idea this wreck should be dated to no later than the first half of the 16th century.

Figure 96. (continues on next page) Wrought iron bombard with carriage, probably the only preserved cannon from the Zeebrugge wreck.

The Zeebrugge Shipwreck

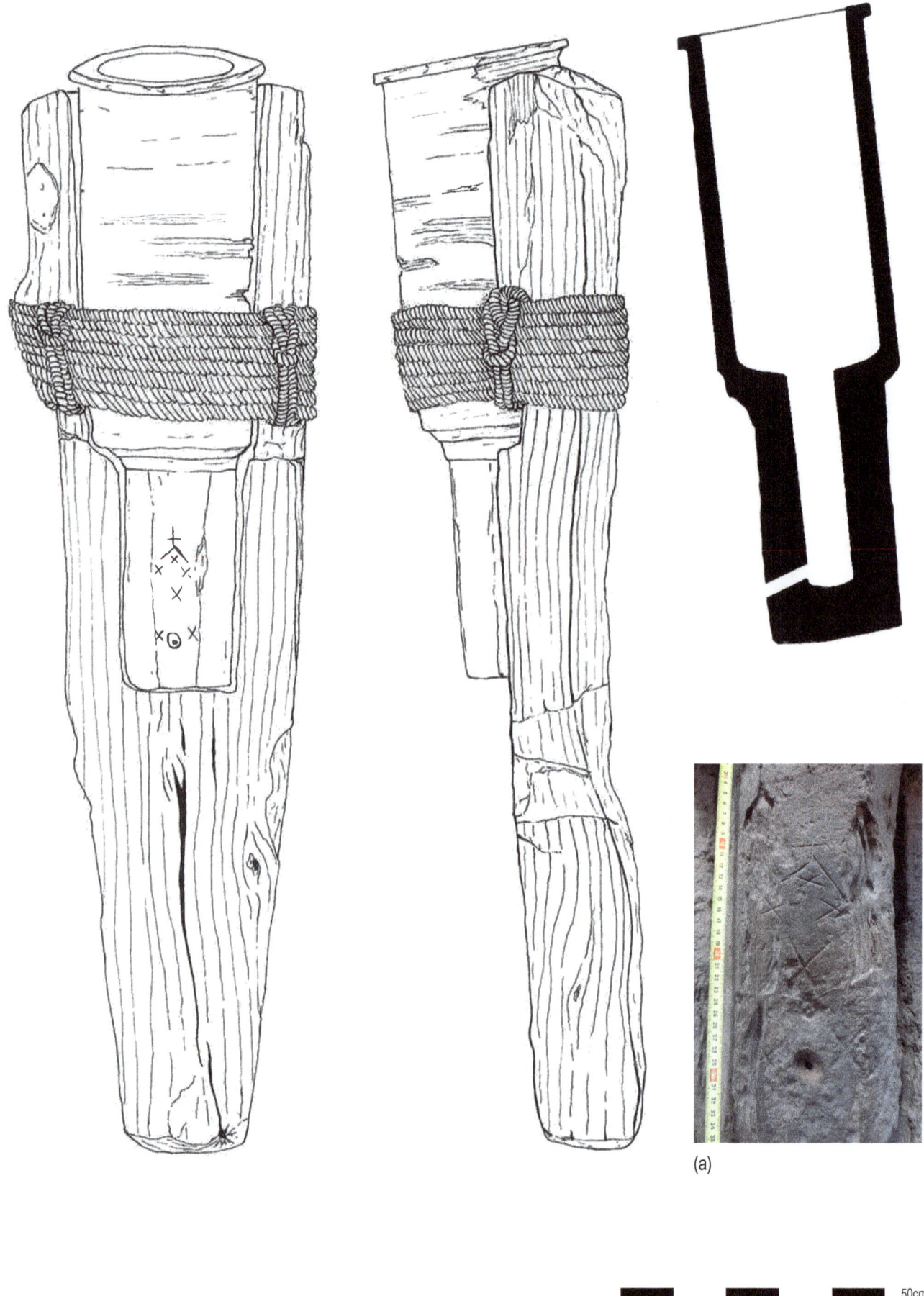

Figure 96. (continued) **Wrought iron bombard with carriage, probably the only preserved cannon from the Zeebrugge wreck.**

3.10. Other finds

Among the finds from the Zeebrugge wreck there are quite a few objects that could not be included in any of the previous groups. Since they could not be classified in a separate, homogeneous functional group either, it was decided to group them together under the name 'other finds'. The main reason these objects were not added to any of the other groups is because they are incomplete and/or their function is unknown. For this reason, most objects in this group cannot be discussed elaborately, yet we will briefly describe them.

A first object in this category is what appears to be a kind of copper-alloy handle, or pull-ring (*Fig. 97.a*). The object is made of different assembled parts. A first part would be the ring. This ring, with a diameter of 3.3cm, is not fully closed but features a small gap. It is attached to the second part, a flat object with stepped sides (length 3.1cm; width 2.9cm; thickness 1.5cm). On top of this object, a punctured protrusion or loop is present in the middle, through which the ring runs. Next to this protrusion, through the surface of this object, another hole is pierced (diameter 0.7cm). On the other side, four loops are present. Parts of a chain are connected to three of these loops. Probably, on the other end, these chains were attached to another unknown part of the object. The ring could than be used to lift, hold, or hang this object. Unfortunately the object itself does not allow further interpretation. No contextual data to add to its interpretation is available either.

Three more parts of chain, similar to the chains attached to this object, are present among the finds (*Fig. 97.b*). They have different lengths (1.9-5.7cm) and all are incomplete. Whether they belonged to the same object discussed above is uncertain. They can be different parts of a same chain, or may have belonged to different individual objects.

Another ring (diameter 3cm) is present in the Zeebrugge collection, together with a small, punctured piece of metal (Length 2.4cm; width 2.2cm; thickness 0.1cm) (*Fig. 97.c*). According to the MAS database these objects belong together and are part of another pull ring. Possibly this is correct, yet the objects themselves do not allow for such conclusive determination and no additional, contextual information is available.

Two copper-alloy handles or support brackets were recovered from the wreck individually. The first handle (*Fig. 98.a*) is horse shoe-shaped and features a ring on top. The ring is not casted together with the rest of the object, but is added separately. The total length of the object is 11.1cm. The length without the ring is 6.8cm. The total width is 8cm. The top of the handle features a stylized decoration. The ends of the handle are pointed sideward, probably fitting in the object it was supposed to carry.

The second handle has a similar shape, but does not feature a ring on top (*Fig. 98.b*). The pierced top indicates a ring may have been attached to this handle as well. The handle

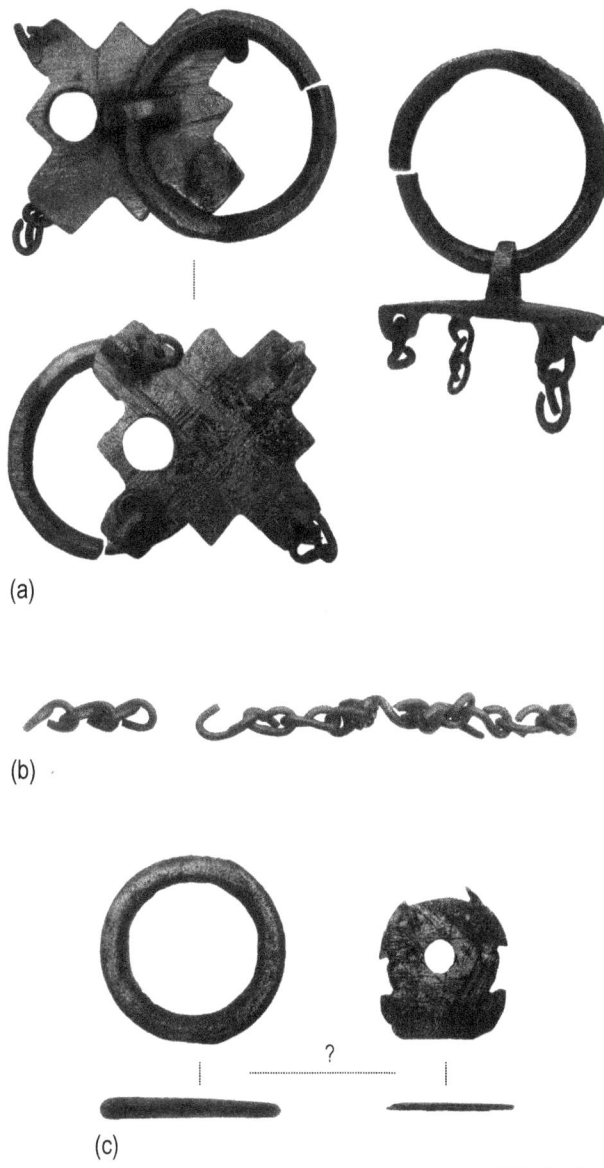

Figure 97. Pullring or handle of an unkown object (a), parts of chain (b) and a copper-alloy ring (c).

has a total length of 8.7cm and a width of 8.8cm. Peculiar is the decoration on top of the handle, in the shape of stylized heads with long ears and pointed noses. These heads may represent stylized zoomorphic figures or fantasy figures. We could not link these handles to any other objects in the Zeebrugge collection. Possibly these handles carried buckets, or they may be linked to the holy water fonts referred to by Vandenberghe (*cf. supra*).

A nicely decorated door or lid (*Fig. 99*) has in the past been interpreted as the door of a lantern (Vandenberghe 1997, p. 89). It has a length of 16.1cm and a width of 6.3cm. It features hollow tubes on the side (thickness 0.2cm) that probably functioned as hinges. The object may well be the door of a lantern indeed, yet no parallels to support such a determination were found by the author.

The Zeebrugge Shipwreck

Another nicely decorated object is a copper-alloy item in the shape of a stylized bird (*Fig. 100.a*). It has a length of 3.7cm and a width of 3.9cm. This decorative item may have been the finial or top decoration of an unknown object.

A small, copper-alloy sheet features a vague mark (*Fig. 100.b*). Unfortunately, the mark is too worn to recognise any image. The sheet has a length of 18.5cm and a width of 9.5cm. It is only 0.04cm thick. Its function is not known.

Furthermore the Zeebrugge collection features two, rather similar, curved metal straps, rounded on one side and flat on the other (*Fig. 100.c and 100.d*). The larger object has a length of 11.8cm, the smaller object has a length of 8.7cm. They both have a width of about 0.8cm and a thickness of about 0.4cm. Square apertures are present on both objects (0.2x0.4cm to 0.4x0.4cm), but they appear to be filled with the same material, protruding on the flat side. For the smaller object, it is clear the ends are damaged. These straps probably were applied to an unknown object.

A small, folded piece of metal (*Fig. 100.e*) is another unidentified piece. Possibly it can be interpreted as a lace chape, which are known to have appeared in this shape (Egan 2002, p. 284) and are mentioned by Vandenberghe (2006, p. 20) too. However, data is inconclusive for such an interpretation. Finally, eight different coloured pieces of what appears to be glass (*Fig. 100.f*) were present among the finds.

Although some of these objects are only bits and pieces, we wanted to include them nevertheless to present the integral collection of objects we were able to study. By presenting this last group, we have discussed all finds from the Zeebrugge collection that were available for study. Now, it is time to see what the combined information of these objects can teach us about the Zeebrugge wreck in general.

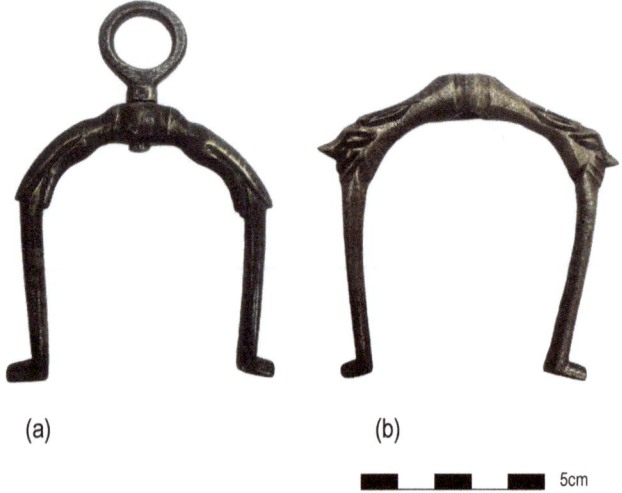

Figure 98. Copper-alloy handles, possibly belonging to holy water pails or similar objects.

Figure 99. Copper-alloy door or lid, possibly of a lantern (a).

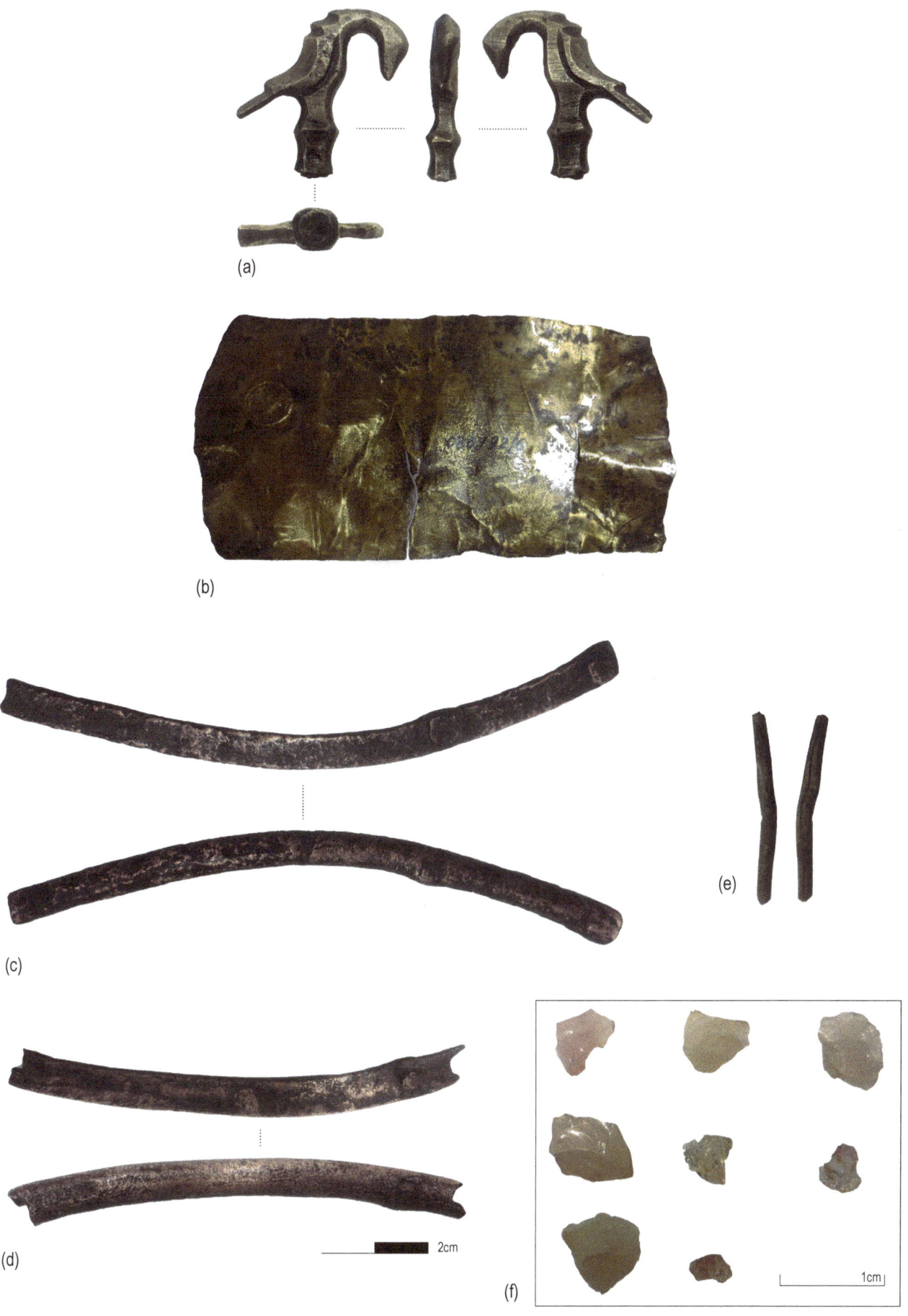

Figure 100. Unidentified objects.

Chapter 4

Discussion

The abundance of finds recovered from the Zeebrugge wreck provides data that can help us interpret and understand the site to a certain extent. Based upon the study of the finds, in this chapter we will propose a relative date for the Zeebrugge wreck and a possible origin. Also, we will discuss a possible destination for the ship. Although the discovery and study of the Zeebrugge wreck may lead to certain insights about our past, it also creates new questions and possibilities for further research. These will be discussed briefly as well.

4.1. Date

The group of 'finance-related objects' is the only category that could propose a *terminus post quem* for several objects. The *medio excelente* was first minted in 1475, and parallels for the related coin weights are dated to 1499. The *excelente de la Granada* first appeared in 1497, and again parallels for the coin weights are dated to 1499. The *forint* was in use over many centuries, yet the maker's mark of the hand, present on the coin weights from the Zeebrugge wreck, was only obligated since 1509. The specific type of Venus counters recovered from the site are identified as early copies that appear from 1500 onwards. Finally, the nested cup-weights from the Zeebrugge wreck may be attributed to Hans Gscheid who became master in Nuremberg in 1507. Additionally, coins ordered by Charles V may provide an even younger *terminus post quem* of 1521. Although this latter statement is certainly possible, it could not be confirmed by the author. When we combine this information (*Fig. 101*), we can date the wreck with certainty in or after the year 1507, and possibly in or after the year 1521.

None of the other finds could provide such specific data, yet their stylistic features do support a date in the early 16th century. For many of the finds parallels are found dated to the late 15th and/or early 16th century. Also, objects similar to some of the finds are depicted on paintings from this period. Based upon this information we can assume the wreck is probably not much younger than the year 1521, although a specific *terminus ante quem* could not be derived from our research. A *terminus ante quem* has been proposed by Vandenberghe in the past, who dates the ship around 1520-1522. Although this certainly is a possible date for the wreck, the data analysed within this research did not allow for such a specific interpretation. Although the ordnance of the wreck certainly needs further study, the nature of these finds seems to encourage a date for the wreck no later than the first half of the 16th century.

4.2. Origin

The 'origin' of a wreck is a rather ambiguous term and can be interpreted in different ways. Origin may refer to the location where the ship was built. Or it could refer to the origin of the crew, or the owner, or the fleet it is part of. In the case of the Zeebrugge wreck, we don't have any evidence to support statements about the above. We do, however, have information about the cargo it carried, which may lead us to another kind of origin: the ship's (last) place of departure.

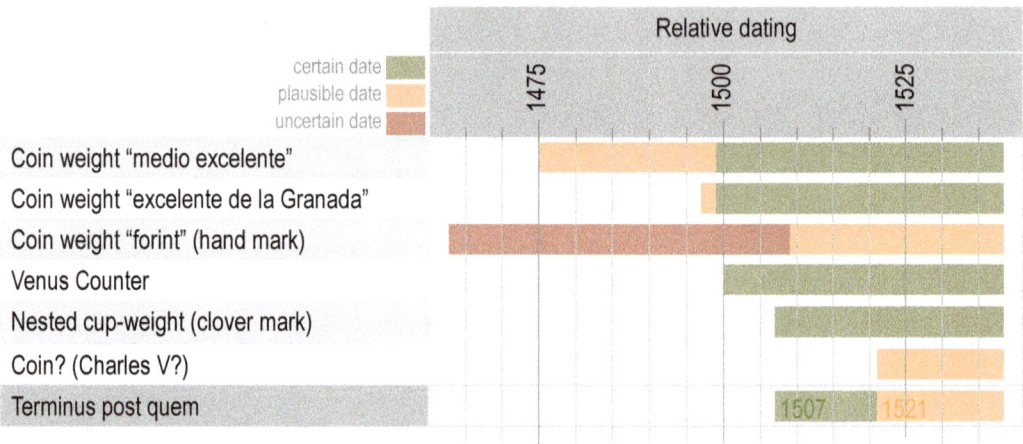

Figure 101. Comparative perspective of *termini post quem* based on study of the Zeebrugge finds.

To determine the place of departure, we should take a look at the actual origin of the cargo. Most finds were produced in the Low Countries or Southern Germany. In some cases their production can even be linked to a certain city, such as Antwerp (e.g. salt holders, coin weights) or Nuremberg (e.g. nested cup-weights, taps) because of maker's marks. Also, some objects were produced overseas in England (e.g. pewter plates) and other objects are made of tropical materials originating from Central-Africa and possibly Asia (e.g. knife handles). If we would plot these locations on a map, this would give a rather dispersed impression.

In the early 16th century, however, all these goods were traded in the city of Antwerp. Since the late 15th century onwards, Antwerp was becoming a leading centre of international trade and one of the most important harbours of its time. Conveniently located at the river Scheldt, it became a 'hub' for international trade, both overseas (e.g. Portugal, England) and with the European hinterland (e.g. Germany). When we consider the location of the wreck, near the Scheldt estuary, in combination with the date of the wreck in the early 16th century and the traded goods, Antwerp, a city connected to the sea by means of the river Scheldt, indeed seems a very plausible candidate for departure of this ship.

The rise and fall of Antwerp as a gateway for international trade has been discussed elaborately in ample academic studies. Often, emphasis is put on the importance of Portuguese, German and English tradesmen for the growth of this city (e.g. Van Der Wee 1963). Already in the 15th century, Portugal was an active player along the African west coast, having several settlements functioning as enterprises there (Blackmore 2008, p. 38 (*after Blake 1942*)). In 1508 the Portuguese installed their *feitoria de Flandres* in Antwerp as an official branch of the *Casa da Indias* in Lisbon. Portuguese colonial products were now first registered in Lisbon and afterwards shipped to their Antwerp stall market for further commercial distribution (Van Der Wee 1963, p. 129; Almodovar & Cardoso 1998, p. 18). Therefore, it should not be surprising knife handles made of African or even Asian wood species were circulating in this city in the early 16th century.

The presence of wealthy German tradesmen in Antwerp around this time has been well attested. Several prominent families from Nuremberg and Augsburg, such as the Fuggers, the Welsers, the Hochstetters and the Tuchers, were involved with the export of copper and silver in Antwerp. Trade routes between South Germany and Antwerp were well established, with a strong focus on the city of Nuremberg (Harreld 2004, p. 128-135). High quality brassware from Nuremberg or other German cities, such as Raeren or Cologne, could have reached Antwerp easily via these same networks.

Finally, the presence of English tradesmen has often been cited as one of the prime causes for Antwerp's 'Golden Age'. The combination of the embargo against English cloth in Flemish cities (e.g. Bruges), and the mutual agreement between the city of Antwerp and the English company of the *Merchant Adventures* to establish this company's cloth staple in Antwerp, was very influential for the further commercial rise of this city (Brulez 1973, p. 3). Although the export of cloth would play an important role in 16th century Antwerp, it was not the only sought-after English export product. As we discussed before, a court-case in 1523 indicates Antwerp pewterers started copying the crowned rose mark to compete with the high-quality English pewter export (*cf. supra*). This is a clear indication the pewter plates recovered from the Zeebrugge wreck were a common and popular trading good in early 16th century Antwerp.

Furthermore, some of the finds are directly related to Antwerp as we can learn from the hand-marks present on some objects. Other finds may be related to nearby cities such as Ghent or Brussels. For some of the finds we can say they were at least known objects in the city of Antwerp (or surroundings) in the early 16th century, since they were depicted by contemporary painters from Antwerp or nearby cities.

Among the very limited publications on the Zeebrugge wreck, only Parmentier discusses a possible point of departure for the ship's final voyage. Although he initially believes this could be Antwerp, Damme, or Sluis (Parmentier 2000, p. 236), he later on makes a case for just Antwerp stating: "the cargo that was found was made up entirely of items that at that time were sold only in Antwerp" (Parmentier 2011, p. 34, 40). We would not say these items were only sold in Antwerp, yet the specific combination of all these items in relation to both the period and location of the wreck, do indeed make a strong case for an 'origin' in Antwerp.

4.3. Cargo

The assemblage of finds recovered from the Zeebrugge wreck provides a unique insight in the maritime trade in the early 16th century. The many objects, mainly belonging to the ship's cargo, seem to be an example of the many goods traded in Antwerp at that time. The cargo of this particular wreck is rather prestigious, with several high quality objects, in some cases nicely decorated. Although no exhaustive contextual information is available, we can still draw some conclusions about the transported goods. Some interesting indications about the possible storage of traded goods were established. Cauldrons of different sizes were transported nested into one another, with straw placed in-between the objects to prevent damage. At least some of the knife handles were wrapped in paper during transport. The many candlesticks recovered from the Zeebrugge wreck provide new insights in regard to trade and production. They demonstrate these objects could be traded as semi-finished products, as large quantities of candlestick stems without bases were found, indicating these products would be finished in a local workshop at their destination. The Zeebrugge wreck seems to provide the first actual evidence for this practice. Other objects were also traded as bulk goods, such as the many hook-and-eye fasteners, assembled by means of a simple metal wire. Some objects appear to be among the earliest known finds of their kind, such as the octagonal plates. Possibly even an early coin weight box was recovered, although this interpretation certainly can be disputed. Although some parts of the cargo may not have been found or may have deteriorated before excavation took place, and the recovered finds may not present the actual cargo in its entirety, the variety of generally high quality pewter ware, nicely decorated brass ware, and even some religious objects, all appear to indicate this was a valuable cargo.

The ordnance and shot present on site indicates this ship was rather heavily armed. Although the ordnance as such certainly deserves further analysis, it proves the considerable effort that was made to protect ship and cargo.

4.4. Destination: context of trade

While Antwerp seems a very plausible 'origin' for the ship based upon different clues provided by the detailed analysis of its cargo, pointing out the destination of the ship appears to be a more complex issue. Early 16th century Antwerp was a transit centre for merchantmen of many different origins and nationalities, and the ship could have sailed virtually anywhere. While for the place of departure we did look at the actual origin of the cargo, the possible destination requires looking at the nature of the cargo, location of known parallels, and available historical and archaeological data. And, even so, we can only make more or less plausible assumptions rather than pointing out an exact location.

Although precise historical data for the export from Antwerp in the early 16th century is missing, a slightly later source, known as the 'hundredth penny tax' (1543-1545)[39], permits a unique insight in the goods exported from Antwerp and their destinations around the mid-16th century. In the period 1544-1545 these destinations are (in decreasing order) Germany, Italy, England, Spain, France, unknown destinations, Portugal, Liège and the Levant. It should be noted that some destinations, such as Germany and Italy, together making about 60% of the total export in these years, were reached over land (Puttevils 2015, p. 27). Although the situation certainly may have changed between the early 16th century and the mid-16th century, this source gives us at least an idea of possible destinations.

Parmentier (2000, p. 236), in his first article on the Zeebrugge wreck, mentions England or the Mediterranean as possible destinations for the wreck. Parallels for some of the candlesticks indeed have been found in England, yet given the fact that a large part of the cargo is English pewterware, England seems a rather unlikely destination. Although the Mediterranean could be a possible destination (again, the ship could have virtually gone anywhere), there is no indication to assume this destination over any other destination. In his second article on the Zeebrugge wreck, Parmentier (2011, p. 34) argues for three possible destinations: England, the Iberian Peninsula, or one of the (colonized) Atlantic isles. His preference, however, goes to the Iberian Peninsula and especially the city of Lisbon, Portugal.

Portugal, indeed, seems a plausible destination for several reasons. First of all, Portugal was one of the main players in Antwerp during the early 16th century, and it was strongly depending on the metal-export of the earlier discussed German families. The Portuguese needed South German copper and silver, for trade in Africa and India respectively (Brulez 1973, p. 3). Such products would be transported as raw material ingots, as encountered in the Portuguese cargo of the St Anthony wreck (Craddock & Hook 1987, p. 202), or the Oranjemund wreck, where the ingots carried stamps referring to the Fugger family and possibly the Welser family (Chirikure ET AL. 2010, p. 42, 44). Although the Zeebrugge wreck did carry high-quality metalware products instead of raw materials, it is not unlikely these goods were traded via the same established network between Southern Germany and Portugal. In addition, the recovery of over 2000 golden coins from the Portuguese Oranjemund wreck, located off the coast of Namibia, did present a majority of Spanish coins depicting the *Reyes Católicos* (*Idem*, p. 46). This seems to demonstrate the Portuguese need for Spanish coin weights such as the ones recovered from the Zeebrugge wreck.

Parmentier (Personal information) informed us Vandenberghe did see candlesticks identical to the ones recovered from the Zeebrugge wreck in a monastery on the Azores. Although we could not acquire any visual evidence to support Vandenberghe's statement, it is known Flemish merchantmen were closely connected to the trade with the Azores (a Portuguese colony) in the early 16th century, as well as with other Atlantic isles such as Madeira or the Canary Islands (Puttevils 2015, p. 39, 41).

Although the Portuguese were certainly important players in early 16th century Antwerp, historical sources do indicate the metal export from Antwerp to Portugal only represents a relatively small percentage of the total metal trade in this period (Brulez 1973, p. 14). Since we should certainly not assume Portugal, Germany, and England were the only players at that time, we would like to propose an additional hypothesis for a destination: Spain.

---

[39] A 1% export-tax instituted by Mary of Hungary on goods leaving the Low Countries (Harreld 2004, p. 9).

A first indication pointing towards Spain would be the presence of Spanish coin weights among the finds, although, as indicated before, such objects could have been useful to other nationalities as well. Secondly, two of the candlestick base-types have designs associated with Spain, probably influenced by exports from the Low Countries. However, it are mainly the multiple parallels found on the island of Hispaniola which support our hypothesis for a Spanish destination. Very similar objects have been recovered from the earliest Spanish settlements on this island, founded around 1500. A look at Deagan's (2002) work on artifacts of the Spanish colonies demonstrates many of the object categories discovered on the Zeebrugge wreck are also well-presented in these early settler societies. Very similar nested cup-weights have been discovered in Concepción de la Vega (1502-1562, Dominican Republic) and also coin weights and copper-alloy counters dating to this period (be it Nuremberg production instead of Low Countries production) appear to be common finds on Hispaniola. Furthermore, similar candlesticks (*cf. supra*) have been discovered here, as well as nicely decorated needle cases, religious pendants, etc. (Deagan 2002, p. 75-76, 195-197; 257-264). Most importantly, however, a wreck with a cargo very similar to that of the Zeebrugge wreck, has been discovered off the coast of Punta Cana, Dominican Republic. Although this wreck, known as the Punta Cana Pewter wreck, dates to the mid-16th century, the similar nature of its cargo is remarkable. A look at the site plan of this wreck (Roberts 2013a, p. 14) shows us the presence of nested cup-weights, mortars, pestles, combs, bells, holy water buckets, copper alloy bowls, casks filled with nails, ordnance, many pewter objects such as flagons, porringers and plates, etc. Although the objects as such are not identical, there certainly are similarities with the objects recovered from the Zeebrugge wreck. Salt holders decorated with an acorn-shaped finial and featuring an Antwerp maker's mark struck under the base, Nuremberg-type nested cup-weights with a (slightly different) *fleur-de-lys* mark or octagonal pewter plates are just some of the many examples in this regard (*Fig. 102*). So far, only a limited part of the enormous cargo has been studied and published (Roberts 2013a, 2013b), but further contributions are to be expected. The available publications focus mainly on the part of pewterware from the Punta Cana wreck that was available for study after conservation. Just as for the Zeebrugge wreck, analyses of marks and styles point to an English and Flemish origin for these objects (Roberts 2013a, p. 51). Although further analysis of this cargo awaits, the similar nature of finds is striking and it makes one wonder whether the Zeebrugge wreck cargo could have been meant for overseas settlers in the New World.

In 1503, the foundation of the *Casa de la Contratación* in Seville was ordered, an institution that, among others, was to supervise the Spanish trade overseas. The registers of this institution start reporting departures to the overseas colonies from 1504 onwards. Although very little data is available for the years 1504 and 1505, we can see

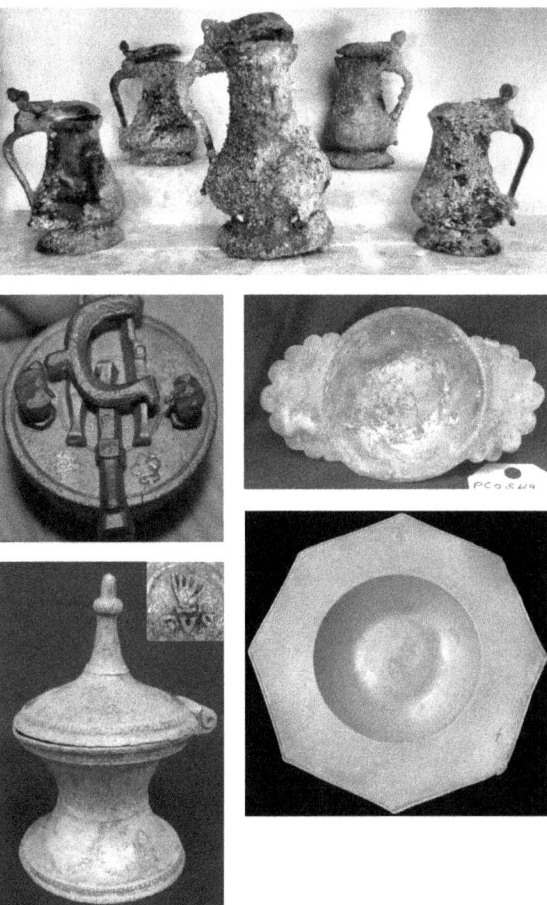

Figure 102. Some of the finds from the Punta Cana Pewter Wreck that demonstrate the similar nature of cargo (images provided by ARS Anchor Research & Salvage Inc.).

increasing numbers of shipments in 1506 (23), 1507 (34) and 1508 (45), mainly heading to '*Española*' or Santo Domingo (Chaunu & Chaunu 1977 PART I, p. 35-36, 42; PART II p. 6-23). Several original registers for ships leaving the port of Seville for the New World in the 1520's are digitally available and provide information about the cargo (Pares 2016). Although these sources can give an idea of the nature of the cargo aboard these ships, our lack of training would have made it too time-consuming to transcribe these registers within the frame of the presented research. However, it has been demonstrated by Roberts (2013a, p. 49-50) similar shipments in 1545 did carry very rich cargos. Here, specific products, such as '*vazos de paylas de flandes*' (Flemish bucket vessels) or '*peltre de ynglatera*' (English pewter) are mentioned among other objects such as combs, thimbles, and knives.

When we look at the increasing number of shipments to the New World since 1504, the nature of their cargos, the remarkable parallels with the Punta Cana Pewter wreck and the archaeological parallels present in the earliest settlements on the island of Hispaniola, it seems reasonable to believe Spain and the New World could have been a destination for (part of) the Zeebrugge cargo. The specific nature of this cargo, including luxurious domestic ware, religious objects, dress accessories, etc., certainly corresponds to the profile of (early) settlers, who soon enough adopted a very rich lifestyle (*Idem*, p. 48).

By the 1520's, legislation was enacted to standardize weights and measures in the New World (*Idem*, p. 259). If indeed this wreck is to be dated to the 1520's, and if indeed its cargo was meant to reach the New World, than would it be possible the cargo of coin weights and nested cup-weights should be interpreted in the light of this new legislation? With such an interpretation we may be stretching the available data over its limits, however, the parallels in the New World and specifically these with the Punta Cana Pewter wreck do indicate links exist in the trading networks of both wrecks. In our opinion, further comparative research in this regard appears to be promising and exciting.

4.5. Further research

As has just been discussed, raising the question about a possible destination for the Zeebrugge wreck almost automatically raises a question for further research as well. If, indeed, the wreck was headed towards Portugal or Spain, research in respectively the *Arquivo Nacional da Torre do Tombo* (Lisbon) or the *Archivo General de Indias* (Seville) may provide additional information. These archives contain information from the former *Casa da Índia* and *Casa de Contratación*, which regulated, among others, overseas trade in the early 16th century. Yet, trying to find this specific ship in any archive would probably be looking for a needle in a haystack, although finding documents for similar cargos may help us in interpreting the further context of this site.

However, the finds from the Zeebrugge wreck as such allow, in our opinion, for further research as well without need for additional historical data. With this research we have provided a broad range of general data for the Zeebrugge wreck. However, the rich cargo of this wreck allows for further in-depth studies of some specific assemblages. This has already been proven by Dumargne, who will include the assembly of candlesticks in her Ph.D. research on this specific topic. The large quantity of pewterware or the roughly 100 knife handles recovered from the wreck certainly allow a similar approach, and also the ordnance may require further analysis. Concerning xrf-analysis, we have only touched the top of the iceberg. Additional quantitative analysis and comparative research of trace elements may indicate a shared production centre for some objects or object groups, or may even lead to the identification of certain production centres.

Furthermore, the nature of the ship itself was not discussed in this paper due to absence of supporting data. This missing information is unfortunate and causes the main hiatus in our understanding of the Zeebrugge shipwreck. Research on site may be continued in the future by the Flanders Heritage Agency, hopefully leading to traces of the actual wreck. The study of any remnants could be of great value for the further interpretation of this site. Of course, any additional existing data that is currently privatised could obviously add, correct, or refine some of the statements made in this paper.

Within the frame of this research we provided an assessment and preliminary interpretation of the Zeebrugge site. One of the main results of this research is the presentation of the large dataset of objects recovered from the Zeebrugge wreck, which is now available for further research, and can be included in the maritime archaeological debate. The specific context of the Zeebrugge wreck, being an early 16th century armed merchantman, provides a unique case that allows us to peek into the international trading networks in this important time of change. Although many academic contributions exist on Antwerp's 'Golden Age', almost none of these studies include archaeological data. Over the last few years and decades, however, several wrecks have been discovered carrying cargos that can be linked to the city of Antwerp as a transit-market, or at least are indicative of the existing trade networks in the early to mid-16th century (e.g. the Zeebrugge wreck, the Punta Cana Pewter wreck, the St Anthony wreck, the Oranjemund wreck, etc.). Unfortunately, most of these cargos have not yet been (elaborately) studied or published. In retrospect, making the archaeological dataset provided by the Zeebrugge wreck generally accessible may have been the main achievement of this research. And, maybe, the main prospect should be the further elaboration of this dataset in comparative perspective to other contemporary wreck cargos. Promising research results have already been established by geographical analysis of data provided by the dispersal of shipwreck cargos and their contemporary production centres (e.g. Matthew Harpster's current research on Mediterranean shipping)[40]. Such a methodological approach applied to ship cargos of the early 16th century may lead to new insights that could be added to, or confronted with, the main body of existing historical contributions in this regard.

---

[40] No publications on this research are available as yet, but a presentation by Harpster at the University of Southern Denmark convincingly demonstrated the potential of this method.

Chapter 5

Conclusion

Within the frame of this research we have been able to collect, study, and interpret a large dataset of objects and information related to the Zeebrugge wreck that has not been published before. This inclusive approach allowed us to appreciate the available data within its own limits, and has led to new insights regarding the excavation and the archaeology of the Zeebrugge shipwreck. The current research results contribute to our understanding of this wreck and hopefully will motivate the further inclusion of the Zeebrugge wreck in the (maritime) archaeological debate. Nevertheless, the further study and assessment of some specific aspects is recommended.

Only limited data allowed us to get an impression of the actual site. Based upon the available information, we can conclude that the site of the Zeebrugge wreck was rather scattered and finds were spread over a relatively large area. The presence of large quantities of ballast stone suggests an east-to-west orientation for the wreck, with the hull tilted to the north. Although reports indicate that no substantive structural parts of the wreck were preserved, the limited present finds in this regard were neither recorded nor preserved by the excavation team. Further surveys are necessary to determine the current state and further potential of this site. If any remains are still present, these are threatened by the widening of the fairway as well as by trawling activity in this area.

The assessment of the collection of finds recovered from the Zeebrugge wreck lead to the positive identification of this wreck as an early 16th-century merchantman. Based upon the analysis of marked objects we can say with certainty that this ship sank in or after 1507. A later *terminus post quem* of 1520 has been proposed in the past, yet due to absent data this could not be verified by the author. Although no specific *terminus ante quem* for the wrecking of the ship could be established, the general nature of cargo and ordnance encourages the hypothesis that this happened in the early 16th century. The vessel carried a valuable cargo and was rather heavily armed. The recovered cargo shows a diverse collection of mainly brass and pewter objects. Products from England (London), the Low Countries (Antwerp, possibly Ghent and Brussels) and Southern Germany (Nuremberg) were identified. Knife handles made of tropical wood species demonstrate the involvement of this cargo in global trade networks.

The particular combination of objects in this cargo, in relation to the location of the wreck near the Scheldt estuary and the date of the wreck in the early 16th century, make Antwerp a very plausible last port of departure. Although a destination for the ship cannot be determined conclusively, Portugal and Spain appear to be plausible candidates. Parallels for several of the finds from the Zeebrugge wreck on the island of Hispaniola demonstrate that this ship may have been involved in trade networks with the overseas colonies. The presence of large quantities of both stone and lead-coated iron shot, as well as the probable presence of at least seven cannon, indicates that this was a heavily armed merchantman.

Other than the assessment and interpretation of the archaeological data from the Zeebrugge wreck, this research has finally made this data generally accessible in an archaeologically substantiated manner, 25 years after the initial discovery of the wreck.

The assessment of the recovered finds in relation to the assessment of data collected by means of archival research and oral history indicates the scientific potential of this site and of the data acquired by vzw Maritieme Archeologie. Although by now their approach is severely out-dated and certain aspects of their approach can be questioned, the initiative to excavate and (to a certain extent) record this wreck while actual legislation in this regard was absent should in our opinion not be criticized but complimented. Although the dataset provided by their work does certainly constitute a contribution to the academic debate, it is also a telling example for the essential need of professional archaeological involvement and guidance in such projects. It is clear that the actual project could have strongly benefited from such involvement in achieving more exhaustive, more consistent, and more accurate archaeological data.

What can and should be criticized, however, is the limited transparency of *vzw Maritieme Archeologie*. Not only does the reluctant attitude of some former members and the privatising of excavation data go against the initial aims of this organisation, but the appropriation of excavation data also conflicts with the essence of archaeological research in general, in which the public interest is inherent. Through privatisation of the data acquired this unique site was destroyed not for scientific but apparently for personal achievement. This unfortunate attitude casts a shadow over the Zeebrugge project, and it seems to impede the appreciation that this project deserves for its pioneering role in Belgian maritime archaeology.

Despite this critical remark, it should be said that the finds from the Zeebrugge wreck provide a unique archaeological dataset for the further study of early 16th century trade. By now, several early to mid-16th century wreck cargos have been excavated that are indicative of the global trade in that period, and some of them can clearly be related to the role of Antwerp as a transit port. We believe the study of the Zeebrugge finds in comparative perspective to contemporary parallels may contribute to our further understanding of trade in this period.

This research has presented and analysed the available data as well as the potential of the Zeebrugge site. However, as yet it has not revealed all its secrets.

Bibliography and archival sources

Abbreviations:

International Journal of Nautical Archaeology: IJNA

Journal of the Antique Metalware Society: JAMS

Journal of the Pewter Society: JPS

Bibliography

Almodovar A. and Cardoso J.L. (1998). *A History of Economic Thought.* London: Routledge.

Andere Tijden, 40 jaar onderwaterarcheologie, jagen op VOC-wrakken. 2002. NPO. 10 December.

Architecture et Patrimoine [No date]. *Architecture et Patrimoine Mobilier.* [Online]. [Accessed 19 November 2015]. Available from: http://www.culture.gouv.fr/public/mistral/memoire_fr?ACTION=RETROUVER&FIELD_1=Cmemo1&VALUE_1=&FIELD_2=Cedif&VALUE_2=&FIELD_3=Caut&VALUE_3=&FIELD_4=Adresse&VALUE_4=&FIELD_5=R%E9gion&VALUE_5=&FIELD_6=Cnum&VALUE_6=&FIELD_7=TOUT&VALUE_7=bougeoirs&FIELD_8=COULEUR&VALUE_8=%20&NUMBER=12&GRP=1&REQ=%28%28bougeoirs%29%20%3aTOUT%20%29&USRNAME=nobody&USRPWD=4%2524%2534P&SPEC=9&SYN=1&IMLY=&MAX1=1&MAX2=1&MAX3=50&DOM=Tous

ARS Anchor Research & Salvage Inc. (2012a). *Global Marine Exploration, Inc. Significant Recoveries of 2011-2012.* Unpublished.

ARS Anchor Research & Salvage Inc. (2012b). *Anchor Research and Salvage. Report of Artifacts Recovered. Pewter Wreck Site – June through August 2012. Punta Cana, Dominican Republic.* Unpublished.

ARS Anchor Research & Salvage Inc. (2012c). *Anchor Research and Salvage. Report of Artifacts Recovered. Punta Cana Lease Area – September through December 2012. Dominican Republic.* Unpublished.

BALaT KIK-IRPA [No date]. *BALaT. Belgian Art Links and Tools.* [Online]. [Accessed 12 November 2015]. Available from: http://balat.kikirpa.be

Bang C. (1995). *The Lear Collection. A Study of Copper-Alloy Socket Candlesticks A.D. 200-1700.* Easton: King's Hill Publications.

Barnard F.P. (1924). The Types of Certain Early Nuremberg Reckoning-Pennies Used in England. *The Numismatic Chronicle and Journal of the Royal Numismatic Society*, 5(4), pp. 261-309.

Bartels M. (1999). *Steden in Scherven. Vondsten uit Beerputten in Deventer, Dordrecht, Nijmegen en Tiel (1250-1900).* Zwolle/Amersfoort: S.P.A. and R.O.B.

Baumgärtel O.A. (1983). Bildquellen für altes Messinggerät. Rotschmieddarstellungen aus Zwei Nürnberger Stiftungen. *Kunst & Antiquitäten*, 4, pp. 36-43.

Baumgärtel O.A. (1997). Zu den Nürnberger Zapfhahnen und ihren Meistermarken. *Mittellungen der Antiquarischen Gesellschaft in Zürich*, 64, pp. 97-120.

Beaudry M.C. (2006). *Findings. The Material Culture of Needlework and Sewing.* New Haven/London: Yale University Press.

Beekhuizen J.F.H.H. (1998). *De Schoonheid van Oud Tin. Een Overzicht van Vijf Eeuwen.* 's Hertogenbosch: Pilkington en Larousse.

Blackmore J. (2008). *Moorings: Portuguese Expansion and the Writing of Africa.* Minneapolis/London: University of Minnesota.

Blake W. and Green J. (1986). A Mid-XVI Century Wreck in the Seychelles. *IJNA*, 15(1), pp. 1-23

Brownsword R. and Pitt E.E.H. (1990). An Analytical Study of Pewterware from the 'Mary Rose'. *JPS*, 7(4), pp. 109-125.

Brownsword R. (2003). Dinanderie. A New Perspective. *JAMS*, 11, pp. 18-20.

Brulez W. (1973). Bruges and Antwerp in the 15th and 16th Century: An Antithesis? In: Brulez W., Koch A.C.F,

Kossman F., Spits C., de Vries J., Geschiere P.L., Carter A.C. and Dhondt J. (eds.). *Acta Historiae Neerlandicae. Studies on the History of The Netherlands. Vol. VI.* The Hague: Martinus Nijhoff.

Camidge K. (2013). *St Anthony. Designated Historic Wreck Site. Desk-Based Assessment.* [Online]. Cornwall: CISMAS. [Accessed 20 January 2016] Available from: http://www.cismas.org.uk/docs/St_Anthony_DBA_Final.pdf

Campbell S.J. and Koering J. (2014). *Andrea Mantegna. Making Art (History).* London: Art History/Association of Art Historians.

Chaunu P. and Chaunu H. (1977). *Séville et l'Amérique, XVIe – XVIIe Siècle. Part I et II.* Paris: Flammarion.

Chirikure S., Snamai A., Goagoses E., Mubusisi M. and Ndoro W. (2010). Maritime Archaeology and Trans-Oceanic Trade: A Case Study of the Oranjemund Shipwreck Cargo, Namibia. *J Mari Arch*, 5, pp. 37-55.

Christie's (2016). *A Franco-Flemish Brass Candlestick. Early 16th Century.* [Online]. [Accessed 24 November 2015]. Available from: http://www.christies.com/lotfinder/furniture-lighting/a-franco-flemish-brass-candlestick-early-16th-century-5653543-details.aspx

Craddock P.T. and Hook D.R. (1987). Ingots from the Sea: The British Museum Collection of Ingots. *IJNA*, 16(3), pp. 201-206.

Dangis T.J. (2014). *Tinmerken van België en Naburige Steden. 15de – 21ste eeuw.* Kessel-Lo: Dangis.

Deagan K. (2002). *Artefacts of the Spanish Colonies of Florida and the Caribbean, 1500-1800. Vol. 2: Portable Personal Possessions.* Washington: Smithsonian Books.

De Francisco Olmos J.M. (1999). La Moneda Castellana de los Reyes Católicos. Un Documento Económico y Político. *Revista General de Información y Documentación*, 9(1), pp. 85-115.

De Hondt Y. (2003). Kandelaars, een Historisch Overzicht. In: Vanloocke D. (ed.). *Steek je Licht op. Van Romeinse Olielamp tot Empire Kandelaar. Volkskundig Jaarboek 't Beertje.* Brugge: Bond van West-Vlaamse Volkskundigen, pp. 9-30.

Demerre I. and Pieters M. (2008). Introduction of the Belgian Test Areas (Flanders). 'Vlakte van de Raan' and 'Buiten Ratel'. *Machu Report 1*, pp. 15-17.

Demerre I. and Missiaen T. (2010). Speurtocht naar het wrak van 't Vliegent Hart. *De Grote Rede*, 28, pp. 2-8.

Demerre I., Van Haelst S. and Pieters M. (2013). *Opvissen van het Verleden. De Bijdrage van Kustvisserij aan de Archeologische Kennis over de Noordzee. Overzicht en Oproep.* Vissen in het Verleden, 29 November 2013, Ostend.

Deweirdt M. (2006). Maritime Archaeological Heritage Legislation in Flanders/Belgium. In: Pieters et al. 2006, pp. 59-64.

Dubbe B. (1978). *Tin en Tinnegieters in Nederland.* Lochem: Tijdstroom.

Dubbe B. (2012). *Huusraet. Het Stedelijk Woonhuis in de Bourgondische Tijd.* Hoorn: Poldervondsten.

Dumargne A.C. (2013). *Chandeliers et Pique-cierges dus XIIIe au XVIIe siècle.* Master thesis, École du Louvre.

Egan G. and Pritchard F. (2002). *Dress Accessories c. 1150 - c. 1450. Medieval Finds from Excavations in London 3.* London: Museum of London.

Egan G. (2005). *Material Culture in London in an Age of Transition. Tudor and Stuart Finds c. 1450 – c. 1700 from Excavations at Riverside Sites in Southwark. MoLAS Monograph 19.* London: Museum of London Archaeology Service.

Euforgen (2016). *Distribution Maps.* [Online]. [Accessed 09 April 2016]. Available From: http://www.euforgen.org/distribution-maps/

Every R. and Richards M. (2005). Knives and Knife Sheats. In: Gardiner J. (ed.). 2005, pp. 144-152.

Farrés O.G. (1959). *Historia de la Moneda Española.* Madrid: [No publisher].

Gadd J. (1999). The Crowned Rose as a Secondary Touch on Pewter. *JPS*, 12(2), p. 1-9.

Gaimster D.R.M. (1992). Frühneuzeitliche Keramik am Niederrhein. In: Krause G. (ed.).

Gaimster D.R.M. (1997). *German Stoneware 1200-1900. Archaeology and Cultural History.* London: The Trustees of the British Museum. *Stadtarchäologie in Duisburg 1980-1990. Duiburger Forschungen 38.* Duisburg: Mercator-Gesellschaft, pp. 330-353.

Gardiner J. (ed.) (2005). *Before the Mast. Life and Death aboard the Mary Rose. The Archaeology of the Mary Rose 4.* Portsmouth: The Mary Rose Trust Ltd.

Gawronski J.H.G. (1996). *De equipagie van de Hollandia en de Amsterdam. VOC-bedrijvigheid in 18de-eeuws Amsterdam.* Amsterdam: De Bataafsche Leeuw.

Goodall A.R. (1981). The Medieval Bronzesmith and his Products. In: Crossley D.W. (ed.). *Medieval Industry. CBA Research Report 40.* London: Council for British Archaeology.

Green J. (2006). Review: Report on the Excavation of the Dutch East Indiaman Vliegent Hart (VOC Anniversary Shipwreck Project). *IJNA*, 35(1), pp. 171-173.

Greenhill B. (2000). The Mysterious Hulc. *The Mariner's Mirror*, 86(1), pp. 3-18.

Groenendijk F. (2015). *Venus op Rekenpenningen, de Naakte Waarheid? Een Onderzoek naar bijna 100 Jaar Venuspenningen.* Zwolle: Spa Uitgevers.

Guérout M., Rieth E., Gassend J.M. and Liou B. (1989). Le Navire Génois de Villefranche, un Naufrage de 1516?. *Archaeonautica*, 9, pp. 5-171.

Guildhall Museum (1903). *Catalogue of the Collection of London Antiquities in the Guildhall Museum.* London: Blades, East & Blades, Printers.

Haneca K. and Pieters M. (2016). *Verslag Houtanatomisch Onderzoek. Collectie Handgrepen Opgedoken nabij de Zeebrugge Site. Rapporten Natuurwetenschappelijk Onderzoek.* Brussel: Onroerend Erfgoed.

Harreld D.J. (2004). *High Germans in the Low Countries. German Merchants and Commerce in Golden Age Antwerp.* Leiden: Brill.

Hicks R. (2005). Navigation and Ship's Communication. In: Gardiner J. (ed.). 2005, pp. 264-292.

Hildred A. (2009). *Weapons of Warre. The Armaments of the Mary Rose. Archaeology of the Mary Rose 3.* Oxford: Oxbow Books.

Holtman R.J. (1999). *Laatmiddeleeuwse Sluitgewichten in Noordwest-Europa.* Unpublished.

Holtman R.J. (2002). Een Muntgewicht met Muntafbeelding op Beide Zijden. *Meten & Wegen*, 117, pp. 2791.

Hoss S. and Grimm G.V. (*in preparation*). *Archeologiche Metalen Vondsten van de Bierkaai, Hulst (working title).* Zaamslag: Artefact!

Houben G.M.M (1984). *2000 Years of Nested Cup-Weights.* Zwolle: Houben.

Houben G.M.M. (1992). Een Muntgewicht met Zowel de Voor- al Keerzijde van de Munt. *Meten en Wegen*, 77, pp. 1814.

Houben G.M.M. (1998). *De Oudste Muntgewichten uit de Nederlanden 1300-1600.* Zwolle: Houben.

Hurst J.G., Neal D.S. and Van Beuningen H.J.E. (1986). *Pottery Produced and Traded in North-West Europe 1350-1650. Rotterdam Papers 6.* Rotterdam: Stichting voor het Nederlands Gebruiksvoorwerp.

Keith D.H., Duff J.A., James S.R., Oertling T.J. and Simmons J.J. (1984). The Molasses Reef Wreck, Turks and Caicos Islands, B.W.I.. A Preliminary Report. *IJNA*, 13(1), pp. 45-63.

Kulstad P.M. (2008). *Concepcion de la Vega 1495-1564. A Preliminary Look at Lifeways in the Americas' First Boom Town.* Master Thesis. University of Florida.

Lockner H.P. (1981). *Die Merkzeichen der Nürnberger Rotschmiede.* Munich: Deutscher Kunstverlag.

Lockner H.P. (1982). Ein Gotischer Tabernakelkronleuchter. Aubau un Konstruktion. *Kunst & Antiquitäten*, 5, pp. 47-57.

Maarleveld T.J. (1993). *Rijksdienst voor het Oudheidkundig Bodemonderzoek. Afdeling Archeologie Onder Water. Jaarverslag 1992.* Alphen aan den Rijn: ROB.

Maarleveld T.J. (1994). *Rijksdienst voor het Oudheidkundig Bodemonderzoek. Afdeling Archeologie Onder Water. Jaarverslag 1993.* Alphen aan den Rijn: ROB.

Maarleveld T.J. (1995a). *Rijksdienst voor het Oudheidkundig Bodemonderzoek. Afdeling Archeologie Onder Water. Jaarverslag 1994.* Alphen aan den Rijn: ROB.

Maarleveld T.J. (1995b). Type or Technique. Some Thoughts on Boat and Ship Finds as Indicative for Cultural Traditions. *IJNA*, 24(1), p. 3-7.

Maarleveld T.J. (2006). The Netherlands. In: S. Dromgoole, (ed.). *The Protection of the Underwater Cultural Heritage. National Perspectives in Light of the UNESCO Convention 2001*, 2nd ed. Leiden/Boston: Martinus Nijhoff Publishers, pp. 161-188.

Maarleveld T.J. (2013). 'Proper and Appropriate' 'Property and Appropriation'. In Prott L.V., Redmond-Cooper R. and Urice S. (eds.). *Realising Cultural Heritage Law. Festschrift for Patrick O'Keefe.* Builth Wells: The Institute of Art and Law Ltd, pp. 63-72.

Malfait A. and Malfait T. (2003). *Zeven Eeuwen Wijwaterremmers & Wijwatervaten in Brons, Geelkoper en Tin.* Kortrijk: Antiqua Nova.

Maritieme Archeologie. (2015). *Zeebrugge wrak.* [Online]. [Accessed on 23 November 2015]. Available from: http://www.maritieme-archeologie.be/WK_Ship_GenView.aspx

Marquardt K. (1997). *Eight Centuries of European Knives, Forks and Spoons. An Art Collection.* Stuttgart: Arnoldsche.

McCune Bruhn H.C. (2006). *Late Gothic Architectural Monstrances in the Rhineland, c. 1380-1480. Objects in Context.* Ph.D. thesis, The Pennsylvania State University.

Mende U. (2013). *Die Mittelalterlichen Bronzen im Germanischen Nationalmuseum. Bestandkatalog.* Nuremberg: Germanisches Nationalmuseum.

Michaelis R.F. (1978). *Old Domestic Base-Metal Candlesticks. From the 13th to 19th Century.* Suffolk: Antique Collector's Club.

Minsaer K. (2007). Archeologische Vondsten onder de Speelplaats. Jonge Soldaten Begraven in de Gasthuisbeemden? In: Scheerlinck K. (ed.). *Mère Jeanne (1824-1907). Stichteres van de Zusters Dienstmaagden van de Heilige Harten van Jezus en Maria. Haar Geestelijk en Materieel Erfgoed.* Antwerpen: Zusters Dienstmaagden.

Missiaen T. (2010). *Akoestisch Onderzoek op de Zeebrugge Site.* Unpublished.

Missiaen T., Demerre I. and Verrijken V. (2012). Integrated Assessment of the Buried Wreck Site of the Dutch East Indiaman 't Vliegent Hart. *Relicta*, 9, pp. 191-208.

Mitchiner M.B., Mortimer C. and Pollard A.M. (1988). The Alloys of Continental Copper-Base Jetons (Nuremberg and Medieval France Excepted). *The Numismatic Chronicle*, 148, pp. 117-128.

Museum Boymans-van Beuningen (1976). *Zout op Tafel. De Geschiedenis van het Zoutvat*, Museum Boymans-van Beuningen, 14 October – 28 November 1976. [Exhibition catalogue]. Rotterdam: Museum Boymans-van Beuningen.

Oosterbaan J. and Griffioen A.A.J. (2015). *Van Vissersdorp tot Havenstad. 750 Jaar Stadsvorming aan de Groote Markt te Vlissingen. Archeodienst Rapport 650.* Vlissingen: Consigna.

Ostkamp S. (2013). *Aen Taefele. Eten en Leven in de Late Middeleeuwen. De Collectie Aad Penders.* Hoorn: Poldervondsten.

PARES (2016). *Portal de Archivos Españoles.* [Online]. [Accessed 12 April 2016]. Available from: http://pares.mcu.es/ParesBusquedas/servlets/Control_servlet?accion=2&txt_id_fondo=1859528

Parmentier J. (2000). Maritime Archaeology along the Flemish Coast. The Case of the Zeebrugge Wreck. In: *TICCIH 10th International Conference, Transactions June 1997, Maritime Technologies – Mining Landscapes, June 1997, Thessaloniki.* Athens: TICCIH Greek Section, pp. 233-236.

Parmentier J. (2011). Un Navire Marchand du Début du XVIe Siècle. In: Anon, *Sur les Traces du Commerce Maritime en Mer du Nord du XVIe au XVIIIe.* Dunkirk: Musée Portuaire, pp. 31-41.

Piasa (2016). *Chandelier en Bronze. XVème Siècle, mis en vente lors de la vente "Haute Epoque" à Piasa.* [Online]. [Accessed 22 November 2015]. Available from: http://piasa.auction.fr/_fr/lot/chandelier-en-bronze-xveme-siecle-1570983#.V0guSN5UsqA

Pieters M. and Schietecatte L. (2003). Maritieme en Fluviale Archeologie: een Nieuw Elan. In *Nieuwsbrief van het Vlaams Instituut voor de Zee*, 10, pp. 3-8.

Pieters M., Gevaert G., Mees J. and Seys J. (eds.) (2006). *Book of Abstracts. Colloquium: To Sea or not to Sea. 2nd International Colloquium on Maritime and Fluvial Archaeology in the Southern North Sea Area, 21-23 September 2006, Bruges. VLIZ Special Publications 32.* Oostende: VLIZ.

Pieters M, Demerre I., Lenaerts T., Zeebroek I. and Monsieur P. 2008. *Maritieme Archeologie.* [Online]. [accessed 04 January 2015]. Available from: https://onderzoeksbalans.onroerenderfgoed.be/book/export/html/2039

Pieters M., Demerre I., Lenaerts T., Zeebroek I. De Bie M., De Clercq W., Dickinson B. and Monsieur P. (2010). De Noordzee: een waardevol archief onder water. Meer dan 100 jaar onderzoek van strandvondsten en vondsten uit zee in België: een overzicht. *Relicta*, 6, pp. 177-218.

Pieters M., Baeteman C., Bastiaens J., Bollen A., Clogg P., Cooremans B., De Bie M., de Buyser F., Decorte K., De Groote A., Demerre I., Demiddele H., Ervynck A., Gevaert G., Goddeeris T., Lentacker A., Schietecatte L., Vandenbruane M., Van Neer W., Van Strydonck M, Verhaeghe F., Vince A., Watzeels S. and Zeebroek I. (2013). *Het Archeologisch Onderzoek in Raversijde (Oostende) in de Periode 1992-2005. Vuurstenen Artefacten, een Romeinse Dijk, een 14de-eeuws Muntdepot, een 15de-eeuwse sector van een Vissersnederzetting en Sporen van een Vroeg-17de-Eeuwse en een Vroeg-18de-Eeuwse Belegering van Oostende. Relicta Monografieën 8.* Brussel: Onroerend Erfgoed.

Pol A. (1989). Noord-Nederlandse Muntgewichten. *Jaarboek voor Munt- en Penningkunde*, 76, pp. 5-143.

Pol A. (1990). *Noord-Nederlandse Muntgewichten*. Leiden: Rijksmuseum het Koninklijk Penningkabinet.

Portable Antiquities Scheme (2016). *The Portable Antiquities Scheme Website*. [Online]. [Accessed 17 January 2016]. Available from: https://finds.org.uk

Puttevils J. (2016). *Merchants and Trading in the Sixteenth Century: The Golden Age of Antwerp. Perspectives in Economic and Social History 38*. 2nd ed. London/New York: Routledge.

Redknap M. (1984). *The Cattewater Wreck: The Investigation of an Armed Vessel of the Early Sixteenth Century. B.A.R. British Series Vol. 131*. Oxford: British Archaeological Reports.

Richards M. (2005). Lighting Equipment. In: Gardiner J. (ed.). 2005, pp. 343-347.

Rijksmuseum [No date]. *Monstrans, anoniem, ca. 1550*. [Online]. [Accessed 14 March 2016]. Available from: https://www.rijksmuseum.nl/nl/collectie/BK-NM-80

Roberts M. (2013a). *The Punta Cana Pewter Wreck. Pewter: Origin, Styles, Makers & Commerce (Edition 1.0, November 2013)*. [No place]: Roberts.

Roberts M. (2013b). The Punta Cana Pewter Wreck. Discursions on a Discovery. *JPS*, 38, pp. 14-31.

Rubin M. (1991). *Corpus Christi. The Eucharist in Late Medieval Culture*. Cambridge: Cambridge University Press.

Rule M.H. (1973). The Mary Rose. A Second Interim Report, 1972. *IJNA*, 2(2), pp. 385-388.

Schiltz B. (2006). Viewpoint of the 'Sport Diver'-Amateur-Underwater Archaeologist. In: Pieters ET AL. 2006, pp. 42-45.

Seliger W.K. and Pritchett III R.H. (2011a). *Anchor Research & Salvage. Initial Recovery Expedition. Punta Cana. May-June 2011. Report of Artefacts Recovered*. Unpublished.

Seliger W.K. and Pritchett III R.H. (2011b). *Anchor Research & Salvage. Recovery Expedition Punta Cana August-September 2011. Report of Artefacts Recovered*. Unpublished.

Seliger W.K. and Pritchett III R.H. (2011c). *Anchor Research & Salvage. Recovery Expedition Punta Cana November 2011. Report of Artefacts Recovered*. Unpublished.

Seys J. (2001). Wrakken voor onze kust. Niet al goud wat blinkt. *Nieuwsbrief VLIZ Februari 2001*, pp. 3-7.

Smolderen L. (2009). *La Médaille en Belgique. Des Origines à nos Jour*. Wetteren: Cultura.

Sotheby's (2016). *A large brass candlestick, probably Spanish 16th/17th century*. [Online]. [Accessed 20 November 2015]. Available from: http://www.sothebys.com/en/auctions/ecatalogue/2007/huntington-antiques-the-journey-of-a-cotswold-antiquarian-early-furniture-works-of-art-textiles-l07303/lot.510.html

Stadtbibliothek Nürnberg (no date). *Die Hausbücher der Nürnberger Zwölfbrüderstiftungen*. [Online]. [Accessed 17 March 2016]. Available from: http://www.nuernberger-hausbuecher.de

Termote D. and Termote T. (2009). *Schatten en Scheepswrakken. Boeiende Onderwaterarcheologie in de Noordzee*. Leuven: Davidsfonds.

Vandenberghe S. (1997). Découvertes importantes datant de la fin du 15e et du début du 16e siècle provenant du fond de la Mer du Nord en face du port de Zeebrugge. In: De Boe G. and Verhaghe F. (eds.). *Travel Technology and Organisation in Medieval Europe: Papers of the 'Medieval Europe Brugge 1997' Conference. I.A.P. Rapporten 8*. Zellik: Instituut voor het Archeologisch Patrimonium, pp. 87-90.

Vandenberghe S. (2006). Major Finds from the Zeebrugge Site. In: Pieters ET AL. 2006, pp. 19-20.

Vandenberghe S. (2007). Belangrijke Vondsten van de 'Zeebrugge site'. In: Zeebroek I., Pieters M. and Gevaert G. (eds.). *Verdronken Verleden, Provinciaal Hof Brugge, September 2006*. [Exhibition catalogue]. Brugge: VIOE & Provincie West-Vlaanderen.

Van den Eynde D., Lauwaert B., Martens C. and Pirlet H. (2015). Baggeren en storten. In: Pirlet H., Verleye T., Lescrauwaet A.K. and Mees J. (eds.). *Compendium voor Kust en Zee 2015: Een geïntegreerd kennisdocument over de socio-economische, ecologische en institutionele aspecten van de kust en zee in Vlaanderen en België*. Oostende: [No publisher], pp. 101-108.

Van Der Wee H. (1963). *The Growth of the Antwerp Market and the European Economy (Fourteenth – Sixteenth Centuries). Vol. II: Interpretation*. The Hague: Martinus Nijhoff.

Van Dromme M. (2006). Conservation of a Cast-Iron Bombard from the Zeebrugge Site. In: Pieters ET AL. 2006, pp. 21-22.

Vangroenweghe D. (2015). *Standaard Sluitgewichten uit Neurenberg – Periode ca. 1450 tot 1800*. Brugge: GMVV.

Vanhoudt H. (2015). *De Munten van de Bourgondische, Spaanse en Oostenrijkse Nederlanden en van de Franse en Hollandse Periode: 1434-1830.* Heverlee: Poldervondsten.

Vlaamse Hydrografie. [no date]. *Wrakkendatabase.* [Online]. [Accessed 12 December 2015]. Available from: http://www.vlaamsehydrografie.be/wrakkendatabank.htm

Watts G.P. (2013). The Western Ledge Reef Wreck: a Preliminary Report on Investigation of the Remains of a 16th-century Shipwreck in Bermuda. *IJNA*, 22(2), pp. 103-124.

Wechssler-Kuemmel S. (1963). *Chandeliers, Lampes et Appliques de Style.* Fribourg: Office du Livre.

Wittop Koning D.A. (1953). *Nederlandse Vijzels.* Deventer: Davo.

Wittop Koning D.A. and Houben G.M.M. (1980). *2000 Jaar gewichten in de Nederlanden. Stelsels, IJkwezen, Vormen, Makers, Merken, Gebruik.* Lochem-Poperinge: Uitgeversmaatschappij De Tijdstroom.

VRT Beeldarchief
Anna Catharina, Journaal, 24/09/1991

Archival sources:

Maritiem Erfgoed Archief (MEA)

    Maritiem Erfgoed Archief RCE archiefnummer 1.853.3.16

Private Archive Bart Schiltz (P.A.B.S.):

    Duik Rapporten (D.R.)

    Folder 'Vergaderingen' (F.V.)

    Folder 'Correspondentie 1' (F.C.1)

    Folder 'Correspondentie 2' (F.C.2)

    Side Scan Image (S.S.I.)

Vlaamse Codex Ruimtelijke Ordening (VCRO)
    Besluit van 17/11/1993: Besluit van de Vlaamse Regering tot bepaling van de algemene voorschriften inzake instandhouding en onderhoud van monumenten en stads- en dorpsgezichten.

www.ingramcontent.com/pod-product-compliance
Lightning Source LLC
Chambersburg PA
CBHW041706290426
44108CB00027B/2877